Family-Centered Treatment With Struggling Young Adults

Family-Centered Treatment With Struggling Young Adults is an indispensible guidebook to the unique set of problems and opportunities that families face when young adults are experiencing difficulty pulling anchor and setting sail. Renowned clinician Brad Sachs, PhD, provides both a conceptual framework for understanding the reasons behind the increasing number of young adults who are unable to achieve psychological and financial self-reliance and a treatment framework that will enable practitioners to help these young adults and their families to get unstuck and experience age/stage-appropriate growth and development. Clinicians will gain an in-depth understanding of the complex psychological challenges that parents and young adults face as the latter forge a path toward success and self-reliance. And they'll come away from the book having learned an innovative approach to sponsoring family engagement at the launching stage—one that reduces tension, resolves conflicts, and promotes evolution and differentiation on both generations' parts.

Brad Sachs, PhD, is a psychologist, educator, consultant, lecturer, and the best-selling author of numerous books, including *Emptying the Nest: Launching Your Young Adult Toward Success and Self-Reliance*. More information about his work is available at www.drbradsachs.com.

Previous Books by Dr. Brad Sachs

Family-Centered Treatment With Struggling Young Adults

A Clinician's Guide to the Transition from Adolescence to Autonomy

Brad Sachs

 Routledge
Taylor & Francis Group

NEW YORK AND LONDON

When case material is being presented, names and identifying details have been changed by the author for the purpose of protecting patients' confidentiality.

First published 2013
by Routledge
711 Third Avenue, New York, NY 10017

Simultaneously published in the UK
by Routledge
27 Church Road, Hove, East Sussex BN3 2FA

Routledge is an imprint of the Taylor & Francis Group, an informa business

© 2013 Taylor & Francis

The right of Brad Sachs to be identified as author of this work has been asserted by him in accordance with sections 77 and 78 of the Copyright, Designs and Patents Act 1988.

Library of Congress Cataloging in Publication Data

Sachs, Brad, 1956–
Family-centered treatment with struggling young adults : a clinician's guide to the transition from adolescence to autonomy / Brad Sachs.
    p. cm.
  Includes bibliographical references and index.
   ISBN 978-0-415-69967-9 (hardcover : alk. paper) —
ISBN 978-0-415-69968-6 (pbk. : alk. paper) —
ISBN 978-0-203-13560-0 (ebk)   1. Young adults—Family relationships.
2. Young adults—Psychology.   3. Parent and adult child.   I. Title.
HQ799.2.S23   2013
155.6'5—dc23   2012017124

ISBN: 978-0-415-69967-9 (hbk)
ISBN: 978-0-415-69968-6 (pbk)
ISBN: 978-0-203-13560-0 (ebk)

Typeset in Garamond
By Apex CoVantage, LLC

Printed and bound in the United States of America by Sheridan Books, Inc. (a Sheridan Group Company).

For Richard, and all who struggle

I was going somewhere and he was seeing me go. I was growing in my own sense of myself and to him I was getting smaller . . . my father did foresee, the glitter in his eyes told me, that time consumes us—that the boy I had been was dying if not already dead, and we would have less and less to do with each other. My life had come out of his and now I was stealing away with it.

John Updike, from his story, "My Father's Tears"

And we didn't know then that remnants of happiness
Are like remnants of every collapse
That you have to clear away to start anew.

Yehudah Amichai, from his poem, "Hamadiya, Memory of Bliss"

Contents

Preface

The family has its own growth.

D. W. Winnicott, *Through Paediatrics to Psychoanalysis*

This book is written for family therapists but should also be of interest to individual and couples therapists, developmental psychologists, human development specialists, family sociologists, and pediatricians and other physicians who treat young adults as well as educators and administrators at the secondary and college levels. It will also have value as a textbook for teaching individual and family therapy in academic and professional settings.

It encourages a clinical orientation that encompasses a family's past and present, with the goal of creating a healthy vision for their collective future.

My interest in this topic is both a current and long-standing one. I pursued several career paths before eventually obtaining my doctorate at the Institute for Child Study and Human Development at the University of Maryland and becoming a practicing psychologist. That was also the point at which my wife, a psychiatrist who had just completed her residency, and I began our family, which eventually grew to include three children.

About a decade ago, I began to notice a significant uptick in the number of parents who were contacting me for assistance regarding young adult children, and since that time I have been reflecting carefully on the contemporary process of making the transition into adulthood. A recent outcome of my thinking was *Emptying the Nest: Launching Your Young Adult Toward Success and Self-Reliance* (2010), which was a guide written for parents who were struggling to understand and successfully address the difficulties that their children were experiencing as they endeavored to cross the threshold from adolescence into adulthood. I also began to frequently lead training workshops for clinicians that detailed the therapeutic approach that I was working to develop, workshops that formed the foundation of the book that you now hold in your hands.

This past decade in my life also entailed the sequential launching of our three children into young adulthood, as well as the expansion of our family as a result of the birth of our first grandchild. So, as usual, I am writing a book not only from a position of passionate *clinical* interest but also of passionate *personal* interest. Sometimes I feel as if it's presumptuous and foolhardy to write about a topic that I have no longitudinal perspective on—for example, it's not as if I can look calmly back on my children's young adult years and sagely comment on what was happening "way back when." On the other hand, I am always hopeful that writing about a developmental stage that I am actually in the midst of injects a certain intensity, immediacy, and relevance into my approach, which perhaps will compensate for my lack of a distant, panoramic view.

It also feels important to note that my own years of emerging adulthood were quite trying. For whatever reasons, I struggled mightily in my 20s to establish relational and professional stability and forge a path forward into life. In some ways, despite being able to easily recall the many wonderful moments and important accomplishments that took place during those years (including, foremost, my wedding), that decade seems to have been the most psychologically bewildering of my life, the one during which I had the least self-assuredness. So it's not surprising that I found myself motivated to write about a stage of life that, for me personally, was filled with prodigies of pain and confusion.

I often joke with colleagues that I wish I could write a letter of apology to all the families whom I treated before I had children of my own—family life, from my perspective as a newly minted psychologist, had a simplicity and clarity to it that was both appealing but also, in retrospect, somewhat delusional. I believe I offered my first patients something useful, but the offer was made with a certain arrogance and certainty that, based on my stage of life and my inexperience, was certainly not legitimate.

That is not to say, of course, that one cannot be an effective family therapist unless one has children—having to directly experience everything that our patients experience would unnecessarily limit all of us. But we need to be constantly aware of the daunting challenges that inhere within any developmental stage, and robustly living through those stages does tend to make this awareness easier to achieve.

Ultimately, this book is designed to help the reader to develop a greater appreciation and enhanced respect for the snarled complexity of family life—the unsolvable pain of childhood, the sacred, ever-shifting matrix of hopes, disappointments, dreams, and anguish that comprise the human condition and the joys and sorrows that individuals experience as they are born, grow, love, and die.

****

The stages in the family's life cycle are generally defined by the exit and entry of its members—the births, deaths, marriages, and divorces that predictably or unpredictably occur over time. It is during these beginnings and endings that the family is at its least stable and most malleable. This book will focus on a stage that is both exit and entry—the separation of children from their family of origin and their admission into the beckoning world of adulthood.

What is important to keep in mind whenever we are addressing a family's developmental stage, however, is that the particular exits and entries rarely do us the favor of occurring exactly when we are *planning* for them to occur or when we are emotionally or financially *ready* for them to occur—and they rarely take the precise form that we would prefer or expect them to take.

For example, an unmarried couple finds themselves expecting a child well before they were prepared to marry, let alone begin a family, while another couple, already married for ten years, spends another ten years as well as tens of thousands of dollars trying to conceive, eventually deciding to begin their family through adoption rather than birth.

Or one set of parents proudly watches their son dating a young woman who is, in their eyes, his perfect match and happily attend the wedding that takes place after two years of their perfectly timed courtship. Then, several years later, these same parents disconsolately watch the marriage dissolve into an acrimonious divorce. Another set of parents wrings their hands as they watch their son marry a woman who is, from their perspective, a complete mismatch. Then, several years later, they silently marvel at how nicely these two have learned to complete and complement each other.

And, of course, in some traditional cultures, the two parents are not standing back and watching at all—they are actively putting their heads together with another set of parents so that the four of them can *arrange* the marriage between their two young adult children.

The leaving-home stage of life tends to be a particularly complicated one because, in a very real sense, that is the entire point of parenthood. A parent's job, as Anna Freud once noted, is to be *there* to be *left*. Mothers and fathers are not entrusted with children so that they can keep them stunted and dependent; they are blessed with children with the expectation that they will raise them to become responsible and self-reliant, to find a way to separate and individuate, to commence their lives as independent adults, and to eventually connect with other independent adults and fulfill the biological and psychological imperative of becoming parents themselves, and starting the cycle anew.

Yet, particularly these days, the process and timing of this renewal of the life cycle have become highly variable and unpredictable, much more so than in previous generations. Taking these changes into account is an essential aspect of effective family therapy—we can never tease apart individual and family behavior from the larger, human ecological narratives of which we are all an inextricable part.

While there is certainly great cultural diversity when it comes to navigating the process of leaving home, and attention will be paid to the ways in which different classes, religions, and ethnic groups manage this transition in unique ways, the focus of this book will be more on what families have in common than on how they differ. Every human language has its unique sound and cadence, yet

all human languages, no matter how different they sound, retain the same elemental structure and grammar. Similarly, while each culture influences, grooms,
and sculpts its families' dynamics such that they are distinct from other cultures'
dynamics, there is still an elemental structure and grammar that broadly defines
family growth and development, a structure and grammar that cut across ethnic
boundaries.

Likewise, while I will be detailing some of the ways in which the passage toward self-reliance is unique for the current cohort of young adults, and in some
ways profoundly different from their generational predecessors, the reality is that
the drama of leaving home is one that has recurred, in structurally similar ways,
ever since the story of Adam and Eve. For better or worse (and I believe it's the
former), there is much more that links us than separates us as humans, be it across
space or across time.

Finally, I want to emphasize the importance of appreciating each family's dis-
tinctiveness. While our work as clinicians is designed to improve the lives of the
individuals and families whom we treat, none of us have a crystal ball, and we
cannot always be certain if the changes that we are advocating for and helping to
facilitate will truly yield those improvements. And a sometimes bruising reality of
family dynamics is that what improves one member's life doesn't always improve
every other member's life.

I do not have on hand a perfect scenario for family development, an ideal
template that every family should feel compelled to follow when it comes to
young adult development. And I steadfastly and strenuously resist the temptation
to quickly classify a family as deviant, dysfunctional, or disordered if they don't
follow or neatly conform to whatever happens to be the culturally dominant developmental script. I have treated too many families, and seen enough evolution
within my own family of origin and family of creation, to believe that there's any
one, "right" way to raise and launch children.

With this in mind, perhaps the best that we can do is to courageously join the
families that we are treating and bring our insight, perspective, and expertise to
bear so that they are as equipped as possible to make the decisions and follow
the paths that they have come to determine—with as much self-awareness as
possible—are best for them.

Acknowledgments

I extend my gratitude to . . .

Anna Moore, who saw the potential for this book before I did and patiently (*very* patiently) worked with me to nurture it into fruition;

Dr. Roger Lewin, whose insights about matters both clinical and nonclinical, professional and personal, have proven to be invaluable as I've worked on this manuscript;

Phyllis Stern, MA, my first family therapy supervisor, whose voice I still carry with me patient after patient, year after year; and

Karen, as always, forever . . .

Introduction

I recently came across a touching article by a 24-year-old, originally from the Midwest, who had graduated from college and was now a government intern in hard-charging, high-powered Washington, D.C. The author had recently gotten engaged to her boyfriend, and her friends and colleagues in the D.C. area could not understand why she was planning on getting married so soon when she hadn't attended, or even applied to, graduate school; when she hadn't purchased her first condominium; and when she had not yet accumulated any significant savings or made any financial investments.

Meanwhile, at the same time as she was getting heat from her cohort in the East, her high school chums were puzzled that it had taken her this long to *get* engaged! After all, most of them were already married, and many had started families. She wrote with bemusement and sensitivity about the ways in which she felt trapped between two very different sets of expectations, depicted as rash and impulsive according to one set of friends, and as dragging her heels by another.

After speaking and working with numerous young adults over the past two decades, I can tell you that this individual's internal experience of feeling hopelessly hamstrung between competing criteria for autonomy and independence is not at all unusual.

I have written this book to address many of the questions that arise as contemporary families prepare to launch their young adult children forward toward productive lives marked by purposeful success and meaningful self-sufficiency in a world that is changing rapidly (even as I write!). Some of these are questions that have been asked in every generation, while others are unique to this current generation, but all are worthy of our consideration. They include:

- What are the typical developmental tasks and challenges entailed with a young adult's separation from his or her parents?
- What are the typical developmental tasks and challenges entailed with parents who are launching their children toward adulthood?

- Why do some families seem to launch their young adult children forward more successfully than others? What are the family dynamics that promote or impede a young adult's separation and liberation?
- Why do some young adults return home after having departed, and what factors account for how that phase of life unfolds and when/whether the young adult is relaunched?
- What kinds of young adult departures tend to endure and lead to self-reliance in the long run, and what kinds of departures are destined, over time, to compromise growth, or ultimately collapse?
- What unique contemporary factors (economic, sociological, demographic, etc.) account for the growing number of young adults struggling to achieve independence?
- What are the changes that parents need to make to raise the odds of their young adult child's burgeoning self-reliance as well as their own vigorous and dynamic adaptation to middle age and beyond?
- How can the relationship between parent and young adult evolve in healthy ways during the separation and liberation process, and what defines a healthy relationship at this stage of development?
- How do evolving young adults navigate between connection to and differentiation from their family of origin and learn to maintain a healthy balance between gravity and flight?

Up until fairly recently in human history, there were basically two stages of life—childhood and adulthood. In preindustrial Western societies, a boy became a man and a girl became a woman simply as a result of achieving sexual maturity and fertility—there were no other distinctions to be made. The intermediate stages of human development in between childhood and death, which were ultimately given names such as adolescence, young adulthood, middle age, and senior, have, to a large extent, been created and defined in response to changing social and economic conditions.

Social scientist Frank Furstenberg (2005), notes, for example, that the concept of a distinct phase of life occurring between the end of childhood and the beginning of adulthood—which we now call adolescence—is a relatively new one, occurring in the United States in the early 1900s during a time when public schooling was becoming widespread, when the economy was shifting away from agriculture in response to the Industrial Revolution, when protective child labor laws were being introduced, and when, as a result, young teenagers were no longer automatically designated as ready or required to enter the workforce.

While the unique characteristics, behaviors, and attitudes associated with adolescence—physiological puberty, rapid physical and intellectual growth, a migration from the family to the peer group, a striving for separation and autonomy—had certainly existed and had been observed for countless generations, it was only at the beginning of the twentieth century that psychologists and educators began to define adolescence as a discrete life stage, a developmental "grace period" during which teenagers could rehearse some of the privileges of adulthood without shouldering all of the responsibilities. As a result, young people were given a longer moratorium from adult responsibilities, enabling them to receive an extended education, explore a wider range of personal and professional possibilities, and create a sense of their evolving identity.

During the early decades of the twentieth century, this newly defined adolescence was established as a relatively brief phase, the short span between early teenager and late teenager. And the reality was that, through the first half of the 1900s, only a small percentage of older teens remained in school, while a much larger percentage had already left their parents' home and begun working, even if marriage and parenthood did not immediately follow.

The Great Depression decelerated the speed with which young people formed families, but by the end of World War II, marriage and childbearing often commenced almost in tandem with the conclusion of an individual's education. The high proportion of men who were in military service in the 1940s, often by the age of 18, further prevented any kind of extended adolescence from taking place, particularly because the multitude of returning veterans were accepted and treated like adults no matter how old they were, and they were provided with government-sponsored support and employment that enabled them to quickly establish financial self-reliance.

And because, in the economic boom that followed the war, high-paying industrial-based employment remained stable and easy to find, most young people did not have difficulty making it on their own by the end of their teen years, even without any formal education beyond a high school diploma. So adolescence had a clearly defined beginning and end, and, from a cultural as well as a socioeconomic standpoint at that juncture in U.S. history, individuals in their early 20s were really not all that different from those in their 30s and 40s.

The current invention of young adulthood is taking place in much the same way that the previous invention of adolescence took place—as an important response to larger social, economic, and cultural forces that conspire to make the simplicity of previous developmental frameworks seem inflexible and antiquated. Just as the smooth, almost invisible transition from childhood to adulthood disappeared in the face of industrialization, leading us to conceptualize adolescence, the smooth, almost invisible transition from adolescence to adulthood is now disappearing as well, making young adulthood a conspicuous and categorical possibility, a life phase that fills what has become a growing gap in human development.

Just as we needed to create adolescence to describe the significant nodal phase between childhood and adulthood, so we have now created young adulthood to describe the new chasm that has opened up between adolescence and adulthood. Like a meteorologist whose vocabulary must expand beyond *hot* and *cold*, we need to expand our own vernacular beyond *child* and *adult*.

It should be acknowledged that there is some controversy in the field of developmental psychology regarding whether young adulthood can actually be considered a discrete developmental stage. After all, one of the criteria for defining a developmental stage is that there is a universality to it, that it is a phenomenon that regularly occurs cross-culturally. From my vantage point, there is not yet enough compelling research and evidence to suggest that young adulthood meets this criterion. However, whether it officially passes muster as a developmental stage or whether it is simply a growing reality that adolescents no longer can instantly become self-sufficient adults once they finish their education or come of age, family therapists must recognize young adulthood as a phase in the family's life cycle that deserves sedulous and careful attention.

One reason for this occurrence is that adolescence is now commencing earlier than it did in the past, partially as a result of the (still difficult-to-explain) earlier onset of puberty that has begun to prevail. From an educational standpoint, many, if not most, contemporary psychologists tend to see the start of middle school—which for some students is at 10 or 11 years old—as the beginning of adolescence.

But not only does adolescence start earlier, its end can no longer be easily determined, and certainly not by chronological age. The transition into adulthood has become much hazier—far less distinct and far more ambiguous—and no longer follows any kind of predictably consistent pattern. So it's as if the starting line for adolescence has been moved back and its finish line pushed much farther ahead, making it much dicier to determine the official conclusion of adolescence and the official beginning of adulthood with much precision.

After all, for example, we may find two different children who are each in school full-time, each living at home, and each completely financially dependent on his or her parents—but one may be 12 years old and the other 22 years old. Can we accurately call them both adolescents? Or we may find two different post-adolescents who have decided to embark on additional education or training that limits them to part-time work for several years and, as a result, puts them in the position of having to live at home with their parents—but one may be 19 years old and the other 29. Can we accurately call them both young adults?

The reality is that it is just not possible for contemporary young people to achieve financial and psychological autonomy as quickly, and with the same certainty and efficiency, as did their parents and grandparents. The fact, for example, that a substantial majority of college graduates enter postgraduate life with debt that averages $22,380 at private colleges and universities and $17,700 at public institutions helps to explain why so many young adults have at least temporarily moved back in with their parents. And nearly 30% of college students who took out loans did not graduate, making them four times more likely to default on their loans.

The timing and sequence of the traditional markers of adulthood—moving out, finishing education or training or apprenticeship, entering the workforce, forming intimate partnerships, marrying and starting a family—also vary wildly, displaying increasingly less uniformity and increasingly more elasticity with each successive cohort of 18-year-olds.

Why has crossing the frontier of adulthood become so much more difficult? Perhaps the main reason is that education and training are far more essential now than they have ever been when it comes to acquiring the cognitive and emotional maturity, social acumen, and job-related skills required in a world that seems to significantly transform itself every year. Most young adults aim for college in one form or another, because they are aware that most of the jobs that will enable them to finally achieve financial self-reliance and establish a home independent of their parents depend on attaining undergraduate, and often graduate, degrees. As a result, college and graduate school, which used to be the exclusive province of the upper-middle and upper classes, have become mainstream institutions, available in one form or another to all socioeconomic groups.

But even if college and graduate school are not options and cannot be pursued for economic, academic, or other reasons, then some sort of extended training through military service, internship, or technical studies is still required to lay the groundwork for eventual self-sufficiency. The greatly extended length of these academic and training periods accounts for much of the growing chasm between the end of adolescence and the solidifying of adult status. And even when these extended training periods have been completed, self-sustaining employment is not guaranteed. For example, according to a recent *Wall Street Journal* article, only 55% of the 44,000-member law school class of 2011 procured a legal job within nine months of graduation, while the average graduate was simultaneously buckling under $100,000 in student loan debt.

But there are other realities that impinge on the longer, more elastic phase of young adulthood, such as:

- Jobs are not as permanent as they used to be.
- College takes much longer to complete than it used to. The federal government noted that fewer than 50% of students graduate in four years at 33 of 50 state universities and that the overall four-year graduation rate is 31% for public colleges and 52% for private colleges.
- Many young adults migrate back and forth between school, the labor force, living at home, and some sort of internship or externship, sometimes participating in more than one simultaneously.
- There is more openness to experimentation and numerous alternatives to traditional developmental paths, such as an increasing number of middle- and upper-class young adults participating in a community-service project before committing to a particular higher-education or career pathway.
- Due to changing and more flexible moral standards, young adults feel freer to live together, to start a family without marrying, to delay parenthood, or to not have children at all. Related to this, the Centers for Disease Control and

Prevention recently concluded that the pregnancy rate for women in their early 20s declined significantly from 2000 to 2008, while the pregnancy rate for women older than 30 increased. In the past 50 years, the average age of first-time parents has increased from 21 to 25 and is even older for college-educated women.

- Beginning and early-career salaries not just for high school graduates but also for college graduates and even for those who have completed graduate school, have not kept up with the cost of living and, consequently, no longer allow young adults to easily afford decent housing or medical insurance.

- College tuition continues to skyrocket at a breathtaking rate—as noted above, undergraduates are completing their degrees with an average of $20,000 in loans in addition to possibly thousands more in credit card debt, meaning that they are forced to enter adulthood paying backward rather than saving forward.

- Broader cultural diversity changes our societal time line—for example, many young adult children of immigrant families are likely to live at home well into their 20s, not only because of economic factors but also out of a culturally bound sense of responsibility to their family of origin.

Census and demographic surveys provide us with data that support these realities. For example, almost half of the individuals who leave home for the first time between the ages of 17 and 20 return to live in their parental household at some point. About a quarter of American young adults do not leave home at all until age 22 or later. In 2000, 56% of men and 43% of women between the ages of 18 and 24 lived at home with one or both parents. In the 1920s, the return rate of young adults was 20%, while in 2000 it was almost 50%. The median age of leaving home is currently 19, which is the lowest since records began being kept in the 1920s, but 25% of young adults do not leave home until 22 years old or later.

So with all these changing realities in mind, the process of firmly establishing an outpost in the uncharted territory of self-reliance is necessarily a much more daunting and self-directed one for modern young adults than it was for their counterparts in previous generations. It is not that these shifting conditions are all good or all bad—surely it's some of both—but that contemporary young adults have fewer familiar stars to reckon by as they journey forward

Of course, it's not just the novel phase of young adulthood that society has given birth to. With the notable and continued reduction in fertility and mortality rates over the past several generations, parents have had fewer children to raise and have thus been able to provide significantly more time and attention to the children that they *do* raise. They are living long enough to see not only their children leave home, but even their grandchildren, and sometimes even their *great*-grandchildren. So this has gradually created new trajectories and another unique life-cycle phase: empty nesters, adults who are young and healthy enough to enjoy an extended period in their lives without any children dependent on them.

But contemporary parents who are trying to empty their nest are vulnerable to, and must respond to, the same mercurial circumstances and morphing scenarios that are affecting their children. For example, parental support in its almost innumerable forms—paying for college and other postsecondary education, providing other financial subsidies and allowances, offering coresidence, taking over loan payments and credit card debt, cosigning leases, purchasing a car, helping with property taxes, extending health insurance coverage—may be vital if some young adults are to have the flexibility to pursue the more extensive education and training required to expand their career options or to marry and start a family in an economic climate that most experts predict will experience very slow growth for some time. The era of hard-working parents being easily able to boost their children to a higher standard of living than they themselves experienced, and to concurrently savor their retirement while contentedly watching the fruits of unstoppable upward mobility, is long gone.

And forget about the *child's* future for a moment—what about the parents'? In the current recession and with their life span (hopefully) extending into a healthy eight or nine decades, what happens if the parents outlive their retirement savings—savings that were depleted not only by economic woes but by a decision to fund one or more college educations? To what extent does helping to pay their child's bills interfere with their paying their *own* bills? What if bankrolling the child's plans and possibilities entails the evaporation of certain plans and possibilities that the parents were dearly counting on? The New America Foundation's Federal Education Budget Project has discovered that in the past five years, as college prices have soared and many families have struggled through financial difficulties, parents have increased their borrowing about 33% through federal Parent Plus loans. The average single-year federal Parent Plus loan was $12,000 this school year, compared with $9,850 in 2007. And the Council on Contemporary Families points out that today, nearly 25% of child-rearing costs occur after age 17.

These kinds of excruciating dilemmas and conflicts mean that parents and their charges have to engage in a different and more complex kind of negotiation regarding expectations and obligations as they grapple with fundamental changes in the nature and texture of the elongating parent–child relationship. And how those negotiations play out has profound influence on both generations' life-course transitions, including the probability of young adults' leaving or returning home, the way in which they form or dissolve relationships with peers and romantic partners, their child-bearing decisions, their level of education, and their professional paths and accomplishments, as well as the maneuverability that parents have when it comes to their own individual, relational, professional, and retirement options.

No matter how we understand the basis for the vastly different timetable that young people follow as they become adults, it has created a new set of challenges to be met, problems to be solved, and questions to be answered for clinicians who are asked to help families light the fuse that will propel young adults toward separation and autonomy. The modern family has become a Petri dish for conflict and consternation during the launching phase, as both generations struggle anxiously to chart a wilderness that has not yet offered up any reliable maps because it is still so new, and still evolving.

For example, a study conducted by the Child Trends Data Bank on more than 4,000 American adolescents born between 1980 and 1984 concluded that the best predictor of their academic and social success was "consistent, high-quality relationships" with their parents. A similar six-year investigation in the Netherlands revealed that there was a positive correspondence between satisfying parent–child relationships and young adults' psychological well-being.

Research led by the National Survey of Student Engagement discovered that students at 750 colleges tended to be more satisfied with their education, more engaged in their learning, more collaborative with other students, and more likely to seek out and interact with faculty members when their parents were more involved in their college education.

The Pew Research Center recently concluded that a significant majority of 18- to 34-year-olds who are living at home are satisfied with their living arrangements and remain positive about their future.

In a changing world in which young adults are already carrying sizable debt and need significant training before they can obtain the kind of job that enables them to be financially independent, returning home for a period of time during early adulthood may not be the result of soft, substandard parenting or spoiled entitlement but instead the outcome of careful planning in preparation for ultimately achieving self-reliance.

And, perhaps most importantly and least surprisingly, young adults who report high levels of warmth and emotional closeness and low levels of conflict and hostility with their parents tend to display nurturant behavior toward romantic partners and eventually enjoy positive relationships with their *own* children when they make the transition into parenthood.

So the case can be easily made that a solid parent–child relationship remains crucial even during early adulthood and can ultimately influence emerging adults' subsequent growth and functioning in positive ways. These findings should not be met with incredulity, because according to much of the world, equating maturity with the repudiation or obliteration of the parent–child bond is a completely alien (and disturbing) concept. In fact, in many countries and cultures (and even in the United States, albeit in previous generations), it is not only common but expected and valued that young adults remain in their original home for a long period of time, even after they have married and started their family, and that they find a way to experience a workable balance between closeness and separateness with their family of origin.

So rather than parents seeing themselves as having somehow failed the litmus test of successful parenthood simply because their young adult child is not yet thoroughly and unconditionally independent, maybe it would be better if families were able to more effectively adjust in a world in which, for better or worse, young adults still require, and *benefit from*, appropriately involved parenting.

This involves finding ways for parents and young adults to maintain effective communication, resolve conflicts, establish clear and respectful boundaries, find pleasurable ways to interact and share activities, and support each other in their ongoing individual journeys toward fulfillment and wholeness—challenges that we, as family therapists, are entrusted to help them meet. It is this task that we will be taking up in the following chapters.

Chapter 1

Fluid Family Therapy

Music begins the moment you listen.

Jean Monahan

Several years ago, I treated a family with two sons, one of whom was an adolescent and one of whom was a young adult, both of them living at home with their parents. The treatment extended over the course of almost a year and addressed a wide range of worrisome behaviors that included underachievement, scrapes with the law, and drug and alcohol abuse. Although most sessions included all four family members, there was plenty of variability within sessions—sometimes I met with the sons together or individually; sometimes I met with the parents without their sons. I also scheduled some individual sessions with each son from time to time, a few parent-only strategy sessions, and one meeting that included the maternal grandparents, who lived less than an hour away and had always had a close relationship with their grandsons.

The treatment produced good results, and by the time we decided to finish up, things at home weren't perfect, but they were a good deal more stable than when the family had first consulted with me. At what was planned to be our final session before taking a mutually agreed upon hiatus, I asked the parents what they had found most helpful about the work that we had done together.

The mom responded by telling me that she was pleased with what we had accomplished, but she had been doing some reading about adolescence and suggested that if they ran into problems again, perhaps they ought to try family therapy.

I was completely taken aback by her comment. "What exactly do you think we've been *doing*?" was the question that I was tempted to ask her. How could they not have known that they had indeed been participating in actual family therapy with an experienced family therapist? But I bit my tongue and agreed with them that that might, indeed, be worth pursuing down the road, if necessary.

After they left, I imagined that, based on the reading that she had done, she must have envisioned family therapy as treatment that entailed the entire family spending every minute of every session together with the therapist. But because there had been plenty of coming and going in our work together—conjoint sessions, individual sessions, split sessions—it could not, according to her criterion, truly be classified as family therapy.

In addition to throwing me for a loop, however, this mother's comment was revealing, because it suggests that the *name* for the work that we are doing doesn't really matter. What ultimately matters is the *actual* work that we are doing—however we name it—and, more importantly, how well we are doing it.

The name that I have come up with for the clinical approach that I will be describing in this book is Fluid Family Therapy (FFT), and I suppose in some ways it's a response to this mother's comment. Adopting a systemic outlook in therapeutic work doesn't have much to do with how many people are sitting in the consultation room. You can be thinking and working systemically with only one, motivated family member sitting in your office, and you can be thinking and working in a linear way with an entire extended family sitting in your clinic, hospital, or office (my first family therapy supervisor, the ingenious Phyllis Stern, referred to this as "individual therapy with an audience").

What follows are the basic tenets of Fluid Family Therapy, but the emphasis is on the *fluid* part of this moniker. I want to emphasize that I am not presenting a concrete, manualized treatment method that can be easily replicated and applied with relevance and specificity to every family that consults with you; nor can I offer a tightly edited list of crisp, definitive clinical aperçus. Families, from my perspective, are human enterprises that are simply too complicated to understand in their entirety—they are complex *organisms*, not simple mechanisms. We who treat families are constantly confronted with confusion and contradiction—it is indeed the very nature of our work.

Instead, I have tried to present a flexible *framework* for treatment that is highly versatile, depending on the presenting problem and the identified patient, and one that is likely to induce the family to get unstuck and follow the paths that their best efforts and instincts creatively forge for them. The range of struggling young adults we will come across is vast—we will be taking care of young men and women who suffer from serious mental illness; who are emerging from the foster care system without any family or societal safety net in place; who have autism-spectrum disorders; who are homeless; who are returning from military service, possibly with injuries; who are recent immigrants; who have succumbed to cults; who are wrestling with sexual orientation challenges; who have grown up impoverished and disadvantaged; whose parents are divorced; who are being launched by grandparents rather than their parents; who are up against medical challenges and disabilities. It would require thousands of pages of inquiry to address all of these situations with an adequate level of analysis.

But because of the power of systemic thinking, family therapy has the potential to be an enormously supple and versatile clinical approach when working with any family at the launching stage of the life cycle, and the more that we maintain our fluidity as clinicians, the more likely we are to trigger growth and healing, no matter what the basis of the family's struggles may be.

ORIGINS

The general treatment approach that I will be laying out in the coming chapters emerges most saliently from Family Systems Theory, which hypothesizes that problems and symptoms are best understood not as existing *within* an individual, but within the web of relationships *between* individuals, and that they are sustained and maintained by predictable, but ultimately changeable, patterns of behavior among family members. We refer to the treatment framework as Fluid Family Therapy because both its *origins* and its *strategies* are fluid.

Regarding its origins, Fluid Family Therapy draws from the following sources:

- *Structural Family Therapy*, as proposed by Minuchin (1974), has taught me to look carefully at the ways in which a family organizes itself—its boundaries, its hierarchy, its alignments—and to find ways to intervene that improve the family's organization such that it is more adaptable in the face of change.
- *Strategic Family Therapy*, as proposed by Haley (1985) and Madanes (1981), has taught me to explore the function that certain symptoms perform within the family system and the importance of understanding the role of the symptom before attempting to ameliorate it.
- *Narrative Family Therapy*, as proposed by White and Epston (1990), has taught me that it is not generally the dilemmas and problems themselves that afflict us but the maladaptive ways in which we think and talk about those dilemmas and problems that can be most deleterious.
- *Bowen Theory*, as proposed by Bowen (1978), has taught me to look at the family through the lens of its intergenerational heritage and to emphasize healthy differentiation as opposed to geographical separation or emotional cutoff.
- *Contextual Family Therapy*, as proposed by Boszormenyi-Nagy (1987), has taught me to attend closely to the family loyalties, both functional and dysfunctional, that illuminate and define every individual's journey toward self-reliance.
- *Attachment Theory*, as proposed by Bowlby (1969), has taught me to reinforce the concept of interdependence, the reality that the path toward independence is always anchored in the ability to maintain close emotional connections throughout the life span.
- *Motivational Theory*, based on the work of Deci (1996), has taught me to understand the intricate connection between autonomy and the capacity to develop self-mobilized and self-motivated initiatives.
- The work of Helm Stierlin (1981) has taught me to understand why healthy separation between parent and child during late adolescence and early adulthood is sometimes imperiled or runs aground.

- The work of D. W. Winnicott (1952) has taught me to be closely attuned to the "empathic ruptures" that are a natural occurrence in individual and family therapy and to use these painful impasses as ways to enhance self-awareness and spur personal and relational growth.
- The work of Monica McGoldrick (2011) has taught me to respect the complexity of the family life cycle and the ways in which each member's developmental trajectory intersects with and influences those of others.
- The work of Froma Walsh (2002) has encouraged me to apprehend the complex multiplicity of family life in a diverse and changing world.

Like most seasoned clinicians, I have also incorporated techniques borrowed from numerous other theorists, practitioners, and schools, including those associated with cognitive-behavioral therapy, mindfulness, and Eastern thought (acupuncture, meditation, yoga, etc.).

FAMILY SYSTEMS

When I was growing up and my brothers and I got sick, my mother would remind us that it will take some time to get the cold "out of your system." While that may be an applicable metaphor when it comes to mild infectious diseases, the reality is that nothing ever "gets out" of the family system—issues, themes, conflicts, and entanglements remain there forever, echoing through the generations in various forms and guises. Our job as family therapists is not to disinfect the family system but to *illuminate* it so that the family can see it more clearly and then make the necessary alterations and find the appropriate antidotes in response to this illumination.

FFT recognizes the uniqueness of each family and does not have as its objective a particular solution to a family problem or a particular definition of healthy family functioning. Its goal is to help families understand themselves better, augment their realization of and access to their own resources, and enable them to use those resources to get themselves unstuck and moving forward. This is accomplished not through engaging in a lockstep, irreversible sequence of assessments and interventions but through the therapist's creative and courageous encounter with the family, his capacity to take the family's psychological pulse, to enter into their darkness and light a single match, to help them slow down and simply have a good look at, and give a careful listen to, each other.

While dramatic transformations and epiphanies may, at times, take place, FFT is designed to foster steady, nuanced shifts in the family's functioning, ones that are more likely to take root and endure over time rather than those that will breathtakingly flare up and then disappointingly disappear. The therapist does this, at least initially, by injecting something new and different into the warm bloodstream of the family through pointing out the recurring patterns of their behavior and how the patterns might be changed to everyone's advantage.

The priority is not whether change occurs but whether change can be *maintained*—and, especially, whether it can be maintained outside of therapy, like a hothouse flower that can also thrive when transplanted into an outdoor garden. This kind of sustained and expanded change is likely to take place only if the family system has changed along with the individuals comprising the system.

In this regard, the goal of FFT is to make the therapist, and therapy itself, obsolete; to empower the family with the capacity to perceive and resolve their difficulties on their own (I like to keep the wonderful Ray Charles song, "I Don't Need No Doctor" in my head: "The doctor say I need rest, but all I need is her tenderness, He put me on the critical list, when all I need is her sweet kiss.")

In FFT, problems in treatment can be anticipated, but it is recognized that they cannot be avoided. Defiance and resistance among family members are not seen as problems or obstacles but instead as invitations to the therapist to become better acquainted with who they are and how they behave. We want to acknowledge and address the power of the family as a whole, or the power of one or more of its members, to defeat us as well as to defeat anyone else who tries to facilitate change, and to see this power not as a headache or a hindrance but as royal entrée into the experience of what it must be like to live with them.

FFT is a patient and deliberate intervention as well. While it is practical and doesn't waste time, it also recognizes that families have limits to what they are able to accomplish and that they are entitled to rest and restore themselves on certain developmental plateaus for periods of time, if they would like, before resuming their march up the continuous mountain of growth. FFT recognizes the wisdom of the family and respects their intuitions regarding how much recalibration of their closeness with or separation from each other can be tolerated. It appreciates that self-defeating behavior may serve a purpose, communicate something important, or protect against even more destructive behaviors.

Patience on the part of the therapist is particularly important, because the emotional skin of individuals and families is always thinner, more tender and vulnerable, at a developmental juncture, and so the likelihood of oversensitivity on the part of one or more family members is magnified. There is an emotional nakedness that we all expose when we welcome someone into the family or experience the loneliness of a farewell. Confusion, compressed thinking, prickly reactivity—all of these are associated with the need to change, and all of them need to be respected and very tenderly palpated.

Our patients are often going into murky, hidden places deep within themselves and yet simultaneously may be available for more open and intimate contact with others than ever before. So there is tremendous room for growth but also tremendous room for clinical error if we push too hard or move too quickly.

Every family is afraid to face certain truths because they are afraid of what these truths will say about them, both to themselves and to others. Our job as clinicians is to help them confront these truths and, as Dorothy and her friends do when Toto pulls the curtain hiding the Wizard of Oz, to realize that these truths are not quite as intimidating and fearsome as the family imagined.

When a confrontation with the family's reality becomes necessary, the therapist does not proceed heedlessly but remains mindful of the vulnerabilities of the family and its members and constantly monitors the level of trust that has been established with them. There is a necessary roughness that may be required to galvanize them but unnecessary roughness deserves a penalty, and the family will be certain to inflict this penalty, in one form or another, on the therapist for this infraction.

FFT gently but firmly guides the family toward a rational assessment of their situation and some prospective changes that might improve it but includes an acknowledgment of what remains irrational and difficult for them, and perhaps even for the therapist, to understand.

It is also useful, in this regard, to make the distinction between curing and healing when treating the family. The reality is that not every illness will be cured, but with the right care, the patient—in this case, the family—can still *heal*, often in psychological, spiritual ways. The identified problem brings the family members into closer contact with themselves and with each other, and this increase in connectedness expands their sense of well-being, even though the problem itself may not be completely resolved.

Finally, FFT acknowledges that people grow and change in many ways without having to be in therapy. There are many events and endeavors that catalyze human development, and the family should be discouraged from believing that clinical intervention is their only route toward safety or sanity.

Despite the aforementioned premises, it should be acknowledged that psychological intervention can never have the precision and predictability of other clinical interventions. In other words, we don't always know why what we do works when it does, in fact, work. I was listening to the National Public Radio program "Car Talk" one morning, and a caller commented that she noticed that she always got better gas mileage after going in for an oil change and wanted to know how oil changes improve gas mileage.

The hosts hypothesized that the better mileage had nothing to do with the oil change, but instead had to do with the fact that the technician probably checked and inflated her tires when she went in for an oil change. So while it was logical for her to assume that it was the oil change that led to the increased gas mileage, it was actually because of what *accompanied* the oil change—optimally inflated tires—rather than the oil change itself that she experienced improved automotive performance.

We may believe that our effectiveness lies in the inventive clinical strategies that we employ or the theoretically sound framework within which we operate, but it is likely that it is what accompanies our strategies and framework—our warmth, our kindness, our optimism, our faith, our endurance—that accounts for improvements in the family's "performance."

THE FLUID FAMILY THERAPIST

The therapist conducting Fluid Family Therapy must maintain a versatility of roles. At times he observes the family from a distance, getting a read on their functioning and their interactional patterns. At times he pulls up beside the family as if in a sidecar and travels along their bumpy roads with them. At times he tries to muddy the overly placid surface of the family lake and induce imbalances in the family's functioning so that they have the opportunity to rebalance themselves in a more constructive way, and at times he empathizes with their struggles and normalizes their problems.

One way or another, though, the Fluid Family therapist becomes an intimate part of the family system. FFT is not seen as counteractant being administered from a distance but as a healing encounter that involves and changes the therapist in the same way that it involves and changes the family. Charles Fishman (1988) refers to this as maintaining a "Janus-like" position in which the clinician remains both inside and outside of the family, simultaneously influenced by, yet not overwhelmed by, the family's pressures—both actor and director.

With this in mind, the Fluid Family therapist keeps numerous therapeutic arrows in her quiver. A Japanese warrior once said, "Never have a favorite weapon," and that is good advice for the clinician as well—relying too heavily or too consistently on one approach can close us off to the potential healing properties of others.

The Fluid Family therapist maintains his humanity, his humility, and his uncertainty in the face of the family's struggles. By modeling an acceptance of these qualities, he helps the family to do the same. We will, on occasion, hit what feels like clinical concrete and find that we temporarily have no place to go, but our candid acknowledgment of that, without doing so in an exasperated, hopeless or hostile manner, can be reassuring to the family, leaving them to better understand and feel less alone with their stuckness or immobility.

Once, after three consecutive difficult sessions during which we seemed to make little headway, I commented to a glum and displeased 20-year-old patient, "You know, you seem to have painted yourself into such an intricate corner that I'm not convinced I can help you out of it." He suddenly smiled for the first time and said, "Good, now you get it. Now you know why I get fucked up every weekend. It's the only way I can get out of my head. Everybody else says they can help—you're the only one who realizes that maybe you can't." I commended him for being able to imbue me with the hopelessness that he had been living with for many years so that I would have a better chance of understanding it, and possibly join him in resolving it—but until I "got it," he apparently was not even going to let me try.

The basis for successful FFT, which is the basis for any therapeutic encounter, is the therapist's capacity to build trust with the family—psychological pilings have to be laid down before a relational bridge can be built. The most elemental way that the therapist builds trust is by being truly present for the family, and the most tangible way of being present is to listen to them—listening with curiosity and open-mindedness and without judgment or condescension; listening not only to the concrete specifics of the problem that brings them into treatment but listening for the ache in their soul, or the heaviness in their heart, or the darkness in their mind.

Virginia Woolf wrote, "Nothing has really happened unless you have described it." The therapist's commitment to hearing the family's description of their past, present, and future provides the basis for their level of trust in treatment. If they don't feel listened to, they can't feel trusting, and without trust, the possibility of healing and change quickly evaporates.

Whatever role he is playing, and whatever techniques he employs, the Fluid Family therapist must find a way to fall in love with the family, which in turn will help them fall in love with themselves—a process that lies at the root of solving problems. Therapy, like education, parenthood, mentoring, or any other significant human relational endeavor, is at its most elemental basis an act of love, and when we find ways to love our patients, to be smitten with them, we vastly increase our growth-promoting capacity.

Still, there will always be times when families engage in behaviors that make us want to tear our hair out. In a session that took place just earlier this week, for example, I was working with a 19-year-old who was regularly abusing Ecstasy. A month ago, he had to go to the ER with racing pulse and chest pains after having taken pills. His parents went into his room later that night and gathered up all the pills they could find.

During the follow-up session, he told me privately that he was giving up pills but was going to go back to smoking pot and had recently bought some. I asked him how he had the money to do so (he didn't have a job). He told me that he used the money that his parents had given him to compensate him for the pills they had confiscated. Apparently, he had raised a ruckus when he came out of his stupor and realized that they had impounded his pills and demanded that his parents financially reimburse him for what they had commandeered—and they had agreed to do so!

But families who come to us for treatment do not need anyone outside of their system denouncing them; they are usually engaged in plenty of denunciation of themselves and each other. Instead, it is crucial to espouse a kind and benevolent conceptualization of the family and their struggles—one that recognizes and applauds their efforts up until now, counterproductive as they may have been, and that also imbues them with bright beliefs about their capacity to advance.

Rather than lecturing these parents on their maladaptive response to their son's behavior or condemn them for being enablers of his drug habit, we instead explored the mixed feelings they had about being forced into playing the role of drug-prevention police while simultaneously wanting to be seen as fair-minded by their vulnerable son.

FLUID FAMILY THERAPY DURING YOUNG ADULTHOOD

I remember, back during the summer of my postdoctoral internship, being given a copy of Jay Haley's *Leaving Home* (1980) by a supervisor. I spent a week's worth of lunch breaks sitting outside at a picnic table in the hot sun, munching on my sandwich and absolutely entranced as I read about the developmental intricacies associated with successfully launching young adults toward self-sufficiency.

I certainly did not agree with everything that Haley observed or recommended in this book, but it remained extremely valuable to me as a clinician (and as a parent), because it helped me to understand how much terror and anguish, how much loss and grief, is likely to be encountered when the process of leave-taking is correctly embarked upon—not just in families that are overly rigid, dysfunctional, and entrenched but in *any* family that has reached that important stage of development.

The work of Haley and other clinicians has also taught me that, as therapists, we need to legislate a wide spectrum of emotions rather than sanitizing or homogenizing the family's emotional life, suggesting that they should be perpetually euphoric or unceasingly content. The more we narrow the family's (or our own) emotional bandwidth, the more we restrict the family's emotional growth.

Every generation of parents faces its own contemporary challenges, challenges that are the one-of-a-kind outcome of the particular culture and chronological era in which they raise their children. But as therapists, we don't want to lose sight of the fact that there are still universal elements to the differentiation process that families of every generation and every culture *have* faced, and will continue to face. FFT is an approach that recognizes that which is ancient and eternal, and that which is modern and unprecedented about the family's effort to complete the job of raising its children and successfully launching them toward new horizons. And, hopefully, FFT will further enable you to intervene effectively when struggling young adults and their families consult with you for clinical guidance.

Fluid Family Therapy during early adulthood is rooted in the belief that the child's relationship with her parents and family remains important even when adolescence has been completed, and that when the young adult is struggling in her efforts to separate and differentiate, it is because the family as a whole has gotten grounded and confounded. In other words, the launching phase of the family life cycle requires the entire family system, not just the individual who is being launched, to reorganize and renegotiate relatedness.

The result of successful launching is not the young adult's complete emotional, physical, and economic self-sufficiency and the concomitant denial, negation, or erasure of his relationship with his family of origin. While this has been our culturally dominant paradigm for young adult development for some time, it completely ignores the realities of longitudinal family life, in which the balanced exchange of intimacy, love, and support becomes one of the foundations of healthy adjustment.

Instead, we will define the goal of the launching stage as each generation discovering the capacity to be simultaneously separate from and engaged with each other, to find and refine a healthy interdependence of functioning that keeps all family members connected to each other in warm and flexible ways and also liberates them to continue to grow and evolve.

To do this, FFT addresses the needs and concerns of at least two generations in the family: the parents and the young adult. The focus with the parents is supporting them through the last stage of hands-on child rearing and helping them to make the adjustments necessary to revolve their lives on other axes besides parental caregiving.

The focus with the young adult is promoting her self-assuredness and self-awareness such that she can become successful and self-reliant as she separates from her family, leaves adolescence behind, and enters the real world under her own power. This kind of differentiation should not be equated with completely detaching from or cutting ties with her family but instead can be best understood as a new way of being connected with them that is predicated on her autonomy and distinctness but that still allows for healthy engagement. By becoming more intimate with her developing adult self, she carves out space within which to become intimate with her family in new, different, and less dependent ways.

When FFT is successful with struggling young adults, the bond between parent and child is not transcended or abandoned but made stronger and more resilient so that it can become the basis for the young adult's relatedness with individuals and his engagement with endeavors outside of the family. The security of the young adult's continued attachment to his parents is what allows him to eventually move his parents to the margin of his life so that he can still turn to them for support, if necessary, but so that he can also create space for peers, colleagues, romantic partners, and mentors to move in.

When it comes to working with young adults, there is also the issue of timing. The common problem that brings families with children of any age into treatment is that the child is, at some level, not *acting* her age—such is the case whether the child in question is 5 or 25. Our dual task as clinicians, then, is to help the family, and the parents in particular, to key in on their definition of age-appropriate behavior and to place that definition within the larger context of our cultural definition of age-appropriate behavior.

As we have already discussed in the introduction, age-appropriate behavior for the parents when *they* were 25 may have been marriage, parenthood, no financial debt aside from a monthly car payment, and the ability to make ends meet while paying rent on their own two-bedroom apartment, and still having a little money left over each month to begin funding a retirement account.

These objectives may not be realistic for their 25-year-old son, who just began a master's degree program in sports industry management after having worked in ticket sales for a minor league baseball team for several years—a job that did not pay him enough to get his own apartment, let alone to chip away significantly at his college loans. This current degree program, which will require two years of coursework, may pay off down the road, because, if nothing else, the networking that he can tap into will enable him to learn about, and possibly qualify for, jobs with increased earning potential. But the program will also delay his economic self-reliance for several more years due to his inability to make much money while he's in school and due to the money that he'll owe on his graduate school loans— payments that will need to be made in addition to his undergraduate loan payments. So it is entirely possible that this young man, even though he is smart, skilled, and hard-working, will still need to be living at home, subsidized by his parents to some extent, until he is almost 30 years old—and that's if everything goes well.

Nevertheless, most would agree that this young man is thus far displaying age-appropriate behavior, even though he has not achieved the level of self-sufficiency that his parents had achieved when they were the same age—after all, he has finished college, he has worked regularly for several years, he is now in a graduate program, and he has a clear understanding of the kind of professional future that he would like to pursue and the steps that need to be taken to pursue it.

On the other hand, a 25-year-old who is still living in her old bedroom, who doesn't hold a college degree, who has been intermittently or underemployed for the last four years, and who has no savings at all is *not* displaying age-appropriate behavior, regardless of whether it is by her family's yardstick or a cultural yardstick that she is being measured.

Rather than locking into too narrow a definition of appropriate or inappropriate developmental timing, we want to help each family find a developmental *range* within which they can comfortably operate and assess each member's progress.

Now that I have laid out the infrastructure for Fluid Family Therapy, let's take a look at one of the core issues that every family at the launching stage is buffeted by.

FFT requires an inclusive, "all-hands-on-deck" approach to treatment. While, particularly during young adulthood, it may not be possible to get the entire family in the consultation room at the same time, no one should be excluded, and anyone who has potential influence over or relevance to the family should be considered as a potential participant.

It is obviously more effective when at least the young adult and his or her parent(s) participate in treatment. There is no substitute for witnessing the family's interactions in vivo. When I ask a mother to have a seat in the waiting room so that I can have some time alone with her 19-year-old son, and she bends down on her way out and stage-whispers in his ear, "Be completely honest with Dr. Sachs; you can say anything you want to say to him," that reveals a tremendous amount about her belief, or lack thereof, in his capacity to handle relationships. When another mother in the same situation tells her daughter, "Remember to tell Dr. Sachs everything . . . *everything*," it becomes easy for me to surmise that there are personal secrets that her daughter has been trying to keep or family secrets that she has been entrusted to carry by others.

"All hands on deck" also applies to other professionals who are involved in the young adult's or the family's lives. Tutors, clergy, physicians, lawyers, probation officers, and others all have a place at the clinical table. One of our goals is to yoke together whatever team is in place and try to ensure that everyone's efforts are aligned and that the different approaches eventually converge, like climbers scaling different sides of a mountain with the goal of convening at the summit.

Having discussed the basic philosophy behind Fluid Family Therapy, we can now proceed by looking for ways to apply it to our work with struggling young adults and their families.

The Six Categories of Struggling Young Adults

Sometimes it's necessary to go a long distance out of the way in order to come back a short distance correctly.

Edward Albee, *The Zoo Story*

Family therapists in this day and age (indeed, in any day and age) must operate with the understanding that psychological separation is not continent upon geography or technology or any other external factor. I have treated young adults who live at home and lead emotionally and financially self-sufficient lives, and I have treated young adults who live away from home but seem unable to function without the uninterrupted emotional and financial involvement of their parents.

I have worked with young adults who are in indissoluble contact with their parents through e-mail, Facebook, texting, and phone calls and who feel confident enough in their separateness that this frequent communication is enjoyably satisfying for both them and their parents. And I have worked with young adults who are in indissoluble contact with their parents because they feel incapable of managing any feeling or making any decision on their own.

I have taken care of young adults who spend very little time with their parents because they are busily involved with relationships and endeavors outside of the family orbit. And I have taken care of young adults who spend very little time with their parents but who simmer in a bitter brew of resentment toward their parents such that they might as well be living at home, since so much of their mental time is spent in a lacerating internal dialogue with their parents.

There are, of course, always going to be young adults who appear to display few difficulties as they leave adolescence, giddily plunging headlong like frisky, fearless canines into the beckoning white surf of their exciting future. But the reality is that for many young adults, there seems to be more fear than fearlessness, more doubt than certainty—in the words of Abbott and Costello, it's a case of "Go ahead, back up." The transition into adulthood may seem more akin to one of those cartoon scenes in which a character dashes off a cliff, stares down in disbelief as he contemplates the depths of the chasm that awaits below, suddenly encounters the force of gravity, and then grasps at a branch during his terrifying descent, clinging desperately to it while trying to figure out what to do next.

The popular sobriquets that are bandied about in an effort to describe and make sense of the serpentine developmental paths of these young adults generally have *some* relevance and explanatory value but tend to sanitize the hazards of young adulthood. American descriptive phrases such as the "boomerang generation" or "Twixters" or "adultescents" tell us little about the basis for young adults' behavior, the origins of their decision making, and the dynamics of their relationship with their family of origin, even if they are, or are about to recommence, cohabitating with them.

Other countries and cultures struggle to pinpoint the right terminology as well. For example, Japan refers to its "freeters" and "parasite singles": young people between the ages of 15 and 34 who are underemployed or unemployed and generally living with their parents. The acronym NEET (not engaged in education, employment, or training) was initially coined in the United Kingdom, but its use has spread to numerous other countries in Europe and Asia. Young adults who haven't left home are referred to as *Mamboende* (those who live with Mama) in Sweden and as *Mammoni* (Mama's boys) in Italy. In Belgium, "hotel families" are those in which parents continue to allow their young adults to live with and be supported by them.

My belief is that it is impossible to come up with just one or two aptly named divisions that most of these "not-quite-ready-for-prime-time" emerging adults could fall into—the range of options and possibilities, of paths and trajectories, of internal and external obstacles is simply too vast. Instead, I have conceptualized six groups of struggling young adults that, taken together, seem to capture the immense variety and complexity of today's undulating journey toward self-sufficiency, illuminating the extent to which that journey can vary from young adult to young adult, and from family to family, in our society:

PROGRESSING

Progressing young adults are moving ahead nicely with their lives and forging paths that are likely to lead to self-reliance but still have some maturing to do and require a degree of parental support and guidance. While their parents sometimes become exasperated, it is usually short-lived, and they tend to not experience great difficulty or conflict accommodating their offspring because their young adult is showing overall signs of positive growth and development.

Twenty-six-year-old Isabelle has just begun a master's teaching program in special education. While she is doing well academically, she is often short on money and tends to run up significant credit card debt a couple of times a year, and her parents frequently have to bail her out. They have lectured her repeatedly about the importance of fiscal conservatism, but, despite consistently agreeing with them on the importance of being more careful, her credit card bills inevitably balloon. The reality is that she never learned to budget because she was never expected to have a job in high school or college, or to save money, or to contribute to her expenses. Instead, for example, her parents encouraged her to spend her high school summers attending an assortment of science programs that they proudly paid for. So it should come as no surprise that Isabelle has poor financial management skills and still counts on her parents to bail her out of debt.

On the other hand, it is difficult for her parents to get terribly upset with her, knowing that she is functioning well overall and that once she finishes graduate school she is likely to find a solid job with benefits. So despite their annoyance, they tend to be more patient and generous than might be advisable for parents to be with someone Isabelle's age—although, as a result, they retard the process of her learning to live within her means.

REGROUPING

Regrouping young adults have forged a leave-taking and established some independence outside of the home but have returned for a short or long period of time to lay the groundwork for their next foray toward self-reliance. They are seemingly taking a step backward, but it is in the service of ultimately taking steps forward. They require some support from their parents during this phase, and there may be some tension as readjustments to the return have to be made by all family members. But because there is still a concrete plan for advancement in place, everyone is able to adapt.

Twenty-one-year-old Shadonya earned a certificate as a nursing assistant after graduating high school and worked in a hospital for a year, living on her own in an apartment with two friends. She recently decided that she would like to go to college and earn her RN degree. She has picked out a program that she would like to attend, but it is unaffordable for her at this point in her life. With this in mind, she has asked her parents if she can move back home for at least a year, and probably two, to save money while continuing to work at the hospital—a plan that they have all agreed to.

Arguments between Shadonya and her parents occur fairly frequently, as her parents had grown accustomed to not having any children at home. Shadonya often has her boyfriend over in the evening, and he tends to stay fairly late—at times, her parents have found him in her bed in the morning. And, while Shadonya likes to cook, she does not always clean up after herself with much conviction. But, overall, her parents are pleased that she's working hard toward a legitimate goal, and she is pleased that she has been given a chance to live rent-free for a while in order to achieve that goal—so all three of them are generally able to share the house without an excessive amount of friction.

MEANDERING

Meandering young adults are also moving ahead with their lives but are not doing so in as direct and straightforward a fashion as those who are progressing or regrouping. Meanderers' growth seems more wayward, proceeding sideways, and sometimes even in reverse, more than forward. Because of this, they tend to continue to need regular support and guidance from their parents. Parents may still feel some hope and optimism regarding their meandering young adult children's academic or professional endeavors but are also starting to wonder when true self-sufficiency will emerge, fearing that they will have to continue to provide emotional and financial subsidies for much longer than they had originally anticipated. The experience of shoving quarters into an unyielding slot machine disquietingly enters their mind.

Twenty-four-year-old Ramin was a marketing major in college, but by junior year he had been seriously bitten by the acting bug and decided that he wanted to make a career of it. He moved to Brooklyn, sublet an apartment, got a job as a server at a midscale restaurant, and started auditioning in New York City, but with little success. His parents then agreed to sponsor his participation in a two-year acting institute that supposedly had excellent connections in the film and drama industry. Despite completing the program, Ramin has thus far not been able to get any regular gigs.

While Ramin continues to work at the restaurant and diligently pound the pavement in search of acting jobs, he still requires monthly infusions of cash to make ends meet, and there is no clear point at which he will be close to having established financial independence. His parents are thinking about setting some sort of deadline for him to begin managing things on his own without any regular support from them, but they understand that the entertainment industry is an unreliable one, even under the best of economic circumstances. They want to give him every chance to make his dream a reality but know that, at some point, they may have to pull the plug and don't know exactly how and when to do so. Meanwhile, the possibility of one or both of them retiring keeps getting postponed as they agonize over their decision making.

RECOVERING

Recovering young adults have also forged a leave-taking and established some independence outside of the home but are returning under different circumstances than regroupers—they have come back home with their tail between their legs to recover from an experience that did not work out particularly well, and there is not yet any clear plan or time frame for their next departure. Because of this, significant support may be necessary, and tension can run high due to the uncertainty of the current arrangement.

Nineteen-year-old Kelvin graduated from high school and got an apartment with his buddy, Stuart, cosigned for by the two sets of parents, while Kelvin and Stuart both got jobs at a local restaurant. The apartment worked out disastrously— Stuart's girlfriend basically moved in with them just a few weeks after they signed the lease and mooched off of the two of them constantly. After they hosted a few get-togethers for their friends, word quickly spread through social networking sites, and many local (and not-so-local) young adults—both in and out of school— began showing up uninvited and partying well into the morning hours, prompting difficulties with the landlord, who was being regularly besieged by complaints from the neighboring tenants. The apartment quickly took on a bombed-out look from the reckless nightly revelry.

Meanwhile, the restaurant that they both worked at fell on hard times and cut both Kelvin's and Stuart's hours in half. Now no longer able to make rent and cover their expenses, the two of them clumsily concocted an ill-conceived drug-dealing scheme that quickly collapsed when an irate and inebriated customer showed up at their apartment waving a gun and demanding that they turn over their cash and their stash. Terrified, and now in a deep financial hole, Kelvin returned home, furious with himself but taking it out on his parents and blaming them for not covering his rent for a few more months while he tried to find a new job.

This naturally created a charged atmosphere, with Kelvin thrashing about, frantically trying to find a way to move out again, and his parents enraged at him now that they were on the hook not only for the last six months of his lease but also for the blown security deposit as a result of all of the festivity-related damage to the apartment.

FLOUNDERING

Floundering young adults have not yet summoned the capacity to embark on any kind of leave-taking and remain developmentally marooned—frustrated and simultaneously frustrating their parents with their perplexing state of suspended animation. They remain adolescent in their behavior and outlook and, because of this, elicit the kind of parenting that adolescents require, leading to a strained climate that ignites high-octane clashes because their parents, for the most part, no longer *want* to raise an adolescent, and the floundering young adult is, for the most part, tired of being *treated* like an adolescent.

Twenty-year-old Kirby has been hospitalized twice in the last year, diagnosed with bipolar illness that has probably been exacerbated by his frequent use of a variety of drugs, including pot, mushrooms, and LSD. He has made several efforts at college but cannot sustain his focus long enough to complete any classes. He recently joined a fundamentalist church and has spent much time trying to convince his parents that they will be going to hell because they are not religiously observant. Kirby writes long memoranda to them, attempting to persuade them to join him at his church, and tries to embroil them in endless theological arguments. Meanwhile, he has no job, nor is he making any effort to find one, and he has made some of the neighbors uncomfortable by sitting on the roof of his house reading in his underwear. His father, from time to time, will lose his temper and kick him out, but because he has nowhere to go, Kirby returns, usually within a day or two. Kirby's parents always relent and allow him back in because of their concerns that he'll endanger himself and "wind up dead in a gutter somewhere."

DRIFTING

Drifting young adults are similar to floundering young adults except that they have few internal or external resources at their disposal. They may not have functional or available parents, or, if they do, their parents tend to be overwhelmed by their own concerns, by the task of simply surviving.

Twenty-one-year-old Jesse, born a crack baby, was placed into foster care by social services on his second birthday because of his mother's inability to conquer her addiction and her resultant neglect of him. Several of his foster homes were warm and caring, but a couple of them weren't, and there was evidence that he was sexually abused in one of them. Now he has aged out of the foster care system, and there is no safety net in place for him. He is severely learning disabled and barely made it through high school. One of his previous foster fathers got him a job on a road crew, but he was fired within a month for being chronically late. He has no home and wafts from friend's apartment to friend's apartment, sleeping on couches and scouring restaurant and grocery store dumpsters for food at night.

These six categories, like any categories that attempt to classify people, cannot be rigidly defined or belonged to, and it's certainly possible that a young adult will inhabit one or more of them at various points in development or will do some straddling of or migrating back and forth between two or more of them. But it is important to keep them in mind as we conceptualize a treatment approach for the range of young adults and families who will be consulting with us for treatment.

Chapter 2

Family Loss at the Launching Stage

And when, solemnly, the evening
From the black oaks falls,
The voice of our despair,
The nightingale, will sing.

Paul Verlaine, *Muted*

Bruce Springsteen's song "Independence Day" tells the story of a young man leaving home and the mourning brought about as both son and father come to grips with the irreversible changes that are faced when separation is embarked upon. At the beginning, there is great defiance in the narrator's words—"Well, Papa go to bed now, it's getting late, Nothing we can say is gonna change anything now . . . They ain't gonna do to me what I watched them do to you." But as the song concludes, there is a bittersweet mixture of empathy and sadness as the son makes the decision to move on—"Papa, now I know the things you wanted that you could not say, But won't you just say goodbye, it's Independence Day? I swear I never meant to take those things away."

Life is a series of lessons in the art of loss. Unless we embrace loss and understand its inevitability and necessity, we are unable to live our lives fully. When young adults and their families are struggling with separating from each other, it is most likely because they are having difficulty coming to terms with what they are losing, no matter what the specific content and nature of their struggles may be.

There is much to be gained for both generations when children leave home, but to reap the benefits of those gains, parents and children have to acknowledge what is being lost. It is the never-ending current of losing that keeps us alive and allows us to experience and discover ourselves and others.

Loss can lead to growth when we come to realize that we may be stronger than we thought and, as a result, better able to survive life's relentless slings and arrows. And when we lose, we create room for something new and different. But even though it may renew us, loss is permanent, and we are perpetually in the position of having to mourn for that which we have lost. Nothing is capable of completely fortifying parents against the loss of their children, against all of the associated and irreducible feelings of vulnerability and sadness.

The loss embedded in separation is profoundly experienced by both generations, which is why I refer to the launching stage as a veritable "feast of losses." For parents, each child strikes a unique chord that resounds in the capacious chambers of their hearts—a chord that will not and cannot be created by anyone else. When children leave, parents are left with the echoes of that chord, echoes that dampen and diminish with each passing year, but echoes that mothers and fathers desperately want to prevent from disappearing completely into silence. As Stephen Sondheim wrote in "Into the Woods," "Children must grow from something you love into something you lose."

Launching means not only freedom from the responsibilities of day-to-day parenthood, it means that the home the parents have built has begun to dissolve around them and that they have to begin to erect a new kind of residence—one that can still be rich and full but that will never be enriched and filled in the same way as the one that was inhabited during the previous decades.

Parents feel wistful as they think back to the time when family life opened up like a vista in front of them, beckoning toward its endless possibilities. Early on, parenthood feels like it is forever, and it indeed does last forever, but, at a certain point, hands-on parenting is over. It is not just children who get homesick—parents can get homesick, too: sick with longing for the home that was once alive with children and all of their unstoppable forces and energies. The heartbreaking reality of being a parent is that it is basically temp work.

When parents are grieving for the departure of their child, they are grieving not just for the child whom they loved and who is leaving but for the part of them that loved that child, because it is the part of us that we love the most that takes the risk of most passionately loving another. Parents want to linger around all that reminds them of their children, attempting to hold on to them and to what they symbolize and have meant, because it is so painful to lose them.

One of the words for home is *dwelling*, from the word *dwell*, which means "to remain for a time." Built into the word is the sense of impermanence, of tarrying, lingering, delaying. Children cannot remain at home forever, and even if they are destined to return home at some point, that return can only be a successful one if the young adult has spent some time venturing forth as a result of having *left* that home.

I was working with a father whose youngest child had recently left for college, an event that was prompting him to reevaluate his life and the decisions he had made. At one point he said, "I guess I've got some real questions about the life I've been leaving," and then quickly corrected himself: "I mean, the life I've been *leading*." But there was obviously great truth to his slip—at this juncture, it's not only about the life that one is leading but also about the life that one must ultimately prepare to *leave*.

I often hear parents express their frustration with a struggling young adult child by exasperatedly admitting, "I'm at a loss." To my way of thinking, there is a sparkling precision to these words, and they point unerringly to what the underlying nature of the struggle may be. Many other parents have told me that they are tired of their young adult "giving me grief." Again, the choice of words is unmistakably true.

The family therapist must always keep foremost in his mind that parents' capacity to come to terms with the losses that accompany their children's growth and departure provides the compass that helps the intergenerational family to productively make their way into the next stage of their lives.

For the young adult, loss at the launching stage has to do with the loss of childhood, what she has to *give* up to *grow* up. While there is much that awaits her as she crosses the threshold that divides adolescence and adulthood—freedom, independence, possibility—there is also much that must be left behind.

No stage in the coming years will ever feel the same as it did when he was a child. No matter how privileged or underprivileged he may have been, he will never be *given* as much, and *excused* from as much, as he was during childhood. Adulthood requires him to say good-bye to being on the receiving end and to begin taking on the responsibilities for providing—at first for himself and, eventually, for others as well. There is a canopy that shades him during childhood and adolescence, but becoming an adult means traveling out from under that canopy and more directly encountering the cut and thrust of life, its beating sun one day and its driving rain the next.

A 20-year-old patient of mine who had made slow but steady progress recovering from a psychotic break and several subsequent psychiatric hospitalizations decided to have the words "no more pain" tattooed on his chest. As we talked about this etymological emblem he told me that he felt that much of what he had recently experienced was a result of his inability to come to terms with the end of his childhood; he was hoping that now that he was moving into the open spaces of adulthood, he would not have to experience that kind of pain again.

It is interesting to me that many of the struggling young adults whom I treat refer to themselves as losers (often using their extended thumb and index finger to make a symbolic L on their forehead that visually signifies their belief). While they may, at one level, be referring to loser in the sense of "losing at the game of life" (such as still living at home or still unemployed or still chemically dependent), I tend to hear it at another level—loser in the sense of losing something very important, some aspect of their identity that is hard to let go of. And the inability to let go and move on invariably stymies growth.

Helping our patients to recognize that mourning for the loss of a *stage* of life, not just for the loss of a human life, is a necessary aspect of growing and changing is one of our primary clinical tasks, yet too few of us do it. And this is not surprising—our culture as a whole seems to work hard to deny death in any form, be it physical or developmental, and we tirelessly emphasize achievement, accomplishment, competition, materialism, and consumerism over acknowledging the complex and painful relationship between the finality of death and the continuity of life. We do not naturally speak the language of grief.

In my work, I attempt to help families understand what I refer to as "healthy developmental grief," since it is sometimes counterintuitive for them to appreciate the fact that the process of mourning has healing and growth-promoting properties, even when everyone in the family remains very much alive.

The components of healthy developmental grief are as follows:

1   **Acknowledging** who/what has been lost
2   **Appreciating** who/what has been lost
3   **Recognizing** the mixed emotions that are aroused by loss
4   **Reciprocally** sharing these emotions with others, both in and out of the family
5   **Envisioning** the new possibilities that this loss has made possible
6   **Evolving**—moving on to explore those possibilities with what you have and becoming able to leave behind what you can't keep
7   **Honoring** who/what has been lost by moving on together as individuals, and as a family

When I am taking care of families at this developmental juncture, I classify them, in my head, in one of three categories when it comes to their capacity to mourn:

- Active grievers
- Reluctant grievers
- Avoidant grievers

Active grievers are families who recognize the authority of loss and who understand that grieving for loss is a natural and essential part of growth—they address it candidly, both within themselves and within the family. I describe them as being willing to "make the time to think about time," as being keenly aware of evanescence, of impermanence, of time's passing. My mother tells me with great fondness that her grandmother had a tender phrase as she anticipated the departure of a family member—"I miss you already." Embedded in this phrase is active grieving, the awareness that even when we bask in the shimmering light of a loved one's presence, there is still the perception of a shadow that will at some point darken our lives.

Reluctant grievers are families who acknowledge the reality of loss and the importance of grief but who have difficulty thinking about it and talking about it. They pay lip service to the reality that time is marching on but drag their heels as they begrudgingly join the march.

Avoidant grievers are families who work assiduously to diminish or demolish the reality of loss and do anything they can to prevent it. They work strenuously to either turn back the clock or to keep everyone petrified (in both senses of that word), reasoning that, "If we don't proceed with our journey, time will stand still, no one will ever have to leave, and loss will never have to be experienced."

We will usually find that it is the reluctant grievers and the avoidant grievers who need to consult with us, because their reluctance or avoidance comes at great expense to their development. They require assistance taking on their grief and allowing it to carry them forward. When grief is hindered, growth is hindered, and at this point a family member—usually one of the dutiful children—will be invited to call attention to the unaddressed grief, which usually involves creating a quiet or loud disturbance of one sort or another.

I thought of the importance of grieving a few years ago when I was going through a phase of frequently straining my hamstring muscle when I ran. I would impatiently take a few days off and then go back to running, and, within another few days, strain it again. I eventually consulted with a friend of mine, Diane, who is a physical therapist and who forbearingly explained to me that while the days of rest were giving the muscle a chance to heal, it was simply healing back to its original, tightened state and thus remained highly vulnerable to reinjury. If I started stretching the muscle more regularly, however, then it would remain more supple and be less likely to go into spasm.

Grieving is a form of psychological stretching; it not only enables us to recover from pain but makes us more supple and less prone to experiencing psychological reinjury.

Many parallels exist between loss that comes about as a result of death and loss that comes about as a result of growth. Both kinds of loss, for example, tend to serve as a catalyst for other changes as individuals and families reorganize and realign themselves in the face of bereavement—changes that may or may not be in the family's best interest.

And, of course, there are many ways in which both kinds of loss coincide and influence each other. As each child leaves home, other leave-takings from the parents' recent or distant past are accentuated, some of which may have been expected and welcomed and some that may have been unexpected and unwelcomed.

Not atypically, for example, parents are contending with the recent or impending death of one of their own parents as one or more of their children are beginning the process of leaving home. The co-occurrence of the two losses may emotionally overwhelm a parent and prompt him or her to cling too tightly to either the older or the younger generational partner. In many families, the departure of a child coincides with the death of a beloved family pet that is strongly associated with that child.

These kinds of synergistic losses do not have to chronologically coincide to exert their power. For instance, a child is often conceived or adopted by a parent partially in an effort to replace a deceased family member and thereby forestall or prevent an acknowledgment of the loved one's demise and the need to mourn. If that mourning never takes place and the child continues to serve a replacement function within the family system, his leave-taking will likely be a problematic one, since it will not only invoke pain and grief in the present but reinvoke the unresolved pain and grief from the past.

For example, 20-year-old Natan was conceived two months after his father's father, Nechama, died—in fact, he was named for his grandfather. Natan's father, Yoel, had a very conflicted relationship with his father, and there was much that was unspoken between the two of them when Nechama suddenly passed of a cerebral hemorrhage at the age of 57. I learned that Yoel never addressed the mixture of feelings that he experienced upon the death of his father and simply went about "trying to be a better father to Natan than my father was to me, which wasn't particularly hard to do, since my father was not a very good father—he had a mean streak and made sure that everyone knew it and felt it."

But the fact that Yoel had never grieved for his father made it very difficult for him to tolerate Natan's departure years later. Because Natan seemed to be playing a stand-in role for his grandfather, and because Yoel had never grieved for his father, he had a difficult time tolerating his son's departure. It was as if he knew down deep that Natan's leave-taking would tear the scab off of his unaddressed feelings about his father and his father's premature leave-taking, so he did little to support his son in his efforts to leave. He conspicuously shifted from being the supportive father that he had been during Natan's childhood and early adolescence to the demeaning, disparaging father his own father had been, constantly putting Natan down and scolding him for his inability to move forward with his life. It was as if Yoel had brought his father back to life by imitating his captious caregiving and kept his father close by chopping away at his son's initiative, ensuring that Natan, his father's impersonator—wouldn't leave.

And Natan, unconsciously obeying his father's wishes, remained in a holding pattern by becoming his own worst enemy, getting jobs and then losing them, starting school and then withdrawing, spending himself into constant debt. Yoel's father had "left home" too soon, while Natan, it appeared, was making it clear that he wasn't going to leave home at all.

It was only when I made some time to speak with Yoel about his own father's premature departure, and when he began to more directly address his relationship with his father, that Natan slowly began to shed the skin of adolescence and move more confidently toward separation. Released from psychic captivity, and sensing that his father had finished some unfinished business, Natan finally felt free to unfurl his sails and voyage out to sea.

The family therapist working with families at the launching stage needs to help parents understand that they are supposed to be in pain—that they are in pain because they are grieving, that they are grieving because they loved, and that a life without love is an empty life, indeed. It is when we are offering love that we are most fully human, but also that we are most vulnerable. We want parents to learn to envision the feelings of sorrow and loss at this phase of the life cycle as a testament to the closeness and attachment that they have nurtured and enjoyed with their children over the years and as a way to reorganize the family into more serviceable patterns of closeness and attachment. We all must travel the tragic arc of life, which can be agonizing, but it is better than the alternative, which is not to travel it at all.

Death is always our lifelong companion, but mortality always becomes more of a presence when children grow and leave and when parents are forced to realize that time moves in one direction only, ferrying everyone forward in its relentless tides. One of my patients once happily commented that "The end is in sight," as he discussed the payment he had just made on his youngest child's junior-year college tuition. Then he paused and said, poignantly, "But I guess that means that The End is in sight, too—you know, The *End*."

Yet while parents need to acknowledge time, they also need to remember that prematurely surrendering to inertia and resignation is unwise, that there is always a future that awaits, even if that future is increasingly foreshortened. As Martin Heidegger wrote, "If I take death into my life, acknowledge it, and face it squarely, I will free myself from the anxiety of death and the pettiness of life—and only then will I be free to become myself."

We also must be attentive to cultural issues when we help families to understand and grieve their losses. Every culture—whether it pertains to family, religion, ethnic group, or community—provides guidelines and rituals for how to behave, how to cope, how to adapt, and how to grow in the face of loss. Clinicians must be respectful of cultural influences and not make the assumption that the family is adapting poorly because they are responding to loss in a way that is not familiar or recognizable to them (McGoldrick and Hardy, 2008). Just as every individual grieves in his or her own unique way, so, too, does every culture grieve in its own unique way.

Our inquiry into a family's culturally prescribed traditions for managing loss can sometimes spur their new or renewed interest in these traditions, which may in turn help them to respond to loss in a more effective, active way.

We have been talking mostly about what I am calling developmental loss, but, as I noted, there will obviously be times in a family's life cycle when a deeper, more permanent loss, a loss through death, comes into play, too. The prospect (and actuality) of a parent's death can accelerate or delay a young adult's decision-making, urging the child to move ahead or to stay behind, in ways that he or she might not otherwise have done. Let's conclude this chapter by examining two case studies in which the impending loss of a parent bore down on a young adult's relational journey with an intimate partner.

Twenty-five-year-old Danielle and 26-year-old Andrew contacted me because they were struggling with marital conflict as they approached their first wedding anniversary. Danielle felt that Andrew had lost interest in her, both sexually and emotionally, over the course of the last several months, while Andrew felt that

Danielle was "never satisfied, no matter what I do, she'll always find what's wrong, what's missing."

I learned that they met in college and dated for several years prior to getting engaged. It was also notable that Danielle's mother, Louise, had died six months ago of pancreatic cancer, having been diagnosed a year before she died. When I was asking Danielle about the impact that her mother's illness and death had exerted on her, she admitted at one point that she had pushed herself and Andrew to solidify their relationship because she wanted her mother to be alive for her wedding.

"I'm the oldest, and the only daughter in our family, so this was really going to be my mother's only chance to see one of her children get married. She had saved her wedding dress for me, and I really wanted her to see me wear it."

"Do you think you would've decided to get married when you did if your mom had not been dying?" I asked.

Danielle stared down at the floor, her cheeks reddening, then glanced at Andrew before proceeding: "I honestly don't know. I mean, I kind of envisioned a future with Andrew as soon as we met, and we had a great thing going. So I guess so . . . I guess the answer is yes." She did not sound entirely convincing to me.

"How about you, Andrew?" I asked. "Do you think the two of you would be married if Danielle's mom were still alive?"

Andrew squirmed in his seat and turned to his wife. "Look, Danielle, you know I had my doubts about this. Not about *you*, but about marriage. I felt like we were rushing it, and I just wasn't sure."

"But you were *never* going to be sure, Andrew . . . whenever we would talk about marriage you would hem and haw."

"We didn't even *start* talking about marriage until your mom was diagnosed, Danielle. I mean, yeah, we would talk about it, but kind of just for fun, not really making plans. But right after your mom was diagnosed, you started pushing us to get engaged . . . and then when we got engaged, you started pushing for a marriage date."

"My mom was going to *die*, Andrew, you knew that!"

"Of course I know that, Danielle. I felt terrible. I loved your mom, too, I thought she was great. She was more of a mom to me than my *own* mom, I can tell you that! And that's why I went along with it, because I knew how hard this was for you; I didn't want to say no."

"So you didn't want to marry me?" Danielle's eyes were filling with tears as she looked at him pleadingly.

"No, no, that's not it, Danielle. Like you said, I kind of figured we might get married at some point, it was just a matter of timing."

"Might?! We *might* get married?! Oh, this was a big mistake; we *never* should've gotten married!"

"Danielle, you're missing my point! I'm not saying I don't love you; all I'm saying is that we rushed things along and maybe moved a little too quickly. It's not like I was interested in anyone else. But think about it, one day your mom has cancer, the next day we're talking about engagement, two months later we move in together, and six months later we're married. It's all been so fast, and I've gone along with it because I care for you, but it's like we jumped onto a speeding train and neither of us checked to see if it was the right one."

"So you're on the wrong train?! Then get off! Get off the fucking train if you don't want to be on it!"

"I want to be on it, Danielle . . . I just didn't think it would be moving this quickly," Andrew said, almost to himself. Danielle shot him a lethal glare.

"How did you attempt to convey your doubts and concerns to Danielle about moving so quickly?" I asked Andrew.

"That's a good question. I think I was afraid to. I could see how upset she was about her mom. And I really *do* love her. I've never met anyone like her, anyone who really *gets* me like she does."

"So what would happen when you tried to bring it up?"

"I guess I pulled my punches a little too much. I never really took a strong stand on this." He paused for a moment, looking uncomfortable and swallowing hard. "Look, there's another piece of this. I kind of screwed around on Danielle early in our relationship."

"*Kind* of?" Danielle wondered, sarcastically, supplying him with another murderous look.

"What was the nature of your screwing around?" I inquired.

"I was still getting together with my previous girlfriend when I started seeing Danielle. We'd hook up from time to time. I shouldn't have been doing that, and, of course, Danielle found out, and it was a big mess."

"It *sure* was," Danielle added, crossly.

"And I put it behind me, but I felt very guilty about having cheated on Danielle."

"So did that make it hard to put your foot down when it came to making wedding plans?"

"Yeah, it did. I mean, I didn't feel like I had a leg to stand on. I'd already betrayed her once, and it felt like it would be another kind of betrayal if I said that I wasn't ready to move ahead with our relationship. She forgave me for cheating on her, but if her mom died before seeing her get married . . ." His voice trailed off.

"Perhaps it might have felt like you were cheating her again?" I suggested.

"Exactly. Exactly. I had already cheated on her once, so it felt like I was cheating her, and her mother, as well, if I held back. It was like a no-win situation." He turned to Danielle, his own eyes now moist: "I'm so sorry about this, I really am."

"I know, Andrew, I know." Danielle seemed to have softened her stance.

Andrew's acknowledgment of the roots of his ambivalence began to break the impasse that they were in the midst of. While Danielle wasn't happy to hear that part of Andrew's motivation to go ahead with the marriage was spurred more by guilt about their past than by excitement about their future, it helped her to understand Andrew better. This, in turn, helped her to be more honest about her own ambivalence.

"Danielle, what was going through your head as you thought about your mom's illness and your relationship with Andrew?"

"It all hit me like a ton of bricks, really. My mom and I were very close—I think I told you, I'm the only daughter. And she'd always been a big part of my life. I mean, we had our fights and everything, and she could be impossible. But she was my mom! And she had basically been healthy! So this completely came out of the blue and was devastating. I mean, I know I'm lucky to have had her as long as I had her, but . . ."

"But it still would've been nice to continue having her," I offered, "particularly as you were moving ahead with your life. She must have been very proud of you."

Danielle began crying. "Why did she have to die? Why did she have to die? She's my mom, why did she have to die?"

Andrew reached out to touch her shoulder, as she continued weeping for several minutes.

"I miss her. I miss her terribly," Danielle admitted, as she dried her eyes. "I wish she were here."

"You only get one mom," I acknowledged. "I don't care *how* old you are when she dies, you still only get one mom, and no one will ever replace her."

"She had been there for everything in my life—parties, dance recitals, graduations, everything! I just felt that she should be there for my wedding."

"Tell me about the wedding."

She brightened and smiled. "Oh, it was wonderful. I mean, she was struggling through chemo at the time, and we kind of knew by then that it was terminal, that she wasn't going to live for very long. But her doctors timed her chemo so that she would be in between treatments and she was actually feeling pretty decent that day. It was an outdoor wedding at the house of some family friends who live in the mountains. And she looked beautiful."

"And did you wear her dress?"

Danielle began to cry again. "Yes, yes, I wore her dress. I wore it. And I loved it. I loved wearing it."

I turned to Andrew. "And how did Danielle look in her wedding dress?"

He smiled at her. "She looked stunning. Absolutely stunning. Like a model." Then he began to cry, too. "Oh, Danielle, so much has happened here. It's all so much."

She reached out for him and they embraced silently, both tearful. Then they both turned back to me.

"Danielle, I'm going to ask you the same question I asked you a little earlier, but I want you to take your time answering it. Was there any part of you that felt, like Andrew did, that things between the two of you were moving a little too quickly?"

She hesitated, then blurted out, "Honestly, yes. I think I went into a panic when I realized that she was going to die. I couldn't believe I was going to lose her. And I just thought, 'the best thing I can do for her—the *only* thing I can do for her—is to make sure she's at my wedding.' That was my first thought."

"And how about second thoughts?"

"Oh, second thoughts, second thoughts. I had a feeling you were going to ask me about that," she acknowledged, with a wry grin. "Of course I had them. I knew I was pushing us ahead, but inside, I knew this was not exactly what I had in mind. Like I said, I always envisioned a future with Andrew, but I really wasn't planning on getting married at 23 years old. That's even earlier than my parents were when *they* got married!"

"If your mom were healthy and alive, how do you think your life would be different?"

"That's a good question. I've thought about that. I'm not sure." She suddenly seemed reluctant to go further.

"Do you think you would've gotten engaged and be married?"

Andrew leaned toward her. She took a deep breath and sighed. "Honestly? No . . . no, this isn't what I had planned."

Andrew seemed to relax, as did Danielle.

"What's it like to acknowledge that?"

"It's painful. And it's scary. Because now I'm wondering if the whole thing was a mistake. That we did this for my mom, not for us."

"The reality, Danielle, is that there's no perfect moment to get married, or to have children, or to buy a house, or to embark on any important life passage. These things always seem to happen too soon or too late, and rarely do two people completely agree that it's the right time. But the thing is, the timing of a decision tends to have little to do with how that decision plays out, since our timing can never be impeccable, anyway.

"I have worked with couples who married precipitously who turned out to have successful marriages, and I have worked with couples who took their time and waited until everything felt just right, and their marriage turned out to be deeply unsatisfying. The key to a lasting marriage doesn't lie in the timing of your wedding day; the key to a lasting marriage is how you *behave* in your marriage— how you talk to each other, how you hold each other, how you share your love and respect for each other. And that's what we have to work on here."

It was important for this young couple to recognize the tremendous pressure that both of them had been under and the mixed feelings that both of them had been harboring and hesitant to share with each other. They had been forced by life events to rocket their relationship forward much more quickly than either had anticipated. Danielle naturally wanted to obtain a lifelong commitment from Andrew as she was preparing for the end of her mother's life. And Andrew, as a result of his guilt for the violation of trust, as well as out of his love for Danielle, hadn't expressed his reservations clearly and hadn't actively tried to slow things down. It was no wonder that their relationship felt so shaky at this point, one year into their somewhat premature marriage, but they had begun the hard work of repairing and improving it.

Another couple that I was treating was in a similar situation but presented with a different dilemma. Twenty-five-year-old Avery was gay and had come out to many of his friends during his college years but had never done so with his parents. He did not believe that his mother would have difficulty with his being gay, but he was convinced that his father would be terribly upset. After several years of unsatisfying relationships, he had fallen in love with 32-year-old Chonglin, and they had now been together for more than a year. Chonglin had recently introduced Avery to his mother, whom he had come out to years before, and felt that Avery should reciprocate by inviting him to meet his (Avery's) parents, but Avery was reluctant to do so, for fear of his father's reaction.

As it turns out, Avery's father had been diagnosed with a rare and incurable blood disorder with a low survival rate. He had been told by his doctors that the disease was likely to end his life, but at this point there was no way to determine how long he would live—he could decline quickly in a few short months at any point, but he could also live for another several years with reasonably good health. And there was always the possibility, his doctors had said, that current research would yield, if not a cure, then perhaps some sort of maintenance regimen that could extend his life even further.

Avery told me that he had given this matter careful contemplation and decided that he wasn't going to come out to his parents, although he would consider coming out to his mom once his father died. This decision was not acceptable to Chonglin, who felt that he had been very patient but was tired of waiting.

"I spent a long time living in the closet, Avery, and I feel like you're still keeping me there by not allowing me to meet your parents."

"And I don't think you should be forcing this issue, Chonglin. Can't we just wait and see what happens with my dad? We might not even have to make a decision at all—I mean, I hate to say this, but he could die very quickly. And then I promise you that I will introduce you to my mom."

"Please don't throw me that bone, Avery. Look, I know this is hard for you, your dad being sick. And I know he could die anytime. But 'anytime' apparently could be five years from now . . . or even longer! Are you saying that we're going to have to wait *years* to come out as a couple to your family? That we would have to wait until your dad dies for us to get married?"

"Several years is an outside chance, Chonglin—let's not get carried away here, it's really not likely he'll live that long."

"But it could be . . . and anyway, call it three years . . . call it *one* year, for all I care . . . I just don't see why we have to wait at all. You're 25 years old, we want to get married, we want to adopt children. Exactly how long are we going to have to keep things secret from your family? I'm already past 30."

"I just don't think this is your decision, Chonglin; I think it's mine."

"Of course it's your decision. But that doesn't mean I have to be happy about it, Avery. In fact, as I've said repeatedly, I'm very *un*happy about it. You're acting like a little kid, afraid of your daddy being angry with you. Don't you think it's time for you to grow up?"

"Oh, come on, Chonglin, I don't need your evaluation of my maturity. This is *my* family, not yours . . . *I'm* the one who's going to have to deal with my dad, not you. So why don't you just let up already!"

"I would let up if you would just agree to invite me to your parents' house for dinner. That's all I'm asking. We don't have to say anything about our relationship. We don't have to say anything about getting married or starting a family one day. We don't have to do anything but have a nice dinner."

"Oh, sure, that'll work just fine. Like my parents won't know what's going on? Like they won't put two and two together? My dad has been wondering for years why I don't have a girlfriend, why I don't date, wondering if I'm lonely. So this so-called casual dinner is going to seal the deal for him—believe me, he's going to connect the dots."

"And so what if it does? So what if he realizes you're gay, that we're together, that we're a couple? So *what*?"

"I just don't want to put him through it. He's already dealing with his illness; I don't want to give him something else to deal with."

"So being gay is like having an illness? Now you sound like one of those homophobic psychiatrists from the 1950s."

"Ha ha, very funny. You know what I mean, Chonglin. This could upset him."

"Sounds like it's going to upset *you* more than him."

"Well, it will . . . I mean if he's upset with me, I'll be upset. Look, my dad and I have had our ups and downs but he's still my father, and we don't know how much time he's going to have on this earth. I'd just as soon keep our relationship with each other as decent and pleasant as it has been, and not do anything to rock the boat. We worked pretty hard to get it to this point, I don't want to disrupt anything. Certainly not unnecessarily . . ."

"It's unnecessary to *you*, I guess, but not to *me*." Chonglin sat back in his chair, sullenly folding his arms, and at this point I jumped in.

"Avery, as you know, not everybody who is gay comes out, and not everyone who comes out, comes out to everyone. So you are correct, it's entirely up to you whether or not you come out to your father, although it sounds safe to acknowledge that your decision is causing some tension in your relationship with Chonglin. With this in mind, what *are* your concerns regarding coming out to your father?"

"Look, my dad is a salt of the earth kind of guy. He's a good person, a caring person, but he's just not that open-minded, and he never has been. I'm not saying he's a gay-basher or anything, but I know from what I've heard him say that he's not comfortable with gays—certainly not with his *son* being gay. My younger brother is straight, he's had a steady girlfriend for a while now, and my dad really likes her, he's always very excited when the two of them visit. *That's* what he has in mind for me, not *this*," he said, gesturing at Chonglin, who rolled his eyes and sighed.

"You mentioned what it would be like for you, and for your dad, for him to go his grave knowing that you were gay. But you didn't mention what it would be like for him to go to his grave not really knowing you, and not knowing how happy you were with Chonglin."

"Being with Chonglin isn't going to make my dad happy, I can assure you of that."

"But knowing that you're finally in love with someone probably *would* make him happy, correct?"

Avery bit his lip, then slowly nodded. "Yes, I guess it would."

"I understand your hesitation to bring this up with your dad, and I'm not saying that you should, or that you shouldn't. There are certainly risks to telling your father that you are gay—it could upset him terribly, it could disrupt your relationship with him entirely. But there are also risks to *not* telling your father."

"What are those risks?" Avery asked.

"Well, you might feel tremendous regret if your father dies without having had the opportunity to meet Chonglin, without his having gotten to know the person who might become his oldest son's lifelong partner. You have seen how much he enjoys your brother's girlfriend and their relationship with each other—perhaps he also deserves a chance to see *your* boyfriend and your relationship with each other."

Avery sat quietly, Chonglin staring at him intently.

"My dad isn't going to go for this," he finally suggested.

"How about your mom?"

"I think she's kind of in a different place than he is. She's a little more on the liberal side of things. He's retired military, an airline mechanic, he works at an army base all day. You know, 'don't ask, don't tell, don't wanna know, will be unhappy if I *do* know' . . . that sort of thing. My mom, she's a librarian and runs with a different crowd, you might say."

"I suppose another option for you to consider would be to disclose this to your mom first, being that you have the sense that she wouldn't be either surprised or disapproving. Then you could ask her what *she* thinks about telling your dad. After all, her opinion should have some weight here. She might really prefer that you *not* tell him if she believes it's going to be very upsetting for him and if she also believes that *she's* the one who's going to have to talk him off the ledge, so to speak.

"On the flip side, she might really prefer that you *do* tell him—she probably has insight into his thoughts about this that exceed yours, and, as we were discussing a moment ago, you don't want to unfairly deprive him of news about something very good and important that is going on in your life. Because, as you know, once he dies, there's no way for you to fill him in. That's what makes this so complicated."

"Avery, you should think about this. I think that's a good idea," Chonglin advised, sounding calmer.

Avery agreed to do so, and he and Chonglin returned a couple of weeks later.

"Well, you were right," he began.

I nodded (even though I wasn't exactly sure what I had been right about): "Tell me . . ."

"I gave it some thought and decided to tell my mom. And it was a very pleasant surprise, because not only did she have the sense that I was gay—and I kind of suspected that she knew—but she said that she and my dad have been talking about this for a while, and she didn't think he'd be surprised, either.

"So then I asked her if he'd be upset, and she said she didn't think so. That when they had first begun realizing this, which was back when I was in college, he had a very difficult time, but she had brought some books home from the library and he had actually done some reading on it. This was several years ago!" he observed, shaking his head in disbelief. "Here I thought I was keeping them in the dark, and they weren't in the dark at all."

"I suppose it's unwise to underestimate one's parents," I commented playfully.

"Yeah, I guess you're right. Anyway, I went ahead and told my dad, and he reacted the way my mom said that he would. He told me that he already had a sense of that, that he had gotten past whatever homophobia he may have had, and that he was mostly worried that I would never find a suitable partner.

"So that was the perfect segue into my telling him about Chonglin and the idea of inviting him over to meet them. So we're going to get together in a couple of weeks so that they can meet him."

"Did your dad have anything else to say?"

"Yeah, he said that he hoped that his being sick hadn't kept me from telling him about this. He didn't want his illness to make things any harder for me."

"So in some ways, you gave him a gift by coming out, and by telling him about Chonglin."

"How so?"

"Well, it sounds like he was feeling guilty that his illness was somehow inhibiting you, or holding you back. But by telling him what you told him, you were also telling him that you were going to live your life the way you wanted to even if he's not going to be able to live his life as *long* as he wanted to."

Chonglin hadn't said anything up until this point, but he was smiling broadly, so I asked him what he was thinking about this turn of events.

"I couldn't be happier. I'm very proud of you, Avery. I know this was a big thing for you to do. And I really appreciate your taking the risk of telling them."

With this young adult, the prospect of a parent's death at first inhibited an important (albeit not essential) developmental step, the act of coming out to his parents. As we explored this matter, though, it turned out that his father's illness actually encouraged him to consider taking this step, and, ultimately, liberated him to do so.

Now that we have laid the groundwork for examining separation by exploring the losses that are an inherent part of that separation, we can continue with the process of creating a clinical scaffolding that will promote multigenerational family growth during young adulthood.

Chapter 3

Beginning Treatment at the Launching Stage

Families typically consult with a therapist at a time of developmental crisis. The crisis may be a sudden one, appearing to have arrived out of the blue without any observable precursors. The crisis may be one that has been building over recent months or even a year or two. It may have been existing in aqueous form, ebbing and flowing for a substantial period of time and finally reaching critical mass. Or it may be a crisis that has been solidly in place for quite some time—many years, perhaps even *generations*—and, in this regard, might be better described as an on-going siege or blockade rather than a crisis.

No matter what form they take, family crises usually have something to do with the difficulties entailed with navigating through change—their inability to facilitate change that one or more of them would like to witness or experience, their inability to adapt to change that is thrust upon them, or their inability to prevent an unwanted change from taking place at all. As a bumper sticker I came across mordantly announced, "Shift Happens."

Crises will generally take place at certain nodal points in the family's development. Most of these nodal points are acknowledged as rites of passage that the family is able to celebrate, honor, or commemorate in some meaningful, healthy, and growth-promoting way—births, deaths, birthdays, graduations, and anniversaries and, of course, the various milestones and accomplishments in human development, often defined by a growing child's "firsts": the first smile, the first word, the first lost tooth, the first day of school, the first paycheck.

However, every family, due to its unique and idiosyncratic vulnerabilities, experiences certain nodal points, certain rites of passage, as challenges to their functioning, and if those challenges are not met successfully, that is when they may ripen into family crises.

For example, a daughter's 18th birthday is a source of joy for one mother but a source of pain for another, who turned 18 the year that her own mother died from breast cancer. This mother, Julie, has no choice but to wonder if the tragedy of a mother dying prematurely as her own daughter, Chloe, turns 18 is somehow going to be replicated for another generation, and so it becomes toilsome for her to enjoy Chloe's springtime birthday celebration. She becomes overly preoccupied with that nagging pain in her chest that has been coming and going for the last several months and concludes that what had been diagnosed as reflux is probably an incipient heart attack.

Julie commences a series of medical consultations with specialists, which makes her even more anxious, as various possibilities are tested and considered. Chloe, looking forward to her prom, her high school graduation, and going shopping with her mother for dorm room supplies as she anticipates freshman year at college, becomes increasingly annoyed with her mother's distractibility and distance. As a result, she starts spending more time with her 17-year-old boyfriend, Calvin, who is excited about this development because he is afraid that their relationship is going to end when Chloe goes off to college and he remains behind in high school.

Meanwhile, Julie's husband, Sid, has had a bad year in his insurance business and is fretting about how he's going to pay for Chloe's first year of college. He wants to be able to talk to his wife about this but senses how anxious she is about her medical worries, so he holds back and tries to manage these worries by himself. He also is hesitant to talk to her as a result of the guilt he feels—one of the reasons that his business is not doing well is because of a decision he made to take on a partner, a decision that Julie had never approved of but that he had gone ahead with anyway. He does not want to admit to her that they're in financial straits because he is now paying this new and underfunctioning partner a salary that is draining the coffers of his business.

So it is difficult for him to celebrate Chloe's upcoming rite of passage, because all he can think about is that he won't be able to pay for the college that she worked so hard to get into. As a result, he not only pulls away from his wife, he pulls away from his daughter, who now has two preoccupied parents and a looming transition that they don't seem to be able to support her in negotiating.

This complicated choreography of three family members dancing away from each other continues until one day in July, a month after Chloe has graduated from high school and a month before she is due to depart for college, when she comes home and announces that she believes that she is pregnant. This naturally creates an uproar, and the family is suddenly in crisis mode. Of course, one of the things that Chloe has accomplished with this crisis even though, as it turns out, she was not pregnant is that she has, in one fell swoop, drawn the family back together. All of a sudden, Julie's medical worries and Sid's financial worries seem insignificant, as they all put their heads together and try to figure out what the next step is . . . and that is when they consulted with me.

No family, no matter how highly functioning, is completely immune to developmental crises. And some families, for various reasons, are crisis-prone and appear to experience almost every developmental event—small or profound—as a catastrophic crossroads.

The family therapist's initial responsibility is to explore the nature of the crisis and to begin the lay the groundwork for helping the family to understand it and to more effectively manage and resolve it. The central goal of FFT is to find a way to define the family's problem in a way that makes it both comprehensible and solvable for everyone in the family. When that has been accomplished, the family is generally more than halfway to where they want to go, but this can only be done systemically.

I do not rule out any intervention when it comes to child, adolescent, or young adult development—I would never want to deprive an individual of something that might be helpful—but I have found that unless these interventions are linked to systemic treatment, they tend to ultimately be ineffective.

There are many oars that we can put in the water to help young adults row themselves from the depths of dependence to the shores of autonomy. These oars can be anything from medication to acupuncture to tutoring to relaxation training—the list is endless. But unless the boat itself is in the water, those oars aren't going to row anyone very far. FFT is what sets the boat on the water so that whatever oars the young adult selects will be ones that can carry her forward.

With this in mind, here are some objectives to keep in mind during initial family therapy sessions.

CREATE SPACE

The family therapist must first work to create a small clearing in the heart of the family, or in the heart of at least one family member. That clearing can then become the theater in which a range of different realities are safely experienced and expressed by all. The consultation room becomes the temporary holding environment in which family members, with the help of the therapist, can see and hear each other differently, talk about complicated thoughts and feelings, and learn to accept and integrate them rather than renounce or dispute them.

Renowned music producer Brian Eno once commented that he sees a recording studio not as a place to simply record musicians in front of a microphone but instead as a place within which to create a new context, a new setting for the musicians so that they play and sound differently than they ever have before. This is an apt description of what we want to try to do with the families that we take care of, encouraging them, in this new setting, to play and sound differently.

This space has to paradoxically be safe enough to not only enter but also to leave. An important component of human development (which will be explored in more detail in a subsequent chapter) is coming to terms with the extent to which young adults are connected to the family and the extent to which they are free, or can be free, to *not* be connected with the family.

When, for example, a young adult patient walks out of a therapy session in a fury (and I have encountered this situation countless times), that should not necessarily be seen as a failure of the holding environment. It might just as easily be understood as the young adult's experimentation with an autonomous departure, one that may very well predict a more modulated and successful separation from the family down the road. Helping the parents and any other family members that remain in the room to see the storming out as a possibly cleansing storm rather than as a sign of immaturity raises the possibility that rage does not have to be the sole precursor to differentiation.

BEGIN WITH A BLAMELESS APPROACH

One of the best pieces of advice I received in my training, and one of the most frequent pieces of advice that I offer supervisees, is the dictum, "No one is to blame, but everyone is responsible." Families may be encouraging or sustaining the problem that they are complaining about, but that doesn't mean they believe that the problem is truly in their best interest; it's just that they have established a pattern that they cannot figure out how to stop, replace, or reconfigure.

So we need to make it clear that the crisis that brings them into treatment is not any one individual's fault; it's not simply because of laziness or selfishness on the part of the young adult, for example, or over- or underinvolvement on the parents' part. On the other hand, we need to emphasize that *every* family member is responsible in one way or another for contributing—intentionally or inadvertently—to the state of crisis, and when these contributions are elucidated and possibly modified, the crisis can more easily pass.

Not only is it accurate to emphasize that every family member has made a conscious or subconscious donation to the current crisis, but putting this out there sets the right tone, alleviating the demotivating feelings of helplessness, powerlessness, and futility that one or more family members may be troubled by and suggesting that that there is reason to be hopeful if an effective collaboration is embarked upon.

With some families and family members who have tended to absolve themselves of responsibility and point the finger at other individuals or institutions, the challenge for the therapist is to *augment* their sense of responsibility without inducing an unhelpful amount of guilt. These individuals and families devote themselves to getting others to change so that they are excused from the hard work of making changes themselves.

With other families and family members, the challenge for the therapist is to *reduce* their sense of responsibility. These individuals and families have convinced themselves that they're responsible not only for what they do but for what everyone else does as well.

Either way, our stance should be one of empowerment. There are rarely victims in families (although sometimes, unfortunately, that does happen)—usually, there are volunteers, recruits, and recruiters, with some family members performing more than one role.

We should also enunciate that progress will be the result of effort. Psychologist Carol Dweck's (2007) research focuses on the importance of attributing success in any endeavor to industry and discipline rather than to innate ability. Telling a child that she solved a difficult math problem quickly because she was smart actually diminishes the likelihood that she will persevere when she is eventually faced with a math problem that she cannot solve quite so rapidly. Instead, telling her that she solved it because she worked hard makes it more likely that she will put forth sustained application of her intellect when it comes to facing subsequent challenges, within and outside of the realm of math.

Likewise, making it clear that the results of therapy will depend on how hard everyone is willing to work together raises the likelihood that one or more family members will summon the strength necessary to break the chains that are holding them back.

ASSESS AND EMPHASIZE THE FAMILY'S STRENGTHS AND RESOURCES

Families do not consult with us unless they are feeling discouraged and disheartened, each generation unceasingly trying the other's patience. So it is of inestimably beneficial when they hear from a professional that there is much that they have done right over the years. This is most easily done by commenting on the strengths that the struggling young adult displays (or *has* displayed in the past) as well as asking into other crises that the family has dealt with and commending them for having at least survived, if not transcended, them.

When I am working with young adults and families who have been through terrible ordeals—for example, multiple hospitalizations or a significant prison term—I will at some point ask them how they were able to manage as well as they did and what kept them going through those very dark times. Even if the challenges have not been quite this traumatic, it is important for the young adult and his parents to hear how much we admire them for having seen their way through distress and tribulation:

"That you got through high school and have begun college despite having to deal with these learning disabilities is a remarkable accomplishment."

"How have the two of you managed to not lose hope or give up on him when it seems as if his drug habit is undefeatable?"

"I'm not sure it was necessarily best for you, or even necessary, to keep your bulimia hidden all of these years, but it shows great compassion on your part in regard to your desire to not worry your parents."

Amplifying the family's strengths for them during a vulnerable time raises the likelihood that they will marshal these strengths and rise to the challenge of growth.

PLACE EVENTS IN A DEVELOPMENTAL PERSPECTIVE

Families are generally feeling significant shame and embarrassment when they meet with us, emotions that can obstruct progress because they generally engender some form of isolation and interfere with candor and authenticity in the treatment room. Putting the family crisis in a developmental context helps to take the edge off of these self-deprecating feelings and leads to a sense of relief, which yields a greater harvest of productive work.

Knowing, for example, that a growing percentage of young adults are unable to achieve financial self-sufficiency makes the existence of a family's struggling young adult less of a shameful secret that has to be buried under the rug and more of a common, garden-variety problem that needs to be solved. Family members can then leave behind whatever purgatory they have exiled themselves to, feel less stigmatized, and begin to behave more like individuals who deserve full and honorable membership in the human race.

This can be accomplished with comments such as:

"Well, you're certainly not the first or last family I've seen with a 20-year-old who has a problem with alcohol. But let's see what the next months and years of maturity bring; I don't know that I would count on his living his life on the street just yet."

"I know that it feels hopeless at times, but I'm not entirely convinced that your daughter's bipolar illness is some sort of psychological 'death sentence.' There are many ways to manage it, and I have seen evidence that some of this instability evens out over time."

"I'm not sure what it is with young men and their desire to take unreasonable risks, and I know you're unhappy about some of the risks that your son has been taking, but I have seen many inveterate risk-takers find safer and more conventional ways to do so as they move into their 20s. It's certainly possible that he'll figure out how to do so as well."

DETERMINE WHO IS DEFINING THE PROBLEM AS A PROBLEM

Successful treatment cannot ensue unless the therapist has a clear understanding regarding the primary motivator for seeking that treatment. Typically, the individual who initiates treatment is one or both of the parents, who are frustrated, angry, and/or worried about their young adult's stalled-out development. Sometimes, it is the young adult herself who initiates treatment, either with or without the parents' knowledge, consent, or support. This often takes place when she is away at college and consulting with the institution's counseling or health center.

Depending on the setting in which we work, there may frequently be an agency or institution outside of the family that has mandated therapy, which obviously changes the context of treatment. If, for example, therapy is required by the justice system as part of a young adult's probation, it cannot be assumed that the young adult and his parents have any skin in the game—one or more of them may see therapy simply as a bureaucratic hoop that needs to be leapt through and completed, no different from the 40 hours of community service that may also have been tacked on as conditions of the probation.

In these situations, I try to acknowledge the reality rather than imagine that they are attending therapy sessions out of their own desire or volition:

"I understand that these sessions are required by law, so in that sense I suppose we're kind of stuck with each other. But being that we're stuck with each other for a period of time, we might as well put our heads together and make the best of this situation by addressing some of the concerns that brought you here rather than pretending that you're meeting with me because you think it's such a terrific idea."

On the other hand, it can't be assumed, under mandated therapeutic conditions, that the family will remain uninterested or unmotivated or that they can't *learn* to be interested or motivated, perhaps wooed into some form of meaningful therapeutic engagement. We have surely all seen cases in which young adults have essentially forced themselves (and their family) into being forced into treatment, because that is the only way that they, or perhaps their parents, are likely overcome their hesitancy about seeking help.

No matter what the presenting problem is, it remains essential for the therapist to attribute expertise to the family when it comes to defining and mapping out the problem's solution. Rather than, "I know better than you do how your family should function," our attitude should be, "You know better than I do how your family should function, but my general experience with and knowledge of many families, including my own, will enable me to help you achieve this if we work together." Allowing the family to call the initial shots empowers them and models for the parents an approach that they may ultimately implement to empower their young adult child.

DETERMINE WHICH FAMILY MEMBERS *NEED* TO BE INVOLVED, AND DETERMINE WHICH FAMILY MEMBERS *SHOULD* BE INVOLVED

FFT during young adulthood may require the clinician to work with the family conjointly, if that is possible, as well as to work with individuals and various subsystems within the family. As noted above, many of the young adults whom we treat will never set foot in our office—we will be meeting exclusively with the parents. At other times, the reverse may be true—parents are not available, or refuse to attend, and it's just the therapist and the young adult.

Either way, a particular flexibility is necessary during this very flexible time in life, when the ground is shifting underneath the family, when each member's role is being redefined and reevaluated, when connections and bonds between family members are being recalibrated and renegotiated.

It is up to the therapist to decide upon the ideal makeup of the therapeutic system, but the implementation of that decision obviously depends on the setting in which therapy takes place. At one extreme, if you are working in a completely independent practice, you can make the final call and simply refuse to work with the family unless they agree to participate on the terms that you have set. At the other extreme, if you are employed by a hospital or agency, you may not have as much say as you would like to have when it comes to who attends sessions—the appointment may have to go on as scheduled even though one parent has decided he or she can't come because he or she has to work late or a sibling can't come because of a social commitment.

In general, though, when the family is in crisis, every family member should be seen as a potential participant, since every family member is contributing to that crisis either by action or inaction. If you get stuck, bring in more people—that way, something's *bound* to happen.

In addition, the identified patient is rarely the only vulnerable, or even the most vulnerable, family member. For example, one or more of the siblings of the identified patient may not appear to be experiencing difficulty because they are not displaying any behavioral, emotional, or developmental problems, but that doesn't mean they are doing fine (despite what they, and their parents, might suggest). It's more likely that they are flying under the radar and will be difficult to diagnose because no explicit difficulties are presenting themselves or because the identified patient's difficulties are so incandescent that they are obscuring other regions of the family's landscape.

Of course, it is safe to say that many families will not be enthusiastic about family therapy. It is much easier for parents, for example, to insist that the therapist simply fix the "broken," malfunctioning young adult rather than to take the time to elucidate the ecology of the family system. Or one or both parents may be harboring dark family secrets and be afraid that these secrets will be exposed if too many family members are allowed to contribute to the process. Whatever the reasons for the hesitancy to create conjoint participation, the therapist must nevertheless run the show.

I remember working with one family and asking the single mother of 21-year-old Dmitri, who had been arrested for stealing cars, to invite her two older daughters to a session.

"They don't need to come," the mom brusquely told me. "They're doing fine."

"I'm glad to hear that, and I want to make it clear that, by inviting them, I certainly wasn't meaning to suggest that they *weren't* doing fine."

"Then why do you need them here?"

"I'd like them to join us so that I can obtain their perspective on their brother."

"Oh, that won't be necessary. I can tell you what their perspective on their brother is. Their perspective on their brother is that Dmitri's screwing up his whole life, and now our lives, too."

"I appreciate your filling me in on what to anticipate, but, nevertheless, there might be advantages to my having some time to hear from them directly."

"They both have jobs; why should they have to give up an hour of work for their unemployed brother?"

"Well, maybe we can set up the session so that they don't miss work."

"I doubt that—*you* work nine to five, and *they* work nine to five."

"So maybe we could schedule it when they have a day off from work and I still have office hours. For example, I work on some of the federal holidays, like President's Day and Martin Luther King Jr. Day. Or maybe they could go in an hour or two late one day, or leave an hour or two early."

"They're not going to be very happy about this, you know."

"I'm not really expecting them to be happy about it. On the other hand, they might appreciate the opportunity to contribute to an endeavor that could help improve their brother's life, along with the life of their whole family."

"What would improve the life of the family is if Dmitri stopped stealing cars and got a real job. What would improve the life of the family is if I hadn't already spent thousands of dollars in legal fees to keep him out of jail."

"I agree, and can certainly understand your point of view. But I'm trying to make sense of this complicated puzzle and the more pieces of the puzzle I have, the better job I can do. Your daughters are crucial pieces of the puzzle."

"But *they're* not the ones who are stealing cars!"

"Thank goodness for that. But their brother *is* stealing cars, and you've asked me to help solve this worrisome problem. The way I go about solving problems is by getting as much information as I can from as many sources as I can. Your daughters are very good sources because they've been an important part of Dmitri's life since the day he was born."

"Okay, I'll ask them, but I can't guarantee that they'll agree to come."

This was a small concession on the mom's part, but I wasn't persuaded that she was going to actually ask her daughters, and, if she did, I suspected that she might do it in a way that would make it very unlikely that one or both daughters would agree to join us. My guess was that the request would be worded along the lines of, "Dmitri's annoying therapist wants you to waste an hour of your time in a fruitless therapy session—you don't want to do that, *do* you?" Nevertheless, I acknowledged this as a first step:

"That would be great. Why don't you go ahead and ask them. But if it turns out that one or both don't agree to come, then perhaps you could give me their contact information so that I can personally explain why I want to invite them. They might hear it differently from me than from you—you know how young adults are with their parents."

Mom reluctantly agreed to this plan and returned for the next session to (almost exultantly, it seemed) announce that her daughters were too busy to come. She did consent to give me their e-mail addresses, though, and, through a brief correspondence, I was able to convince one of them to free up some time to meet with us.

From my perspective, family therapy is a highly ethical treatment endeavor precisely because it looks at the entire system rather than any one individual. Treatment that is solely individually based can certainly be helpful to the individual, but it may ignore the risks to or the distress of the individual's other family members. For example, 52-year-old Jennita contacted me to address her problem drinking, which had recently led to a reprimand at work as well as increased marital discord. I learned that her 19-year-old daughter, Rye, had recently left home for a college out of state after completing a year of community college and that the decision had been made in consultation with a therapist with whom the daughter had been working with individually. However, Rye was not doing well at college, and there was a strong possibility that she would be failing her classes.

After getting permission from Rye to speak with her therapist, Dr. K., I gave him a call. Dr. K. told me that he had indeed pushed the daughter to take the risk of leaving home and attending college because "that is the only way that she is going to survive, to get out of that crazy family—she's a great person, but the typical child of an alcoholic, she and her mother are so codependent. It was time for her to sprout her wings and fly away if she's going to have any kind of future."

When I asked about any family consultations, I learned that Dr. K. had not scheduled any—"Why would I bring them into treatment when the goal is to get her disentangled from them?"—and so was unable to help the parents psychologically prepare for, and adjust in the face of, Rye's departure.

Without that preparation in place, I hypothesized that Jennita succumbed to more heavy drinking, which in turn was jeopardizing her marriage, along with the job that was helping to pay for her daughter's college expenses. Of course, it was not impossible for me to follow this train of thought and imagine that greater dependence on alcohol was Jennita's way of reining her daughter back in and forcing her to return home to fulfill what appeared to be her function as the mother's "private duty nurse." Rye was already giving signs that she was going to succumb to this undertow by underachieving at school to the extent that she might induce a mandated leave of absence.

My concern here was not that this young woman was encouraged to leave home—Dr. K. had clearly been effective in promoting her independence. My concern was that the daughter was encouraged to leave home without the therapist having a clear understanding of the reconfiguration that would be necessary for her to leave home *successfully*, and for that leave-taking to be an enduring one. Without that reconfiguration in place, the stage was set for Rye to be pulled back home by her mother's drinking.

From the moment of initial contact with the family, the therapist must attempt to make sense of the developmental forces and transition points that have led to whatever instability prompted them to get help. When treating young adults, there is obviously a strong likelihood that the instability is emerging from the family's inability to broker a healthy separation. However, families are complicated enterprises—sometimes, as we all know, one symptom masks another symptom, or the identified patient is protecting the family member who is most vulnerable.

So while we need to, at least initially, address the presenting problem, we also need to be on the lookout for the problems that may for now lie dormant but that will blossom once the presenting problem has been resolved. Autonomy is always being sought against the backdrop of the family's systemic and individual life cycle changes, which may challenge the achievement of that autonomy. That is why the therapist needs to maintain an outlook that is as comprehensive as possible, which is best achieved with conjoint participation.

FFT does require the therapist to be nimble as he jockeys back and forth between the generations. Many times, the struggling young adult who is the identified patient will refuse to come to treatment even if she is in the area, but that doesn't mean that treatment cannot take place. I often tell parents with young adult children who refuse to come for therapy, "I have treated many young adults successfully, some without their ever having entered this office." My point is obviously not that I have magical powers but that change in one generation or family member invariably triggers change in another generation or family member.

When I prescribe a tough intervention for parents to implement—the cessation of a subsidy of some sort is a typical one, or calling the police when there has been an extreme violation of the rules at home—they often respond with something like, "If we follow through on this, our son will be so angry with you that he'll *never* come back to therapy." In these cases, I explain that that's perfectly okay and that unless they are prepared to follow through in firm and unyielding ways, no amount of therapeutic engagement with *me* will ever solve the problem that he displays with *them*.

Likewise, there are always issues of confidentiality to sort out. I try to make it clear from the outset that while I will maintain confidentiality, there may be times when I believe that sharing something with the young adult's parents could be important and helpful to her. I emphasize that I will never do so without her permission and that I will do so in whatever format she prefers—revealing it on her own, asking me to reveal it for her, or suggesting that it be revealed during a conjoint session—but that she should consider trusting my belief that she will ultimately benefit if this information is shared. If she declines, I will, of course, respect her decision while discussing the pros and cons of keeping the matter under wraps.

A difficult predicament that often presents itself in family therapy with young adults occurs when the young adult wants to terminate with me and the family remains worried about him and thinks that termination is a mistake. Unless the young adult is unremittingly self-destructive, I generally support the young adult's decision while making it clear that I'll remain available to him and that I can continue working with the parents during his hiatus if they would like to keep me informed of his progress or continue to obtain guidance from me on how to manage.

Nineteen-year-old Allison decided that she had gotten all that she was going to get out of treatment and wanted to finish up. She reminded her parents and me that she was now a legal adult, that it was never her idea to enter into family therapy, and that therapy "had never really helped" her anyway. Her parents were hesitant to agree, as she'd been hospitalized three times in the past two years and they didn't feel that she had made it out of the woods—she still was out late most nights with her friends, she still did not have a job, and she still hadn't mapped out a fruitful plan for her future.

On the other hand, we had worked together for 8 months, and she hadn't been hospitalized during that time (they were referred to me by the partial hospitalization program that Allison had participated in for several weeks after her most recent hospitalization, which was 10 months ago); she was taking her antidepressant medication as prescribed; she was confining her use of pot and alcohol to weekends and one or two weeknight evenings; and she had enrolled in an acting class at community college, which she was enjoying.

With this tangible progress in mind, I supported her wish and remained available to her parents if they wanted to consult with me without her, which they did.

WORK WITH THE FAMILY TO DETERMINE THE GOALS AND ENDPOINT OF TREATMENT

The previous case study reminds us that the beginning of every treatment endeavor requires the therapist and the patient to ask each other and themselves, "How will we know when we are done?" In other words, what are the behavioral, developmental, and emotional markers that signify that progress is being made, enough progress that treatment can begin to be reduced, spaced out, or finished up, either for good or for the time being?

It is important for the therapist to address this issue with the family early on and to try to be as specific as possible. Vague comments such as, "when he is standing on his own two feet," "when she is acting like a 23-year-old, not a 13-year-old," or "when my parents get off my back and stop bugging me" simply won't do.

Often there is a quick consensus on both generations' parts—the parents answer by stating, "We want him to get a job, become financially independent, and move out of our house," and the young man eagerly agrees—"That's great, I can't wait to get out of there, I *hate* it there, so the sooner I leave, the better."

But it's important to delve a bit deeper to determine exactly what everyone means. For example, does "financially independent" mean "*completely* financially dependent," or does it still allow for a certain amount of underwriting on the parents' part, perhaps to cover car or health insurance, legal or medical bills, car repairs, perhaps a security deposit on an apartment?

And if the young adult does, in fact, become financially independent in some agreed-upon fashion, would that change the importance of his moving out, either from his or his parents' perspective? Would the increased level of responsibility and maturity associated with getting a job reduce the tension to the extent that their continuing to reside together becomes a more workable, or even satisfying, arrangement?

Of course, many families will experience great difficulty determining, or agreeing upon, the goals of treatment, and the efforts to resolve the question (deservedly) take some time—that process, in fact, becomes one of the cornerstones of their treatment. Perhaps a young man is burning to get any job he can find and accrue the money necessary to get his own place and move out of the family home, but his parents would prefer that he get some college credits under his belt, which he's more likely to be able to accomplish if he's still living at home. In this case, they may be less likely to help subsidize his move if some financial assistance is necessary, and there may be a conflict when it comes to establishing the endpoint of treatment—for him, it's the day he moves out; for them, it's his agreeing to stay put.

Or the parents have as a goal their daughter's decision to break up with her "knuckleheaded" boyfriend, while *her* goal is to get her parents to accept this relationship and grow to like him. Or the parents have as their goal that their son won't smoke pot anymore, while *his* goal is to get them to accept his use of pot and see it as a harmless, perhaps even helpful at times, habit.

Sometimes, a young adult who is dragged into treatment kicking and screaming will angrily cede goal-setting to her parents. In these situations, she'll tend to adopt either an actively defiant outlook or a passively unhelpful demeanor. Her attitude will be aptly crystallized in the following kinds of statements:

"I don't know what the goals should be. Why don't you ask *them, they're* the ones who scheduled the appointment."

"I'm here because they're making me come. But it's all *their* problem, not mine. I'm not planning on making any changes; I'm fine the way I am."

"They ought to be more worried about my sister than about me; she's the one who's headed for trouble, and they don't even see it. How come *I'm* here and she's not?"

When I run into this kind of obstruction, I will usually ask for some time alone with the young adult and see if I can elicit some sense of what would really make things better and how he believes I might work on his behalf to help accomplish this.

Frequently, the difference in goals does not exist between the two generations but between the two parents. In one family I worked with, the parents discovered that their son was dealing drugs. This prompted Dad to immediately demand that he leave. "We don't want to be arrested because of your drug involvement; we don't want some maniac with a gun coming into our house because of a busted drug deal," was his understandable and clearly stated sentiment.

Mom, however, while certainly not approving of their son's drug dealing, felt *more*, rather than less, compelled to allow him to continue to live at home based on this discovery. "If we kick him out, he's going to need to get involved in even more drug deals just to make enough money to live. He might get arrested, or put in jail, or maybe even killed! At least while he's living here, he's safe, and maybe we can get him to stop, and if he does stop, he'll still have three meals and a roof over his head. Kicking him out will just make him more desperate."

Putting the family in the position of having to determine the objectives of treatment is not only an essential part of the opening phase of treatment and a way to focus and direct the work but also a tremendously useful assessment tool, revealing much about the family's dynamics.

It is also necessary to keep in mind that the process of determining therapeutic goals ultimately lies in the hands of the family, not the therapist. The therapist's job is to help the family broaden their definition and understanding of the problem that brings them into treatment so that they are better able to naturally discover their own solutions to that problem. Just as the parent must trust the young adult to figure out her own unique way of navigating forward, the therapist must trust that the family can figure out *their* own unique way of navigating forward. Similarly, the therapist must also trust the *pace* with which the family approaches problem solving, even when that pace is slower or faster (and it will usually be one or the other) than the therapist thinks would be best.

It is tempting to believe that we know best and to become overly purposeful and invested in a particular therapeutic outcome, to try to mold or direct the family to interact or grow in a certain way. But to do our job, we have to remove ourselves from the family's trajectory—similarly, again, to the ways in which parents must do the same with their young adult children.

DON'T BE AFRAID TO MAKE A FIRST MOVE

It interests me that one of the primary metaphors for psychotherapy remains the image of the couch. Contemporary psychoanalytic theory and practice remains vibrant, but the number of patients who participate in traditional psychoanalytic treatment is surely dwarfed by the number of patients who participate in the many varieties of face-to-face treatment that have become more common. Yet the visual shorthand for psychotherapy remains a patient lying on a couch with the therapist seated stoically and silently behind him, pen and clipboard dutifully in hand.

This shorthand shows up in our vocabulary as well. A recent column about my favorite football team in the local sports section suggested, in its opening paragraph, that the players don't need more practice time but more time "on the couch" so as to understand why they sometimes underperform against their weaker opponents.

With this in mind, it is not surprising that despite various evolutions and revolutions within the mental health care industry, families come to us with certain expectations about treatment, one of which is that it will be built along the lines of their stereotypical understanding of psychoanalytic treatment—that is, it will be expensive, time-consuming, directionless, and without any concrete end. And, of course, because some of the families who are consulting with us may have had previously unproductive treatment experiences that neatly conformed to these negative expectations, even if they weren't traditionally psychoanalytic in structure, these same expectations accompany them into our office and need to be productively violated.

Establishing goals for treatment, as we just discussed, is one way to do this. Another is for the therapist to set a different tone right off by offering at least one suggestion or recommendation by the end of the initial session. While it would be unwise to leap into action and prematurely prescribe a change in behavior that could destabilize the family and make things worse rather than better, it would be equally unwise to conclude the initial session without providing the family with something to work on, with a new take on their situation or an assignment that might get them thinking even slightly differently.

Often, to do this, I will ask family members to make lists that assemble the substructure for change and construct the necessary crucible of shared responsibility and accountability.

For example, I might say to the young adult, "I would like you to make two lists—one is a list of the behaviors that you are currently displaying that make it clear to your parents that you are ready for a more independent life, and one is a list of the behavior that you are currently displaying that suggests to your parents that they need to continue to worry about your ability to manage well on your own. You are to bring both lists with you for our next appointment, as they will form the basis of our next conversation—and I do not want to rely on mental lists, so please bring the list with you on paper or in electronic form."

To each of the parents, I might say, "I would like you to make two lists—one is a list of ways in which you are making it clear that you believe in your son and his capacity to manage well on his own, and one is a list of the ways in which you may be explicitly or subtly suggesting that he still needs your assistance. You are to bring both lists with you for our next appointment, as they will form the basis of our next conversation—and I do not want to rely on mental lists, so please bring the list with you on paper or in electronic form."

If you don't think you have established enough of a connection with the family to assign something this thought-provoking and concrete, you can always fall back on, "I would like each of you to take a step outside of yourselves between now and when we meet again and observe what you are doing, or not doing, that is contributing to the currently conflicted state of affairs."

Of course, while we should have suggestions to offer, both initially and throughout treatment, unless those suggestions are concrete and implementable, they won't do much good. A patient of mine who is a health educator advises the parents with whom she works, "Food that is not eaten has zero nutritive value."

In other words, no matter how much potential nourishment is embedded in our recommendation or advice, nothing will be achieved if that nourishment is not taken in and digested by the family.

LEND STRUCTURE TO THE THERAPEUTIC ENTERPRISE

By the end of the first meeting, it is wise to offer an initial framework within which treatment will unfold. Even if you decide to revise this framework later on, the family deserves to have a tangible sense of how you envision the work progressing. Doing so will not only increase the likelihood of their buy-in, but it also builds their confidence in your capacity to be the beacon who will guide them toward their preferred destination.

To a family of three, you might say: "I would suggest that we meet every other week and that the three of you be present for all subsequent meetings, although I will be making sure that I have some time with you [the young adult] individually and some time with the two of you [the parents] without your daughter."

To parents whose struggling young adult refuses to attend and believes that therapy will be a waste of time, you might say, "Before we insist that she join us, let's meet a couple of times without her, come up with a game plan, put it into play, and then see how she responds and what happens. At that point, we can decide if it's useful or necessary to ask her to join us."

To a struggling young adult who has made it clear that he doesn't want to be in the same room as his parents, you might say, "That's fine for now. I can understand that you want some individual time to address the important matters that are on your mind and that rehashing dusty old arguments with your parents in my office is unlikely to be productive. So why don't you and I meet a couple of times individually and let me meet with your parents a couple of times without you, and then we can all decide together if a conjoint meeting is worth our time."

REFRAME THE PROBLEM AS A SOLUTION

Many parents have told me that the most valuable insight that they have gleaned from me is my belief that the child's solution is his attempt to solve a problem. The idea that every family member is trying to solve a problem, and that some of the solutions that are conceived may simply be maladaptive or disadvantageous, can quickly change the family key from minor to major and move the generations from occupying adversarial, opposite sides of the fence to sharing the collaborative, same side.

With this in mind, reframing the presenting problem or symptom as something that has a function or value and providing it with a positive connotation is essential to establishing the right therapeutic climate. We will be exploring this in more detail in subsequent chapters, but trying to set the process into motion as early as possible can change the family's perspective and quickly open up new dimensions for them.

DIRECTIVE FEEDBACK

I do not advocate being directive in the sense of literally directing patients to behave, or to *not* behave, in a certain way and then sitting back and expecting them to do so. Instead, I mean being directive in the sense of being clear and *direct* with them about the impact, and likely results, of the behavior that they are, or are not, engaging in. It is imprudent to underestimate the capacities of our patients, but it is equally imprudent to overestimate them. Many parents, and many young adults, through no particular fault of their own, simply do not understand with much sophistication both the observable and the invisible apparatus of human relationships.

Not only might a father not understand how constantly hectoring his son to get a job is reducing the likelihood that his son will actually get a job, but he may also not understand how the specter of his long-unemployed and underfunctioning brother is fueling the intensity with which he hectors.

Not only might a young adult who lives with her parents not understand how her coming home visibly inebriated is reducing the likelihood that her parents will help pay for the apartment that she has found for her and her girlfriend to move into, but she may also not understand how her binge drinking is an effort to call attention to her concerns about her mother's nightly consumption of a bottle of wine after dinner.

It is always worth taking advantage of our neutrality to discuss the likely outcome of either generation's behavior without sitting in judgment of it or insisting that it be altered.

CONTAMINATE THE FAMILY'S THINKING

One of our major tasks as clinicians is to bump up against whatever rigid (and possibly misguided) beliefs that the family has adopted, either as a result of previous clinical encounters or as a result of their own patterns of thought and behavior. This rigidity often expresses itself through a medicalization or pathologizing of the identified patient.

I pay very close attention to the words that patients use to describe their problems, because those words often suggest the tenacity of their beliefs. Most of us, for example, have heard parents say, "My son is ADD," suggesting that "being ADD" is the essence of his identity similar to an observation that "My son is male" or "My son is athletic." The concept that their son is a complex individual with *many* strengths and weaknesses, *one* of which is ADD, gets completely lost in that verbiage.

Recently, though, I heard another version of this. I was working with a 19-year-old and her parents, and the daughter tended to be spacey and distracted. When I asked the parents how they understood the origin of her inability to focus, the mother suggested that perhaps her daughter had "ADD of the brain." This phrase really puzzled me. After all, ADD is, by definition, a brain-based disorder—in what other part of the body could ADD possibly show up? It would be akin to saying that she had "laryngitis of the throat" or "diabetes of the pancreas." The best explanation I could come up with was that ADD has become such a common part of our parlance that it no longer has any specific diagnostic meaning and is simply a natural state of affairs that can show up in any bodily system any time it wants to.

A 20-year-old college student met with me for an individual consultation at her parents' behest. When I asked her why her parents had scheduled the meeting, she replied that they had told her that she has "self-esteem." I had to pause for a moment before making sense of this one. In other words, it's no longer "problems with self-esteem" or "low self-esteem," or "self-esteem issues"—it's simply "self-esteem." What used to be a good thing—self-esteem—now sounds like it is a bad thing.

Related to this, I often hear "self-esteem" prefaced with "the," as in, "Our son has the low self-esteem"—in this case, the "the" appears to me to set "self-esteem" off as if it's an actual entity or disease, as in "*the cancer* has spread" or "*the seizures* need to be managed more effectively."

No matter what descriptive language is being employed, the reality is that many of the struggling young adults we see have been struggling before, possibly for quite some time, and, as a result, many of them have been diagnosed or labeled—correctly or incorrectly. Sometimes, of course, a label or diagnosis can be quite helpful and provides a welcome reprieve from self-loathing. We have all probably worked with students who were convinced that they were stupid or dumb because they couldn't read well and who learned, through psychoeducational testing, that they had dyslexia. The diagnosis provided them not only with solace and explanation but also with a potential solution.

On the other hand, labels and diagnoses can easily interfere with a young adult's self-regard and disempower the family at the same time. Many parents have been convinced by various clinicians that there's nothing they can do to influence their child because he or she suffers from a (not always well-defined) mental disorder. For example, if I had a dollar for every young adult who arrives in my office with the diagnosis of "chemical imbalance," I would have a nice little nest egg set aside by now.

Another phrase that I hear more and more frequently is "self-medicating," as in, "My daughter is using pot to self-medicate for her ADD," or "My son is using alcohol to self-medicate for his depression," or "I am using chocolate to self-medicate for my anxiety." When exactly did recreational or illegal use of drugs and alcohol, or even a *food*, become equated with a physician-prescribed clinical intervention? Again, the danger of this language is that it suggests that medication is the solution to every psychological problem and that almost anything that is ingested can be defined as medication.

So one of our most important jobs is to perforate the belief system that the family came into treatment with so that new possibilities and potentials can be contemplated. And this has to be done thoughtfully and strategically, because we don't want to put the family in an uncomfortable position, asking them to suddenly abandon the beliefs that they have been carrying along for many years or to reject the perspective of clinicians or other professionals from the past who surely were attempting to be supportive and helpful with their labeling or diagnosis.

Sometimes I will do this by substituting a word that, to me, is more accurate but that also doesn't contradict the diagnosis, as in, "I think your daughter is more *oppressed* than depressed." Sometimes I will do this by focusing more on behavior than on diagnoses, as in, "Your son may have schizophrenia, but he still will have to learn to control his temper and his thinking if he's going to be able to take advantage of his substantial intellect and become a success in life. You want that for him, don't you?"

Successful family therapy counters dire predictions and bleak prognoses and infuses the family with a realistic but indomitable hope—and sometimes that means carefully questioning assumptions and beliefs that have left them feeling patently hopeless.

LISTEN

As noted in the previous chapter, listening is the key to the therapeutic relationship, but it needs to be listening in its purest form rather than listening that is designed only to acquire enough information to make an assessment or prepare a rebuttal.

A 25-year-old patient of mine came in for an individual session and provided me with a litany of the liabilities of his girlfriend of four years and why he needed to break up with her. I did little during that session but hear him out, as I sensed that he really needed an opportunity to put his feelings into words so that he would be able to do what seemed best, which was to end the relationship.

When he returned for his next session several weeks later, he surprised me by cheerfully telling me that he and his girlfriend were now engaged. As it turns out, getting things off his chest was, in fact, helpful to him, but not in the way that I anticipated it would be. We finished up our work shortly afterward, so I do not know if he did get married and, if he did, how their marriage has been going. But, looking back, it would obviously have been a mistake for me to quickly join in during the previous session and chime in with enthusiastic verbal support for his negative feelings about his girlfriend. Life for families, and for young adults in particular, is quite mutable, and we have to be careful not to jump in too rashly and take a position that later becomes difficult to reverse.

STAY CALM (OR AT LEAST AS CALM AS POSSIBLE)

Difficult as this may be, it is best to avoid being stampeded by the family's urgency. Few issues require a right-this-second decision, and usually we will find, particularly with a problem-saturated family, that they have somehow endured and survived many trials and traumas in the past. So it's always best to buy a little time and see if you can maintain your maneuverability rather than get hijacked by a family's overwrought imperatives and be forced into making recommendations under duress.

Plus, we want to model as much as possible a calm, deliberate, thoughtful approach to problem solving rather than a desperate, knee-jerk reactivity, so that they begin to practice this approach themselves. When we remain implacable in the face of serious problems or temporary regressions, we convey to the family that there may be better ways to respond, which in turn can prevent the frequency and intensity of these problems and regressions in the future.

We also have to maintain a balanced response in the face of change and growth, not just in the face of calamity and commotion. We certainly don't want to minimize or ignore even the slightest positive departures from the family's dysfunctional pattern. On the other hand, we don't want to get overly euphoric and exuberant either, because sometimes what looks like change may actually be nothing more than a slightly disguised repetition of previous behavior, a flip side of the same coin, so to speak. Or we will run the risk of inadvertently quashing the first, tender shoots of change by overreacting to them in a positive way, flooding them, so to speak, with our gushing approval.

MAINTAIN A LONG-TERM OUTLOOK

Parents will often be hesitant to adopt a recommendation that may make things temporarily harder or worse for their young adult or for themselves. One of our responsibilities is to keep them thinking longitudinally rather than focusing too specifically on the immediacy of the situation. For example, while I rarely advocate a dramatic sink-or-swim approach to child, adolescent, or young adult problems, I will often recommend some form of disengagement. In response, one of the parents (but usually not both) will express some version of, "But if we don't keep her afloat, she'll drown!"

For example, if I suggest to the parents that they leave the young adult's academic progress in her hands, that they really have no control over it anyway, one of them might say, "But we *tried* that already back in high school and she failed all of her classes that semester. If we back off now, the same thing will happen, and it'll be worse, because now she's in college and we're *paying* for it!"

My response will likely be, "That is a possibility, although I hope it doesn't happen . . . but while I know that you've tried this before, there may be a way to do so this time that is a little more carefully calibrated, better tailored to her level of development. And if she does fail some or all of her classes as you pull back, which *is* a possibility, she may learn some lessons that are more important than the content that she is currently not learning in school anyway. But the reality is that while I cannot guarantee you that she'll succeed if you back off in the way that I am advising, I *can* guarantee you that she'll continue to underachieve if you don't take the risk of doing something different. So it's up to you . . ."

****

We have been discussing recommendations for the beginning of treatment. But for treatment to continue in a positive direction, therapists must ensure that they are accurately assessing the hindrances to the family's growth that led to the crisis that brought them into therapy. That will be the focus of our next chapter.

Chapter 4

Family Assessment at the Launching Stage

The breaking of a wave cannot explain the whole sea.

Vladimir Nabakov

A family is composed of individuals, and every individual has his or her unique matrix of strengths and weaknesses, endowments and eccentricities. But even though the family is composed of separate organisms, it is also an organism unto itself, and when we help families to embrace the complexity of their organism, they are much more likely to fly through whatever turbulence they encounter and maintain a stable flight pattern.

We fall into a bottomless pit when we succumb to the spurious belief that everything about the psychology of individual and family life can be reduced and explained, that human relationships are ultimately mundane, mechanistic enterprises that simply have to be observed and described to be understood and changed for the better.

That is not to say that the acquisition of information about our patients is useless—only that such information leads us to the *beginning* of knowledge, not its conclusion, and that our ability to utilize that knowledge in healing ways depends on not losing our sense of wonder and curiosity as we attempt to divine the mysteries of human relatedness.

Our goal as clinicians, then, is to formulate the right questions, which are designed not only to elicit data but, more importantly, to create a framework and prompt family members to think differently about themselves and about each other. We are looking for something larger than facts—as Amos Oz wrote in his memoir *A Tale of Love and Darkness*, "Sometimes the facts threaten the truth."

One of my wife's favorite stories from medical school is about two classmates of hers who were conducting their first physical examination of a live patient, which took place in the school's teaching hospital. The duo nervously but earnestly performed all of the procedures that they were trained to do with a middle-aged man and then wrote up their evaluation for their supervisor to comment on. The attending physician told them that he was impressed with their thoroughness but mentioned one important fact that they had neglected to include—a fact that, as it turns out, they were not aware of, even after all of their assiduous poking and prodding: the patient whom they had assessed was a quadriplegic. All of us, no matter how experienced or inexperienced, can become so preoccupied with assessing patients properly that we sometimes miss the bigger, and most important, picture.

One of the reasons that I don't ask my new patients to fill out basic questionnaires in the waiting room or in my office during the initial session is that I don't want them, or me, to get overly caught up in the facts. I can always get that information later, if necessary; I would rather see what emerges first without the scaffolding of data-collection in place. Also, I like to see and hear—to witness—the process by which information is shared, and this can't be easily done if the disclosure is silently or privately completed on a piece of paper or computer screen.

We also need to keep in mind that family history is never objective—it is always a mythic tapestry woven of remembrances, wishes, fantasies, and fears. And the highly (and sometimes hyperbolic) distortions and misinterpretations that inevitably abound as the family shares their history with us should be of as much, if not of more, interest to us than the actual facts are. The family's stories will not begin at the beginning, nor will they end at the end, because there is no true beginning and no true end—they begin in the mists of the past and extend into the haze of eternity.

Because of this, we are better off assuming that we not only *can* be deceived by the family's initial presentation but that we *will* be deceived by this initial presentation. We simply need to remain aware that this is happening, even if we are not immediately, or even eventually, able to detect the nature of the deception.

Families tend to ignore the subconscious themes that lie below the intellect, because it is troubling to be reminded that thoughts, feelings, and behaviors are often guided by forces of which they are not fully aware. It's one thing for us to enter shadowy, primitive, illogical dreamworlds when we are asleep, because we are comforted by the reality of our awakening. But what about the shadowy, primitive, illogical dreamworld that we inhabit when we are awake, one from which there really *is* no true awakening? How disruptive it is to our comforting (albeit delusional) sense that we completely control our own destiny when we are forced to come to terms with the extent to which we become irrational and "beside ourselves" among the ungovernable tumult of family intimacy.

So, as therapists, we have to function as the family's fearless guides through the symbolic underworld that lies below all of us. Donning our miner's headlamp and illuminating the sometimes menacing lures and obstacles that inhabit this underworld neutralizes their danger and makes them less detrimental to the family's real-world functioning.

But despite our best efforts, there is only so much we can come to know about the family. The theologian Abraham Joshua Heschel usefully distinguished between the unknown and the ineffable. They are different from each other because the unknown may at some point become known, but the ineffable is "that aspect of reality which by its very nature lies beyond our comprehension, and is acknowledged by the mind to be beyond the scope of the mind." For Heschel, we sometimes must rely on apprehending more than comprehending, encountering realities that may lodge beyond our ability to describe, understand, or categorize but that can still be felt nevertheless.

From my perspective, psychotherapy does not exist without an acknowledgement that some aspects of human existence remain beyond our understanding. But this can be an emancipating realization, not a limiting one, because in recognizing our limitations, we are better able to come to terms with them.

In FFT, assessment and treatment cannot be distinguished, because the nature of the assessment that we perform, if done well, has curative properties. The questions we ask, the ways in which we respond to answers, and the hypotheses that we formulate as a result determine our clinical success.

Families, of course, will vary significantly on the extent to which they participate in the assessment, just as they will vary significantly on the extent to which they participate in treatment as a whole. Like certain novelists who for stylistic reasons don't furnish or authorize the "who, what, why, when, and where" very easily, many families behave similarly. Our job in these situations is not to get exasperated or to become absorbed with "getting the facts, ma'am" and relentlessly pursuing them like hunted prey, but to realize that the hesitancy to disclose in and of itself discloses a great deal and provides us with more useful and important testimony about the family than specific evidence might. People always reveal a lot by how little they reveal—through not being forthcoming, something important is still coming forth.

Along these lines, some families will be *so* withholding that we're left simply guessing as to the circumstances that led up to the crisis. Here's a recent interchange from an interview with an 18-year-old patient who had been referred to me by his doctor at a day hospital:

How did you originally come to work with Dr. L., the doctor who referred you to me?
I was sent to him by the hospital . . . he worked at the day program that I had to go to.
How did you wind up in the hospital originally?
The police took me to the ER, and the ER sent me to the mental hospital.
Why did the police come in the first place?
I think the school called them.
Why did the school call them?
I don't know, I guess they were worried.
What were they worried about?
I don't know . . . you'd have to ask them.
Can you imagine what they might have been worried about?
No, not really. Everything was fine, then all of a sudden I'm being taken to the ER in handcuffs.

How long were you in the hospital?
I'm not sure—a couple of weeks, I guess.
Did you get anything out of being there?
Don't remember much.
Did you like being there?
It was okay . . . not really.
What was okay about it?
The people.
What about the people?
Just the people.
What was not *okay about it?*
The food.
What kind of food did they serve you?
Lousy food.
Miss being there at all?
Not really.
Glad that you're out?
Yeah, I guess.

Here's an excerpt from the interview with the mother of this patient. It was difficult for me to ignore the similarities in their verbal stinginess.

Why was your son originally hospitalized?
I don't know, I can't really remember exactly . . . it was a couple of months ago.
Do you remember anything about it?
Not really . . . I think the school told me I had to take him to an ER.
What were they worried about?
I don't know . . . I think he was cutting classes and smoking pot.
Were you worried about this, as well?
I don't remember . . . I guess I was . . . a lot was going on back then.
What was going on?
All kinds of things.
Such as?
I don't know . . . I think that's around the time my father got sick.
What is he sick with?
A stroke.
Is he still alive?
Yeah.
How's he doing?
Not so good.
Is your father close to your son?
Sort of . . . I guess so.

Are you close to your father?
Not really . . . he wasn't much of a father.
What might have made him a better father?
Being around more.
Why wasn't he around more?
I don't know . . . he left my mom when I was little . . . he wasn't much of a hus-
   band, either.
Is your mom alive?
Yes.
How is her health?
Pretty good.
Is she close to your son?
She used to be . . . not anymore.
Why not?
I'm not sure, you'd have to ask her.

In situations like this, I find myself recalling John Lennon's lyric: "All I want is the truth, just gimme some truth." On the other hand, we will sometimes encounter the family that provides so much information that you can't formulate any hypotheses or make sense of any of it. I have a patient who is a veterinarian and who told me that her staff constantly has to remind dog owners that when a stool sample is requested, they do not require a Tupperware container filled to the brim with steaming feces to be plopped onto their counter—a pinch or two of sample will suffice for whatever testing is going to be done.

So just as some families obscure the truth by saying too little, other families will obscure the truth by providing too much information. But it's worth listening carefully nonetheless to see where the narrative flow is heading—often there are numerous treasures hidden beneath the sand of a long, rambling story. For example, in my initial interview with Charise, the mother of 22-year-old Marcellus, I asked her about the challenges of raising Marcellus when he was younger. She began:

> We've always had a hard time with Marcellus, even when he was little. I mean he was the kid who would kick at me when I tried to nurse him, and that wasn't easy for me because my mom didn't think nursing was such a great idea anyway. She was from the day when you wean the kid as quickly as possible because you want to stay attractive to your husband and not give your breast over to the baby, although I always wished that Joe had seen me as attractive when I was nursing, but that didn't seem to ever be the case. He wasn't all that supportive. He didn't like the little bags of frozen breast milk in the freezer, he found that kind of strange, and so did his mother, who also wasn't crazy about me nursing the baby either. She was from a different era, too, and she lived with us for the first month when Marcellus was a baby, but she really wasn't much help. She would sort of sit around and wait for me to ask her for

help, but I was so busy with the baby I didn't know what kind of help to ask for, what did I know? So it was awkward, and I'm not sure she was of much help to me, and I think I might have offended her because it was a while before she came back, although she got pretty sick for a while, she was dealing with gout, and that makes it hard to travel, I guess, or at least that's what she said . . . or at least that's what Joe said. He said I shouldn't be angry with her for not coming to visit . . . and my mom, she doesn't live too far away even, but she always has an excuse for why she can't visit. It's like everything is too damn hard for her . . . with her, it's her job, she thinks she's so important that she can't ever take a day off of work, and then on the weekends she's busy with her church activities . . . so even though there are two grandmothers in the picture, they're not really in the picture, if you think about it.

I kept waiting for her to get back to Marcellus, but she never quite looped back to him, at least not on her own. On the other hand, without even asking for it, I certainly was able to get a good feel for the extended family, including the role that the two grandmothers played and some of the coalitions that had taken root in the family. This ultimately did help to explain why Marcellus, who I actually heard little about at first, had been such a handful for so much of his life.

The assessment begins with the very first contact, whether it's a telephone call, voice mail, or e-mail. Who is calling, how does he sound, what is being requested—there is abundant information embedded in the first interaction between family member and therapist. But we have to be careful not to get too comfortably locked into some of our initial hypotheses.

For example, I recently retrieved a voice-mail message from the stepmother of a 21-year-old stepson who was "depressed". Part of me instantly wondered why the stepmother was making the initial contact rather than the father or the mother. I could speculate that the father had abdicated parenthood and shunted the responsibilities over to his new wife. I could also speculate that the son and his mother had become estranged from each other and that the stepmother had stepped in to fill the caregiving void. As it turns out, the former was true, but the latter was not—the mother and stepmother had conferred and agreed that the stepmother would make the first call because she was better able to receive return calls at work than the mother was.

The assessment process as a whole is designed to generate hypotheses that explain the family patterns that lie at the root of the problem that brings them for treatment. As the work unfolds, the family members' responses to subsequent questions help the clinician to validate or rule out these hypotheses and ultimately to sharpen the ones that remain viable.

We want to make sure that we key in on the *family's* assessment of the situation and give it due process, even if it doesn't make perfect sense or seem wholly legitimate. A parent might say, "We have concluded that Thom will never be able to move out and live on his own because of his hemophilia," to which we might think, "There are people with hemophilia all over the world who figure out a way to move out and live on their own." But before we can challenge the family's reality, we need to understand it, and understanding it begins with carefully listening to it and contemplating it.

As much as possible, we want to move beyond questions that suggest linear sequences, such as, "When did your son last hold a job?" or, "What tells you that your daughter has been promiscuous?" These queries may be necessary to ask at times just to pin down certain realities, but they ultimately steer the treatment into a dead end.

Instead, we want to focus more on the family's systemic patterns, how they are responding to each other in the face of their crisis, such as, "In what ways does your son's unemployment affect the family as a whole?" or, "When you are worried about your daughter sleeping around, how do you express or manage that worry?"

But linear hypotheses are appealing because they wrap things up into such tidy little psychological packages. It is easy to conclude that 19-year-old Hal is not moving forward with his life because his parents are "too controlling," and he will be happy to convince you that that is the case. It is harder to take note of the ways in which Hal engenders the very protective and controlling behaviors that he so detests by withdrawing from school and limiting himself to part-time work at a pizza place while crushing his Adderall and snorting it at night. Likewise, it is easy to believe that Hal is not moving ahead with his life because of a congenital cardiac abnormality that required surgery at the age of 5 days, and two electrocardiograms per year until he was 10 years old. It is harder to take note of the ways in which Hal's father, John, has not responded with relief to the medical all-clear sign that was given to them when Hal was 10 because John's father died of a heart attack when John was in high school, and that, as a result, John still overplays his son's cardiac vulnerability and subtly discourages him from moving on and moving out.

When we distance ourselves from the realities that the family brings to us and help them to consider alternative possibilities, then innovative ways to see and resolve problems will naturally present themselves.

Part of the challenge of assessment during early adulthood is that each generation's story can vary significantly, and young adults and parents may accuse each other of engaging in revisionist history. For example, 20-year-old Lindsay tells me that she was tired of playing the violin by the end of middle school but felt compelled to continue with it for fear of disappointing her teacher and parents. That is one of her best explanations for why she doesn't invest in anything at this point in her life—"I'm afraid that if I do something, I have to do it forever, even when I'm no longer interested in it."

However, Lindsay's mother indignantly refutes that story, explaining that Lindsay loved playing the violin until she graduated high school and even anticipated playing in the orchestra when she went to college. Lindsay angrily denies this, while her mother counters with further evidence that supports her version of the story. Both stories can obviously not be true in the objective sense, but both stories are still important to listen to because they shed light not only on what might have happened in the past but also on what is taking place in the present between mother and daughter.

With this in mind, another important aspect of FFT assessment is the ability to adroitly maneuver between an assessment of the past and an assessment of the present. Our assessment of the past is necessary, even though we sometimes find ourselves struggling to make out the vaguest of shadows that lurk in the midst of the family's half-lit thickets. But we have to help the family to see, and ultimately to slough off, the sheaths of family history that may be keeping them bound, and the latter depends on the former. Every family has ghosts that billow up from the past and whisper their seductive guidance, sometimes for the better and sometimes for the worse—for the family to progress, some of those whispers deserve to be amplified, and some of them need to be muted. Nevertheless, it's also important to resist imagining that, like the therapist in a satisfying but simplistic TV movie, you will always find the Rosetta stone that immediately explains all that has been inexplicable and dramatically mitigates dysfunctional behavior if you just keep digging beneath the family's stubborn soil.

On the other hand, families come to us feeling distress in the present, and they need to know that we're not going to spend their valuable time and energy on some endless exploration of the past. That is why our assessment has to also focus on the present, because that is where their distress is occurring, even if it has its roots in the past. After all, the only components of the family's past that clinicians are given the key to are those that have been called forth by the context of events and the constellation of dilemmas that they are currently in the midst of. And, as we have noted, their recollection of the past is not impartial or unbiased but more like a toy kaleidoscope that transfigures with each slight turn of the tube.

The key to assessment in the present is understanding the family hydraulics that either permit or prevent constructive change from occurring. This change can result from a number of different interventions, but it most reliably occurs when there is a perturbation in the family's belief system—once we alter the perception of a problem, we have automatically increased our ability to *solve* that problem in a better way. That is where the fossa and contours of our assessment in the present become relevant.

Because of this, in its most elemental form our assessment must address five major, interlacing issues:

1   Why has the family crisis occurred now?
2   What is the basis for the family's inability to change or grow that the crisis is designed to call attention to?
3   Which family members are standing in the way of growth, and what tactics and strategies are they utilizing to do so?

4   What needs to happen now so that the crisis has a chance to resolve itself and the family is free to once again commence growth?

5   What are the individual and family fears associated with growth recommencing?

With these primary issues in mind, I have listed below a compendium of questions that I have found to be particularly relevant when working with struggling young adults and their families. Some of them are my own, and some of them I have learned from others, and it is impossible for me to know which are which at this point, so I haven't made any distinction or provided any footnotes. All the questions can be easily modified or made more precise based on the situation that your patients are in the midst of.

It is obviously not my belief that all of these have to be checked off as part of a solid family assessment—a stimulating, well-timed question may take an entire session to answer well, and the best questions lead not only to answers but to more questions. Also, what is more important than the specific questions that we ask is the *way* in which we ask and respond to these questions—hopefully with genuine curiosity and care rather than with implied criticism or a desire to affirm our pre-fabricated assumptions. But the list will give you a feel for the kinds of issues that deserve to be explored when assessment and treatment become linked during the launching stage.

For example, let's examine one simple question and what could lie behind the answers: "Who in your family does your son remind you of?"

The presence of a child invariably casts a magic spell over the family. The expansion of a family always represents a new beginning, but that beginning reverberates to the incessant, and sometimes barely audible, rhythms of the family's past. Every child represents the rebirth of some aspect of the family's soul and spirit, and the family and the child determine collaboratively which soulful, spiritual aspects she is entrusted to embody.

Parents make attributions to each of their children, assigning qualities and characteristics to the child that may or may not be accurate and that conspire to define who she is. Why do parents do this? Why don't they just calmly and patiently allow the child's personality to unfold and allow the child to become her own person on her own terms? The reason is that parenthood requires us to engage in the range of extraordinary compromises, investments, and accommodations that accompany child rearing. And to summon the strength and commitment to do this, we must have some identification with the child—we don't make these kinds of sacrifices for a stranger. The quickest way for a parent to identify with the child is to authorize to her an identity that is familiar, either in good ways or in bad ways.

That is why new parents (even adoptive and foster parents) will instantly note that the baby has "his uncle's eyes" or "his mother's hair" or that "she smiles just like her father" or that "she gets cranky just like her grandmother"—these may or may not be positive connotations or recognitions, but either way they help us to see this somewhat formless, dependent lump of protoplasm as a special someone who is deserving of care and attention.

So when we ask parents who in the family does this child remind you of, we are getting a sense of the ways in which the child has been molded or shaped to represent someone in the family.

Part of the answer to that question will depend on what was taking place in the family at the time of the child's conception, gestation, birth, infancy, early childhood, or acquisition through adoption, foster care, or step-parenthood. For example, if the child's grandfather died as a result of emphysema shortly after his birth, it should be anticipated that one or both parents may associate the child with the grandfather and, as a result, become highly reactive if and when the baby displays respiratory problems as a result of colds, allergies, or asthma. This reaction, in turn, might link the baby to grandfather in other, psychological ways as well.

Many religious traditions adhere to the idea that the when an individual dies, the body is lowered into the ground but the spirit is lifted away. But *psychological* tradition tells us that when an individual dies, the spirit continues to hover and haunt—the spectral presence of a deceased family member is sometimes more powerful and influential within a family than when the individual was materially present.

So who the child reminds the parents of always provides us with a window into the family system—the warp and woof of their perceptions of each other and the ways in which their behavior might be conforming to those perceptions.

One final comment about assessment is that, as I noted in the preface, we have to energetically resist the tendency to have an ideal or normative yardstick in place that we hold the family up against. It is the family's job, not ours, to determine when growth and functioning are sufficient. Sometimes there are cultural biases that we bring to our work. For example, not every culture places the same premium on moving out of the family home when it comes to establishing autonomy and independence. So just because we are treating a family who happen to be living in a multigenerational home, that does not mean we are dealing with some form of thwarted autonomy on the part of one or more generations.

Likewise, there are generational biases that we need to attend to. I began working as a psychologist almost 30 years ago, and if you had told me back then about a student who had left home for college but still spoke to her mother every day by phone, I would have concluded with great certainty that this was a dysfunctional arrangement and that this young woman's individuation was imperiled. Yet a recent study by the student health agency at an Ivy League university revealed that over 50% of freshmen had phone contact with one of their parents (either via text, e-mail, or voice) on a *daily* basis. One can assume that most of the freshmen attending a prestigious college are indeed accomplished and individuated young adults, yet clearly there has been a shift in what is considered normal contact between parents and young adults.

So assessment, at its best, is a process that depends on an awareness of both the clinician's inner world as well as the outer world.

Questions for the Initial Session(s)—Either Conjointly or with the Young Adult and Parents Separately

- What is your perspective on this problem and how and when it began?
- What impact has this problem had on you, and on your family as a whole?
- What was the lead-up to this problem?
- Who tends to be most worried about this problem? Who tends to be least worried?
- Who in the family is aware of this problem, and who is not?
- How do you understand or explain the origins of this problem?
- What have you already tried in an effort to solve this problem? How well did your efforts succeed? Is there anything that you've thought of trying but haven't put into place yet? If so, what has made you hesitate to do so?
- When was the family in its best shape?

Family-Based Questions

- What is the most productive way for the family to be functioning at this time?
- What is the appropriate amount of closeness or separateness that each of you believe would be best to have with each other at this stage of life?
- What has the child's role in the family been? How long has this been her role, and how stable has the role been?
- When was the child anointed as the family savior, or when was the child cast out as the family scapegoat? What were the conditions under which this took place?
- How hard has it been to play that role? What have been the advantages and the disadvantages for the child of taking on this role? What sacrifices did he or she have to make?
- What have been the advantages and disadvantages for the other family members of the child's taking on this role?
- Who displays courage—the capacity to take risks—in this family, and how do they display it?
- How will you find ways to express love and care when you're no longer living together as a family (or now that you're no longer living together as a family)?
- How will you find ways to let each other know that you miss each other when you're no longer living together as a family?

Questions for Parents

- What regrets do you have about yourself as a parent as you look back? What are you proudest of?
- Is there something that you believe needs to happen in your own life before your child will leave home?
- In what ways have you fulfilled your parents' expectations for you?
- In what ways have you made good on the promises that you made to yourself during your youth? In what ways have you defaulted on those promises?
- What is the best or worst advice you've been given when it comes to child rearing, and who gave it to you?
- How did you manage your own transition into adulthood? What were the hardest parts?
- What were the parts that you feel proudest of as you look back?
- Who was helpful to you and in what ways?
- Who was unhelpful, or even obstructed your progress, and in what ways?
- How did your relationship with your parents change as you left home/left adolescence behind? In what ways was this for the better and in what ways for the worse?
- Which decisions did your parents have the most difficult time adjusting to or coming to terms with?
- How did you decide to start a family?
- How did this process come about (conception, adoption, step-parenthood, foster care, fertility treatments, etc.)?
- What were the biggest challenges you faced during pregnancy or early parenthood?
- What were the biggest challenges you faced during middle childhood?
- What were the biggest challenges you faced during adolescence?
- Who in your family does your son/daughter most remind you of?
- If your parents are still alive, what is your relationship with them like these days?
- How did it change when you became an adult? How has it continued to change in the subsequent years?
- What would you want to be different about your relationship with them now?
- What have you tried to do to make that difference come about?
- What do you miss about your child's childhood?
- What will you miss about your child when he or she leaves?
- What are you most looking forward to no longer having to deal with?

Questions for the Young Adult

- Is there something about you that you feel the need to correct or improve before you leave home?

- Is there something about your family that you feel the need to correct or improve before you leave home?
- Now that you've left home, what aspects of your family are you still concerned about (or what aspects will you remain concerned about when you do leave)?
- When do you first recall asserting yourself with your parents, expressing your own point of view? How did you do so, and how did they react?
- When do you first recall expressing displeasure with your parents? How did you do so, and how did they react?
- When do you first recall disappointing your parents? How did you do so, and how did they react?
- When do you first recall feeling guilty about something you did? What was it, and how did your parents react if or when they learned about this?
- What family stories do you remember hearing about becoming independent and making your way into the world?
- In what ways do you want or expect your parents and family to continue to be supportive of you as you begin the process of leaving home (or now that you have left home)?
- What else would you need from your parents and family that would enable you to feel like you could leave home with a "full tank"—that you had been given all that was necessary for you to be given?
- How did your obligations and contributions as a family member change since you started high school? Over the past years?
- When it comes to your parents, what do you think is the biggest disappointment in each of their lives? To what extent do you believe that you might be expected or obligated to help make up for that disappointment?
- What's the best advice you've been given about your current situation, and who gave it to you?
- What do you see as your weaknesses, and how have you learned to compensate for them?
- What do you see as your strengths, and how have you decided what strengths to cultivate? How did you decide what to excel in?
- What sparks your interest? When do you feel most passionate and alive?
- When do you feel most dead inside?
- What is the most annoying thing about your family life? About life outside of your family?
- What is the most intriguing thing that sets you apart from others?
- What do people like about you? What have you heard that people don't like about you?
- What are three things about you that your parents or your friends would be surprised to find out?
- Who is the person you admire most?
- Who is the person you dislike the most?

- Who is the person you are most afraid to become like?
- Who is the person you are already afraid you've become like?
- What do or will you miss about leaving home?
- What will you be happy or relieved to leave behind?

Because in most of the families who consult with us, one child performs the role of the identified patient, one of our areas of inquiry needs to be why this particular child was recruited to and/or volunteered to play this role and, given that the child is now a young adult, why he or she has decided—consciously or subconsciously—to continue to do so. This leads us to ask questions such as:

- How did you get selected to be the problem child?
- Do you remember having been asked to play this role?
- Do you remember who asked you?
- When did you first experience the awareness of having been asked to do so?
- What did you do once you became aware?
- At what level is your awareness right now?
- What are you afraid would happen should you relinquish this role? Who would suffer? In what ways would *you* suffer? How would you claim or re-claim importance, both in your own life and in the life of the family, were you to resign from this role?
- Were you to relinquish this role, who would step in to fulfill it? What do you think would happen if no one stepped in?
- How guilty will you feel if you turn your back on your family by relinquish-ing this role? How will you manage this guilt? How will you expiate this guilt should you decide that it's not worthwhile to feel guilty?

THE ASSESSMENT OF LOSS—CASE STUDIES

Because, as noted in chapter 2, we cannot live our lives without loss, and because anticipated and unanticipated losses often derail the family's journey and detour them into our office, it is impossible to effectively assess the family without under-standing the recent, distant, and historical losses that they have sustained.

Whenever a child has gotten stuck at a particular stage, for example, it is important to inquire as to whether there is a recent loss that is still being dealt with or a critical loss from the past that one or the other parent may have expe-rienced when he or she was the age of the struggling young adult. This inquiry may provide a context in which to understand the genesis of the young adult's difficulties.

For example, the Kaciske family met with me because their 21-year-old son, Armand, had run aground. He had finished his first two years of college without difficulty but couldn't seem to get through his junior year. He passed only one class in the first semester and didn't pass any classes in the second semester. Now he was on academic probation and not allowed to reenroll until he completed a successful semester of community college.

The family was befuddled as to why this very bright young man had suddenly stopped achieving. In delving into the family's history, however, I learned that Ms. Kaciske had had a brother, Bruce, who died in a car accident when he was 21. Bruce was never spoken of, either by Ms. Kaciske or by her family. In fact, Armand was already 14 years old when he first learned about Uncle Bruce—as part of a genealogy project in middle school he was making a family tree, and his mother casually mentioned that there was an uncle whom he had never met.

What was particularly fascinating to me was that Armand had, in the past year, decided to grow his hair out, to the point that it was now shoulder-length. This had surprised his parents, as Armand had traditionally kept his hair short and neat. When I was asking Ms. Kaciske about her brother's tragically shortened life, she mentioned at one point that he was "the first hippie in our high school" and said that he had had long hair beginning in high school and into college. She did not take note of her own son's suddenly long hair as she recounted her brother's appearance.

Sadly, Bruce had died before finishing college, so it was impossible for me to ignore the ways in which Armand seemed to be mimicking Bruce's life—growing his hair out and truncating his academic career without even knowing he was doing so. Further exploration revealed that Bruce was not talked about much because there had always been some suspicion on the family's part that the car accident in which he had died was his fault, as he had a tendency to drive fast and had regularly accumulated speeding tickets since acquiring his license. So there was tremendous shame associated with Bruce's life, which made it difficult for the family to acknowledge and fully mourn his death.

Our work together involved psychologically disinterring Uncle Bruce from the underground vault in which he had been sealed so that Armand was no longer in the position of having to subconsciously resurrect his uncle and keep his forgotten memory alive.

Another loss that commonly presents itself with struggling young adults is the premature death of one of the parents. Alta's father died when she was one year old, and while she was aware of this, she did not know the details—she had grown up being told that he had died of a heart attack. Her mother consulted with me because Alta, now 24 years old and bisexual, had recently been involved in a sequence of destructive relationships with older women, most of whom were either alcoholics or drug abusers.

During our initial session, I learned that Alta's father had not died of cardiac disease—in fact, he was a heroin addict who had been knifed during a drug deal gone bad and left to bleed to death in a public park. As with Armand's Uncle Bruce, the family was unable to grieve because of the terrible stigma attached to the loss. And just as Armand had subconsciously found a way to resuscitate his dead uncle, Alta was creating a replication scenario by seeking out older partners who demonstrated the same chemically dependent behaviors that her deceased father did, thus symbolically bringing him back to life.

In the Broadus family, Vonte, now 22, had lost his father to cancer when he was 16. Mr. Broadus was a deeply religious man with a large and altruistic heart. He had organized a yearly church mission to build houses in inner-city Baltimore and, although not a wealthy man, regularly donated a tenth of his salary to a variety of charities. Vonte had been close to his father, and the family was prepared for the death—Mr. Broadus had been diagnosed with a virulent form of lung cancer two years before he died, so there had been plenty of time to address the impending loss. The problem in this family was that Mr. Broadus was so deified upon his death that Vonte felt flattened by his father's legacy, doomed to be unable to measure up to the saint that his dead father was now lauded as having been.

Vonte became increasingly discouraged by the constant veneration of his father by family, church, and community members and seemed to be taking the opposite tack in a desperate effort to distinguish himself—his deepening self-absorption appeared to me to be an attempt to counterbalance his father's generosity of spirit. One day, he was apprehended for stealing cash from the church's donation box. It has been said that the only thing harder than *being* a saint is *living* with one—one might add that the only thing harder than *living* with a saint is being *raised* by one, and this was Vonte's combined blessing and curse.

Some of our work together, which included his paternal grandparents, entailed helping Vonte to understand that his father was, indeed, no saint and that much of Mr. Broadus's beatific striving may have been an attempt to make up for a youth characterized by drug dealing, which resulted in an eventual arrest and a year of jail time when he was 22.

While we don't always have the luxury of taking the time to do an extensive family history, particularly when struggling young adults and their families are in a crisis, it is best to obtain information as quickly as possible that tells us which of the family's losses have been most profound and impactful and when and why the mourning process for those losses may have been aborted.

STIMULATING SELF-ASSESSMENT

One of the most important outcomes of the assessment process should be stirring the young adult's and the family's capacity to assess *themselves*. Our goal should be to ask questions in a way that attracts each family member's curiosity regarding why they do what they do, so that they begin to evaluate their own behavior, which becomes the foundation for changing it. When we make our inquiries without presumptions and with an eager and genuine desire for understanding, they tend to internalize this approach and do the same from within—we want to embark on inquisitiveness, not on an Inquisition.

A father I worked with was upset about his 26-year-old daughter's often slovenly appearance, one aspect of which was her chronic halitosis, which was the result of never brushing her teeth or going to the dentist. "It is actually hard to be with her, her breath is so awful. She complains about not having any dates, but who would date her when she smells like that? It's gotta be a turnoff; no *wonder* she's single."

When he asked her why she didn't display better dental hygiene, which he did regularly, she always blew him off with, "That's none of your business." But when I modeled a subtler approach during a family session, such as in the following exchange, he eventually became better able to engage her on his own:

"Hayley, it is clear to me that you take care of yourself in *some* ways—for example, I love the way you have your hair cut, it looks great—but, according to your father, not in other ways, such as when it comes taking care of your teeth. How do you decide what you're going to address and what you're not going to address?"

"Huh?"

"How do you decide what you're going to take care of and what you're going to let go of?"

"I don't know . . . I don't think about it."

"So I'm guessing maybe it's not a conscious decision but maybe one that you're not aware of?"

"I'm not sure . . . I said, I don't think about it."

"But at some level you must be making a decision about which facets of your appearance you're going to focus on and which you're going to disregard."

"I *do?*"

"Sure you do. Why else would you devote yourself to *some* things but not to others?"

"Whatever."

"How concerned are you that you would become too attractive if you took care of every aspect of your appearance?"

"What?! Why would *that* be a problem?"

"Well, maybe you'd then have too many guys interested in you. *That* could present a problem, you know."

"I'm sure my father has told you that I don't have *any* guys interested in me right now. *That's* the problem."

"But that leads me to wonder if you are concerned that too much attention from guys might not be such a good thing for you."

"Too many guys is *not* a problem."

"Well, it *could* be—there'd be some choices to make, and it might distract you from other things."

"I could live with that problem."

"Maybe . . . but I wonder if you keep your breath bad and your teeth stained just to be sure that you don't attract too much attention from the opposite sex."

"Are you saying that's why I don't have a boyfriend? Because I don't brush my teeth?"

"I actually have no idea why you don't have a boyfriend. But if it bothers you that you don't have a boyfriend, I have to say I'm puzzled as to why you don't take care of your breath and your teeth—that's pretty basic stuff when it comes to being more alluring."

"You think it's that simple?"

"I doubt it's that simple—why people are or are not in relationships is always complicated. But you seem to be going out of your way to limit your appeal—so it makes me wonder if part of you doesn't want to be too appealing."

"You think if I brushed and flossed I'd have a boyfriend?"

"I'm not sure. I do find myself wondering, though."

"Hah! That would be something."

Clearly the outcome of our conversation was not going to be Hayley leaving my office and calling to make a dental appointment. But our conversation did get past the "It's none of your business" roadblock and prompted her to examine her behavior differently and see it as something more interesting than simple self-neglect. Her father followed up on this line of inquiry in the subsequent weeks and reported back that Hayley was gradually beginning to display better hygiene.

The same approach can be applied when drug dependence or abuse is an issue.

For example, what I generally see with chronic pot use by young adults is one or more of the following:

- increased irritability, sometimes bordering on paranoia
- diminished motivation and initiative
- exaggerated self-justification of drug use

The clinical challenge, of course, is that all three of these issues are difficult to assess and discuss in depth with the young adult, precisely because of their very nature. When an individual is irritable, suggesting that pot use might be contributing to her irritability will generally make her more irritable. When an individual is unmotivated, she will generally do anything she can to avoid that depiction and focus instead on the circumstances that prevent her from getting ahead. And when an individual is convinced that drug use is good for her, it's provocative to suggest that it might be bad for her.

I generally do not take a stand on whether pot is good or bad, since most young adults have already received numerous lectures on this from their parents and other adults and have captained their own extensive exploration of this topic with friends and on the Internet. I focus instead on being realistic regarding the extent to which their parents are going to accept their use of pot if they are still living at home and very gently beginning the process of questioning whether it's as beneficial as he believes it is.

Regarding the former, I will frame the discussion in the following way:

"It's understandable that you would like your parents to see your use of pot the way that you see it. But the reality is that they're entitled to their opinion and you're entitled to yours, and, based on my conversations with them, they are not giving me any indication that they're going to be changing their minds soon. You can certainly continue to try to convert them, but it seems to be taking up a tremendous amount of your time and energy that might be better invested in your education or your job.

"You're entitled to be unhappy that they're not supportive, but you still have several choices that you can make: you can work very hard to save enough money to move out and then no longer have to deal with their disapproval; you can work very hard to prove them wrong by becoming successful while continuing to smoke pot, which is probably the only way to convince them that they're incorrect about its liabilities; or you can accept the difference of opinion between you and them and just be as discrete as you can about your use of pot for whatever period of time you remain at home."

Regarding the latter, I will frame the discussion in the following way:

"You mentioned that you did just fine in high school when you were getting high every day, but you also told me that you're not doing very well at college so far. Perhaps you were able to manage the academic demands of high school while getting high, but now that those demands have changed, it's worth another look at what you're doing or not doing."

Or, "I don't really have any idea if pot is good for you or bad for you—it seems to vary from individual to individual and we're not really very sophisticated when it comes to understanding the workings of the brain, whether it's on or off drugs. You are indeed correct, though, that there do seem to be successful individuals who smoke pot and unsuccessful individuals who don't.

"So I suppose what we have to figure out is whether *you* are as successful as you'd like to be while smoking pot every day. Are you achieving your objectives? Are you accomplishing all that you believe you can accomplish? What are the ways in which pot seems to enhance your ability to reach your goals, and are there any ways in which it seems to be getting in the way?"

When young adults sense that you're not looking to proselytize them to an anti-pot stance, and instead are interested in helping them make decisions that work for them, they tend to engage in a more collaborative discussion of this matter. This approach can obviously be used when it comes to exploring the use of alcohol or any other street or prescription drug as well.

ASSESSMENT OF THE THERAPIST

Part of the assessment of the family involves the family's capacity to assess *us*. Like delicate seismographs that perceive the faintest rumblings from within the core of the family, we need to constantly be alert to implicit or explicit feedback that enables us to make midcourse corrections and better adjust to the family's changing contours.

This should be done at regular intervals by making sure we are asking the questions that key in on this process, such as:

> What did you think about today's session?
> Do you have the sense that we're making progress here, or at least have the potential to make progress?
> In what ways did you envision this going differently?
> In what ways is this process not meeting your expectations?
> Would you have any hesitancy to tell me if this process was not meeting your expectations? If so, what is your hesitancy based upon?

The process of calling forth the family's assessment of the therapist not only provides crucial information to the therapist, but her receptive willingness to hear all about her faults and weaknesses suggests that the process of being evaluated doesn't have to be a harsh, threatening, or demeaning one—instead, it can be welcomed and learned from. This, in turn, makes it easier for everyone in the family to evaluate themselves and each other.

This chapter has obviously not provided a comprehensive approach to assessment. My goal has been to delineate how to evaluate the family's status at the launching phase, not how to evaluate individual family members from, for example, a psychopathological or psychoeducational perspective. And there are, of course, numerous structured assessment strategies—both published and unpublished—that clinicians can use in addition to the actual interview (such as genograms, sociograms, and family time lines).

Anything that provides you with a holistic view of the family and its behavioral and relational patterns is useful, but what needs to be kept in mind is that there is no substitute for the actual assessment-based *conversation* that takes place between clinician and family, and promoting that conversation has been our focus.

In addition, it should be emphasized that one of our greatest challenges when working with young adults and their families is trying to distinguish between the sometimes disturbing but not uncommon or unexpected realities of young adult life (having to do with recreational use of drugs and alcohol, sexual permissiveness, use of the Internet, etc.) and actual problems that reveal psychopathology. Making the distinction between discomfort and disorder is worth a textbook of its own and has also not been covered in depth in this chapter. Again, though, while there are numerous resources to utilize when embarking on this aspect of assessment, we also want to avoid adopting a linear outlook and linking problems too closely with assumptions that don't lead us in the direction of systemic solutions.

We can look at our patients through many lenses, and each one, like the lens of a telescope, necessarily obscures certain realities while focusing on and magnifying others. Keeping a systemic lens in place, and viewing the family compassionately through that lens, is the basis for successful assessment.

The following chapter will build on this process by examining some of the family dynamics that are likely to breed struggling young adults.

Chapter 5

Family Dynamics at the Launching Stage

I recently came across a cartoon that depicted an imposing adult chicken admonishing a little chick, "You're free-range when I *say* you're free-range." The definition of when or whether a child is "free" varies from family to family, but it is one that has to be worked at continuously, from the newness of infancy into hoary old age.

Liberation is an essential developmental task, and the process of healthy liberation rests squarely on the process of healthy separation, a process that begins at the moment of birth. This separation requires the family and its members to summon the past, gather up the present, and move into the future in ever more complex ways, and the process reveals itself as a gradually expanding spiral of growth, maturation, individuation, and differentiation on the part of both generations, increasingly leading all parties toward a healthy balance of self-reliance and interdependence.

Leaving home and establishing self-sufficiency is not so much a day of reckoning for young adults and their families, but an ongoing "phase of reckoning," a multifaceted transaction that at some point will challenge every constituent of the family. It will comprise intense and unavoidable periods of mutual hurt and reconciliation, anger and forgiveness, anguish and joy, loss and discovery, grief and healing, all co-created by the fateful overlap of the struggles, conflicts, and dilemmas of every family member.

In every generation, and in every culture, this extraordinary drama is played out on a unique stage for the highest stakes, for it illuminates the most elemental aspects of human development—the nature of love, loyalty, connection, freedom, responsibility, and selfhood.

And, as with any nodal point in human development, it can easily go awry. Establishing a healthy separation between parent and child is one of the most daunting of family challenges and thus is often impeded and perturbed by various forces. Instead of an even, continuous, and irreversible evolution, distressing detours and frustrating regressions are the norm. Instead of steady, observable growth, there may be long periods of frozen, immobilized stalemate, a developmental deadlock in which growth appears to be completely stymied.

Over the course of my many years working as a family psychologist, I have become enduringly acquainted with the many ways in which the separation process can proceed in growth-promoting or growth-inhibiting ways. While it is easy to fall into the seductive trap of blaming one generation or the other for a confounded separation, these difficulties are invariably the result of the *shared* contributions of both parent and child, who, through acts of omission and commission, add to the push and pull, the swirls and eddies, of intricate and contradictory family forces. Parents cannot help but draw their young adult children into their own personal matrix of conflicts and problems, just as their young adult children cannot help but draw parents into *their* own personal matrix.

Nevertheless, some families successfully launch their young adults and some do not, and an understanding of the family's dynamics helps us to understand why a mutual and respectful separation between parent and young adult child may sometimes be hindered.

In my almost three decades of practice, I have heard parents at every stage of development convey to me their desire for their child's ultimate separation and independence. In fact, a family's dismayed, disconcerted response to their off-spring's behavior, or misbehavior, is often rooted in a fear that the child's journey toward separation and independence is being thwarted.

> "When will he be able to sleep in his own bed?"
>
> "Will he ever stop nursing?"
>
> "When will he be able to wake up in the morning and get his own bowl of cereal without waking me up?"
>
> "When will I be able to drop her off at a birthday party without having to sit with her the whole time?"
>
> "When will she and her brother figure out how to play together nicely without getting me involved in their fights?"
>
> "When will he stay at a sleepover without calling me at midnight to be picked up?"
>
> "When will she learn to handle not getting her way without losing her temper and throwing a tantrum?"
>
> "All of his friends go to sleep-away camp each summer, but he refuses."
>
> "Will she ever learn to organize her schoolwork, or will she always need me to go through her backpack for her?"
>
> "Will he ever read a book and complete a book report on his own, or am I going to be editing his essays in college?"
>
> "Will he ever be motivated to get a driver's license so I don't have to drive him everywhere?"
>
> "Is she ever going to apply to college?"
>
> "Do you think he'll ever start dating?"
>
> "Will I always have to remind her to take medicine?"
>
> "I told him to get a job because he's going to have to pay for his books at college, but he won't get off his butt and find one."
>
> "Will he ever, just, you know, *grow up*?"

The achievement of autonomy is one of life's great triumphs, but autonomy is not easily won. While there are always differences between individual children when it comes to how rapidly they become autonomous, what I have noticed after many years of careful observation is that the climate that the family creates at home has much more to do with how quickly and completely independence is achieved than a child's temperament.

While that climate will always, to some extent, result from the interaction between the generations, parents are often surprised to learn the many ways in which they are actually supplying the very chains that ultimately tether a child to the family's orbit, creating a climate that can make it inordinately difficult, if not impossible, for a young adult to be launched, or to launch herself, into a new and distinct trajectory.

The relationship between the struggling young adult and his parents resembles for me the philosopher G.W.F. Hegel's consideration of the master–slave dialectic, in which the master and slave depend on each other and, as a result of this mutual dependence, are unable to achieve full self-consciousness because each of them inhabits one of these self-limiting roles.

What interests me when I'm working with these families is that each generation perceives its role in completely opposite ways—the young adult believes that his parents are enslaving him by explicitly or implicitly making it hard for him to leave, while the parents believe that the young adult is enslaving them by determinedly *refusing* to leave.

No matter how things are perceived, however, parents cannot help but assign roles for children to play in their middle-aged emotional theater, just as children cannot help but assign roles for their parents to play in their young adult emotional theater. And it is when these roles start to intermesh and conflict with each other that some form of enslavement ensues, and the healthy separation and individuation of both generations is hobbled—self-consciousness, as well as self-realization, become hopelessly halted.

One way to understand and clarify this reality in the context of family treatment is to imagine that every family struggles to find a fluid symmetry between centripetal (pointing inward) and centrifugal (pointing outward) forces. *Centripetal* forces are those that are exerted in an effort to imbue the new generation with a sense of togetherness, loyalty, and tradition—they function as the glue that holds the family together and accounts for its continuity.

Centrifugal forces are those that are exerted in an effort to imbue the new generation with a sense of independence, initiative, and innovation—they function as the lubrication that enables the family to remain a family while allowing its members to move forward into and productively adapt to a changing world.

Both centripetal and centrifugal forces are necessary for healthy functioning and growth, but the contest between the two sets of forces is not always optimal for healthy functioning and growth. In fact, the reality is that all families will teeter back and forth between too much centripetal force, too much centrifugal force, or some conflicted combination of the two. As long as the imbalance is temporary and alterable, significant or enduring difficulties tend not to arise. However, when an imbalance or conflict between centripetal and centrifugal forces sets in, takes root, and begins to establish permanent residency, healthy functioning and growth inevitably become compromised, and symptoms in one or both generations begin to assert themselves.

With this framework in mind, the struggles that young adults experience when they are striving to separate can be best understood not as a flaw or defect in them, or in their parents, but as a symptom of an imbalance or conflict between these centripetal and centrifugal forces.

In my experience, families with struggling young adults tend to fall into one of the following three categories:

When *centripetal* forces dominate, young adults feel overwhelmed by their loyalty to their family—they are not able to successfully leave home, because leaving home is tantamount to a deep, cureless and uncorrectable betrayal of their parents, and any significant life that is lived outside of the family's tight structure is experienced as a violation of love and trust. The guilt that these young adults feel as they consider growing beyond or turning away from their family is excruciating and overpowering enough that they regularly and inventively find ways to sabotage their own development.

When *centrifugal* forces dominate, young adults feel neglected—either rejected or ejected from the family orbit—and they become unable to successfully leave home because they don't believe that they have absorbed enough of the psychological nutrients of love, support, nurturance, faith, and hope necessary to make the daunting journey toward self-reliance.

When centripetal and centrifugal forces are *misaligned*, young adults find themselves in intractable conflict—they are not able to successfully leave home, because they are being asked to fulfill divergent missions for their parents—missions that embroil them in various forms of confusion and ultimately suspend their movement forward because they cannot effectively navigate between these incongruous assignments. I call these Mission-Impossible families.

One of the realities of child development that I find most fascinating, and most relevant, is that children are innate problem solvers and that what we define as a child's problem is actually and invariably a child's attempt to solve a problem. As adults, we often think of children in problem-based modes, but children are generally thinking in solution-based modes.

So when we treat a struggling young adult, the struggle appears to one or more family members to be a *problem*, but, from a systemic perspective, it is a *solution*. The struggle is a solution to the imbalance or conflict of centripetal and centrifugal forces that characterize the family, albeit a maladaptive solution that may (and usually does) work at the expense of the young adult's growth and autonomy.

It is important to remember, as we discuss this triumvirate of family force fields, that all three of them play significant roles in *healthy* child development and ultimate separation and liberation. We often suggest that parents need to provide roots and wings for their children, and what I'm describing isn't really all that different. Centripetal forces are the roots that help children to feel anchored and safe as they grow and develop, and centrifugal forces are the wings that help children to leave the nest and soar away to new and exciting horizons. And, of course, all parents have expectations for their children, wanting them to embody their hopes, dreams, and wishes; wanting them to make good on all the promises to themselves that they may have defaulted on over the years. So the fact that sometimes parents provide children with mixed messages regarding these expectations isn't really avoidable.

In reality, it is not that a well-functioning family is characterized by the complete absence of any of these forces, it's that these forces are well balanced and, over time, are consistently calibrated and recalibrated in response to the child's temperament and developmental stage.

Early on in family life, for example, centripetal forces will most likely hold sway, since children need to be protected, both physically and emotionally. It obviously would not make much sense, for example, to expect a three-year-old to make her own meals, select her own clothes, manage her own social life, and set her own alarm clock to be up on time for preschool.

Later on in family life, centrifugal forces will most likely hold sway, since, as children get older, they need to be able to summon their own resources in preparation for breaking away. With a 16-year-old daughter, it obviously would not make much sense to remain in charge of making her meals, selecting her clothes, managing her social life, and waking her up for school.

We also have to acknowledge that while a good amount of parental consistency is optimal, there will always be differences between parents when it comes to wishes and expectations for their children at any stage of development—that is one of the major advantages of a child *having* two parents (as well, hopefully, as extended family members and other important adults), so that she can experience two sets of regrets and two sets of hopes, two sets of cautions and two sets of inspirations, so that she can ultimately synthesize all of these into a distinct and unique whole.

But when these forces are inappropriately timed, excessively intense, or at war with one other, the separation/liberation process inevitably begins to buckle. When parental nutriments—the roots and wings—are consistently not offered in the right ratios, a child will begin to employ certain survival strategies at the expense of her growth and, as a result, begin to mortgage her future. And this mortgage always comes due as she struggles to cross the threshold into young adulthood.

With this in mind, let's take a closer look at each of these three types of families to see what we can learn about their inner workings and how, ultimately, to rebalance and improve them.

THE CENTRIPETAL FAMILY

A 19-year-old patient of mine once mentioned a movie that he had recently seen that employed tremendous special effects. When I asked him if he had viewed it in a theater, he said, "No, I watched it at home with my parents, during family bondage time." I chuckled to myself at his slip—I'm sure he had meant to say "family *bonding* time," but the membrane between bonding and bondage can be a very thin one in certain families.

In the Centripetal family, the young adult is suffused with the belief that leaving home creates more problems than it solves, which places a corset around his development. Age-appropriate movement toward relative autonomy is seen as a threat, a stunning act of sedition, and is squelched as quickly and fully as possible. Any attempts to individuate, in thought or deed, and any efforts to find joy and meaning by turning away from the family, raise the titer of his parents' fears and anxieties, prompting them to redouble their efforts to terminate the insurrection and fetter him to them as closely as possible.

Both the parents and the enwombed young adult operate under the (usually unspoken) assumption that the family is the ultimate source of all satisfaction and gratification and that seeking such satisfaction and gratification outside of the family is perfidy, a violation of the family code. In this context, members are either totally in the family or totally out of the family—there is no middle ground. As songwriter Shawn Colvin sings, "Wherever you go, you better take care of me."

One of the primary developmental tasks that young adults must master is the transfer of loyalties away from parents and family, and toward friends, sexual and marital partners, mentors, and colleagues. This transfer requires the young adult to attenuate his relationship with his parents so that he can build relationships with people outside of his family of origin and consider adopting values different from his family of origin without experiencing an inhibiting amount of guilt or a sense of being dishonorable to his lineage.

In the Centripetal family, this transfer cannot be accomplished, because the parents exploit their young adult's conscious or subconscious loyalties. She cannot outflank the barricades and remains a helpless captive despite her desire to disentangle herself from her family. I often find myself thinking of Aeschylus's play *Prometheus Bound* when I am working with Centripetal families. The young adult, without necessarily being aware of this, is chained to the family rock and experiences helplessness and torment in the face of powers that she cannot surmount. Yet her willingness to be sacrificed is in some ways her ultimate and most powerful response to being bound.

At its most extreme, the Centripetal family transforms one or more offspring into lifelong, self-sacrificing victims, for whom the very thought of, let alone the attempt at, psychological separation is proscribed and likely to elicit harsh punishment in one form or another from the parents, and possibly from other family members (siblings, grandparents) as well. For parents who operate from a centripetal standpoint, the most gratifying thing that their young adult can do is to stonewall or circumvent her own growth and development—in essence, to *regress* rather than progress.

Many of the struggling young adults that I treat have, over time, internalized that punishment and taken over the process themselves. They regularly and ingeniously thwart themselves without understanding why, without even being aware that they are doing so. If they are socially or intellectually capable of journeying forth from the family, they find ways not to, flapping their wings madly but without attaining any elevation or ascendance because their feet are still tied to the family cage. If they are socially or intellectually insecure or inadequate, they make sure that they don't find ways to use the strengths that they *do* have to compensate for their weaknesses. Meanwhile, their parents, who have already done the "dirty work" over the course of the previous years, sit back, truly mystified, and wonder why their young adult is still just treading water.

Parents keep these centripetal forces in place in many different ways. Sometimes they do this by ignoring and invalidating their child's thoughts and ideas and imposing their own, resulting in a child who never learns to trust and depend on his own perceptions, insights, and interpretations. Boundaries between parent and child are blurry and distorted, and the child is denied any privacy or autonomy in thought or action, while the parents are impervious to the reality that their child has desires and beliefs of his own.

Sometimes parents create self-fulfilling prophecies that are built on the premise that the child is not capable of autonomy—he is "sick" or "weak" or "disabled"—prophecies that interfere with the child learning to transcend whatever weaknesses he does have and harness his assets in the service of self-reliance. The child is destined, as a result, to remain functionally helpless, ruling out any possibility of eventual escape from the airtight family.

Sometimes parents keep life overly centripetal by avoiding direct conflicts with their child, preventing him from learning how to articulate a separate and distinct position, which is the sine qua non of becoming one's own person. Disagreements are generally ignored, suppressed, or too quickly defused by a retreat into a fraudulent state of consensual agreement and harmony, and she enters the world like a cat without claws.

Sometimes parents induce fear in the child, creating an image of the world at large as hostile, dangerous, and forbidding and the (xenophobic) family as the only reputable haven within which to hunker down. One mother whom I worked with repeatedly told her son, "No one will ever love you the way we love you."

Sometimes centripetal parents promote their child's dependence on them, convincing him that he cannot survive without them so he dare not attempt to move on with his life. Through indulging, coddling, and constantly gratifying their child or through constantly supervising and scrutinizing him, they ensure that he never develops the skills and self-assuredness to make it on his own. He may become spoiled, infantile, and manipulative, but, insatiably demanding and dependent as he may be, at least he never leaves—or if he does, he is doomed to fail and eventually return home, because he remains at the mercy of the tyranny of his desires.

Sometimes parents exert centripetal influence by overtly or covertly noting how much they have sacrificed for their child, making it clear not just that they live only *for* him but also that they only live *through* him. "Her life is my life. I would throw myself in front of a bus for her. I've felt that way from the moment she was born," was how one mother expressed this thought to me.

This guilt-inducing enterprise can turn the child into a lifelong vassal, a martyr who experiences merely the thought of, let alone the movement toward, separation as a crime for which only the most draconian sanctions—ostracism or exile, for starters—will do. Diligently pursuing self-undermining and a steadfast shunning of success and self-reliance become the most reliable ways of assuaging this overpowering guilt.

Some parents criticize their young adult, making sure that he adopts a hopeless, defeatist attitude, snuffing out any self-confidence that might be tentatively poking its head above the surface. One 18-year-old patient, a high school senior, confessed to me, "I don't even pour my own cereal for breakfast because my father has convinced me over the years that I'm doing it wrong. Either I'm taking too much, or making a mess. I don't even bother at this point; I just wait for him to do it for me."

And some parents insistently declare the extent to which they depend on their child for their own identity, even for their own existence—in other words, the ways in which they have lived their own lives through their child's life. In the words of one father, "Every goal he scored in lacrosse was like a goal that I scored. I can't tell you how proud it makes me when I see him on the field. I don't know what it will be like once he's done playing; it's as if I was on the team *with* him all these years, suffering through every loss, screaming with every victory."

No matter how centripetal forces establish dominance, however, the potential for the young adult's growth and eventual separation decreases in direct proportion to his strength. The family siphons off the young adult's spirit and ambition with their implicit or explicit demands, and he becomes a confirmed failure, like a horse that runs in ever-smaller circles until he is essentially running in place. Struggling to find freedom from the unholy alliances that distinguish a relentlessly Centripetal family is generally limited to the following developmental options:

- Reluctant to provoke unhappiness or displeasure on his parents' part, he will prune back his initiatives and sacrifice his ambitions, capitulating to the family's ceaseless gravitational pull and becoming submissive and compliant. Self-determination will evaporate in the face of his efforts to remain loyal to his parents, and he will live a life of spineless appeasement to his family and to others.
- Consumed by the constant conflict between her own desires and those of her parents, she will try to numb the pain resulting from this inner strain,

often relying on drugs and alcohol or endless electronic entertainment to assist her in the anesthetizing process.

- Desperate to find some niche that feels like it's his own even though he's still compelled to remain physically close to his tangled family, he will retreat into a fantasy world that replaces the real world of living peers and potentially useful adults (mentors, teachers, etc.), often becoming immersed in the cyberworld of video and computer games, Facebook, and so on.

- Feeling completely impounded, she will create a dramatic expulsion in a desperate effort to break the centripetal deadlock. However, because the expulsion tends to be *impulsive* and *explosive*, it tends not to be well thought out, resulting in an eventual return to the original stalemate. This is often seen when suffocated young adults excitedly cook up half-baked plans for departure that eventually fall through precisely because they are poorly designed.

- He may arrange for a force stronger than his own family to facilitate his leave-taking, such as enlisting in the armed services or breaking enough laws enough times such that where he resides winds up being in the hands of the justice system rather than in his own hands or the family system's hands.

- Overcome by powerful waves of guilt for forging ahead with her own life despite the mandate that she remain home, she maneuvers herself forward anyway but engages in regular self-destructive behavior in an effort to assuage that guilt.

- He will engage in what is often called "malicious obedience," following his parents' directive but making them pay for it in one way or another with his attitude or behavior.

- She will "soil the nest" and make life at home as unbearable as possible for her family, such as by coming in at all hours of the night, not cleaning up after herself, and smoking in the house when her parents have made it clear that this was forbidden, especially when her 80-year-old grandmother with chronic obstructive pulmonary disease is visiting from Florida.

- He will fight off the control by refusing to take care of himself, thereby proving that he, not his parents, is the one who is ultimately in control.

- She will resist by not resisting, by simply succumbing to the undertow that drags her back into a deep ocean of inertia.

An additional challenge to the centripetally bound young adult is that some of the techniques utilized to keep him lashed to the mast of the family ship make it difficult for him to leap into the waters of possibly growth-promoting peer relationships and maintain his seaworthiness. For example, if, as noted above, a child is made to feel dependent on her parents through being spoiled and coddled, if she has been raised by a mother or father who seem constitutionally incapable of being displeased with her, she is going to have difficulty finding same-age friends and romantic partners who are likely to put up with her childish demands or narcissism for very long, making a rueful return to the safety of home all the more attractive and alluring.

Or, without having been given the opportunity to learn to hold his ground and advocate for himself, he will be much more vulnerable to being manipulated, exploited, or rebuffed by others. The limited skills that he learned and the erroneous assumptions that he incorporated from his family's amoebic, stultifying culture will seem completely useless in and bewilderingly irrelevant to his peer culture, and the resultant culture shock that is experienced will become overwhelming, prompting a flight from the inhospitable foreign land of independence back to the familiar province of dependence.

It should also be noted that after many years of unrelenting centripetality, it often becomes completely unclear to the family who is binding whom. The young adult will complain that his parents are suffocating *him*, while the parents complain that their young adult is suffocating *them*. The cycle can become so entrenched and routinized over time that there is no longer any observable beginning or end, no longer any distinct actor or reactor, and the chain that binds them to each other begins to seem unseverable.

THE CENTRIFUGAL FAMILY

One of my saddest memories from elementary school took place when our second-grade class was studying the butterfly life cycle, and we watched a caterpillar grow and change into a chrysalis. One day, we were passing around the chrysalis as the date of its transformation into a butterfly neared. Perhaps it was from the warmth conveyed by several dozen eager students' hands, but the butterfly suddenly began to emerge from the chrysalis, to excited oohs and aahs from its ardent observers. However, because it was premature, the butterfly was not completely formed and unable to successfully extricate itself. Our teacher quickly scooped it up and deposited it on the windowsill, much to our collective disappointment and chagrin.

Later that day, as I was coming in from recess, I saw the butterfly on the windowsill, still struggling futilely to extract itself from its pupa, unlikely to survive and become the beautiful winged insect that it was meant to be.

I think about that image as I write this section because young adults who grow up in Centrifugal families are similar to this unfortunate butterfly, thrust out of their cocoon before they are ready, forced into a premature autonomy that may not allow them to psychologically survive. The steps forward that a young adult from an overly Centrifugal family take feel less like those of a prisoner leaving jail because he has finished his sentence and more like those of a prisoner leaving jail because he is heading off to an execution. If the Centripetal family affords zero degrees of separation, the Centrifugal family affords infinite degrees of separation—so much separation that there is no sense of connection.

In Centrifugal families, the young adult is seen by the parents not as a source of pride but as a hindrance, a distraction from or obstacle to the achievement of their long-delayed or recently evolving objectives and satisfactions. The child is exiled and extradited in important ways by her parents and shoved toward autonomy whether she is *ready* or not, and whether she *wants* to be or not. As Dr. Seuss's Marvin K. Mooney insists, "Just go, I don't care how!" Meanwhile, the young adult struggles to stay put rather than move on, futilely straining to extract psychic sustenance from the family's now-paltry waters.

Sometimes, the centrifugal process begins early in life. The child, for various reasons, is never found to be sufficiently important, interesting, or worthwhile—he never really feels "at home" at home. At other times, the centrifugal process begins to take over later in childhood or during adolescence or early adulthood. The parents feel as if they've put in their time and now believe that they are entitled to be relieved of child-rearing responsibilities in any form. The idea that their young adult child still wants or needs them in significant ways feels like an intrusion, an imposition.

But whenever centrifugality establishes too much dominance, these parents make it clear that they've reached the point at which they care less and less if their child is bound to them or not and, in the process, fail to establish the age-appropriate attachment that may be necessary to support her during her strivings toward autonomy. In trying to solve whatever issues they are personally in the midst of, they adopt a "the sooner, the better" attitude when it comes to her leave-taking, whether well grounded or not.

I often see this happening when parents feel like it's time to make a fresh start in life—ending a marriage or beginning a new one, starting a new professional direction or retiring, living more simply or peacefully or inexpensively or extravagantly. With these goals in mind, they come to view their young adult child as more of a liability than an asset—parenthood feels burdensome, and any remaining dependent children feel like expendable nuisances. So the child is forced to leave home lacking the sense of being important to his parents and instead feels as if he is nothing more than an annoyance.

Because of this, the young adult in the Centrifugal family is not freighted by the loyalty burdens that are assumed by children in the Centripetal family and thus is not prone to being exploited in the same way. In fact, from the outside, she may appear to be footloose and fancy free, easily able to move out and move on, less entangled and conflicted and floating through the world like an unhindered helium molecule. But this is often a mask for feeling banished, cast away, excommunicated, or kicked to the curb. The apparent ease with which she separates ultimately can become a problem, because she knows, at some level, that leaving home is a matter of sink or swim. Either she makes it on her own out in the roiling currents of the real world, or she drowns—there is no life preserver to keep her afloat, no life raft that she can climb onto and row back to shore should she run into trouble. She moves around and outside of the margins of the family like an errant planet that is forlornly exempt from the family's gravitational forces.

The push toward premature autonomy—the sense that his parents have everything to gain and nothing to lose when it comes to his moving on—actually prevents him from experiencing the opportunity to grow through and resolve the normal family conflicts that need to be sorted out to establish the basis for a more mature version of connectedness and intimacy in his young adult life. This usually means that subsequent relationships will suffer as a result. In being dismissed from the family too quickly, he will tend to enact with others—friends, romantic partners, colleagues, employers—the unsatisfied needs that were not met by his family, which usually overwhelm and alienate them, leaving him feeling angry, victimized, and, ultimately, lonely.

Parents often keep centrifugal forces in place by exaggerating their child's self-sufficiency, proudly (if not smugly) defining her as precocious and independent so as to justify an early eviction. They also tend to blithely rationalize their neglect, rejection, or ejection as "teaching her to be independent," "toughening her up," or "not wanting to hold her back." This helps them to expiate their guilt about not providing her with the shelter, guidance, and care that she still needs before being able to survive exposure to the sometimes wintry winds of life on her own.

Centrifugality also manifests itself when the young adult has taken on the role of family scapegoat—members dump their sins onto him, and he symbolically cleanses the family by trudging off into the wilderness, carrying their burdens, while they are now free and unladen.

Centrifugality can be maintained when parents conclude—often with the support, if not insistence, of professionals—that they are ineffective parents and that others with supposedly more experience and expertise need to take over, absolving them of responsibility. This is when socially sanctioned institutionalization may often be recommended, which could be anything from a psychiatric hospitalization to a drug rehabilitation program. I see this when families are told by an educational or therapeutic consultant to send their struggling young adult to a wilderness program or boarding school or therapeutic boot camp. Eager to do right by their young adult child and without being given an opportunity to understand the complexity of their family's plight, they naturally conclude that shipping him out so that other (sometimes questionably trained) adult guides and mentors can take over his life is really the best thing for him. Sometimes, the results of this kind of exile are disastrous.

But even if it goes relatively well, the reality is that the young adult generally returns home to the same force field that was the precursor to her temporary deportation because the same debilitating dynamics will resurrect themselves. So the family's revolving door will inevitably thrust the young adult back out toward another establishment.

No matter how these centrifugal forces are maintained, however, the potential for the young adult's growth and eventual separation are imperiled. Struggling to survive an untimely expulsion will typically lead her to travel one or more of the following paths.

- She will behave in nefarious ways that provoke the very expulsion that she anticipates and fears, thus providing her with a sense of having some control over this process rather than remaining a submissive victim of it.
- He will preemptively expel himself, which also gives him a feeling of control over the ejection process.
- Unable to get what she needs at home but unable to make it on her own, she will just drift dismally along, her life flowing on without any rhyme or reason, without any pattern or direction, barely getting by and cleverly leaving her parents in a state of uncertainty regarding whether they can close the book on parenthood and move on with their lives.
- In an act of punitive protest, he will steadfastly dig his heels in and either actively or passively refuse to lay the groundwork for leaving home, resisting any efforts to dislodge him until he feels as if his importance has been recognized and his needs for nurturance and support have been granted and guaranteed.

THE MISSION-IMPOSSIBLE FAMILY

When we were children, my brothers and I were allowed to stay up late on Saturday nights to watch the weekly TV show *Mission Impossible*. I remember the catchphrase as Mr. Phelps listened to the tape that described the daunting task of that week's episode: "Your mission, Jim, should you choose to accept it, is . . ." The difference between Mr. Phelps and a child growing up in a Mission-Impossible family is that the child, being a child, believes that he or she has very little choice other than to accept what might be an impossible mission.

The Mission-Impossible family occupies an intermediate position between the Centripetal and the Centrifugal family and has similarities with and differences from both. As in the Centrifugal family, the young adult is entitled and encouraged to leave the parental orbit, and, as in the Centripetal family, the young adult is still viewed as someone who is loved and valued and who continues to be tended to and nurtured in meaningful ways as he struggles forward.

The child trying to exit from a Mission-Impossible family tends not to be centripetally suffocated nor centrifugally exiled, which leaves her room to develop a wider and more integrated range of skills, motivations, and ambitions. She is usually able to move successfully into the interpersonal world outside of her family, unlike centripetal young adults, and carries with her a reasonable set of expectations for these relationships, unlike the centrifugal young adults. These realities raise the odds of a successful embarkation.

What is uniquely complicated about the Mission-Impossible family is that the young adult is both released and pulled back at the same time, allowed to leave but still manacled to the family because he is entrusted with a mission that can never be successfully accomplished. Like a faithful canine retriever, he is not truly independent but must report back to his parents on some sort of regular basis, and the report that he provides needs to be one that satisfies his masters.

It is completely natural for parents to invest in children their dreams and wishes, for them to ask their offspring to honor and expand the family's legacy and bring joy, meaning, and satisfaction to their, and their forebears', lives. All parents want to replace themselves with a better copy. However, these expectations are appropriate only to some extent and only up to a developmental point. At a certain juncture, parents have to unfasten their child from being expected to belatedly live out aborted aspects of their own unlived life, to carry the burden of exaggerated and frustrated aspirations that they will not and cannot realize themselves. This release may force them to confront issues, dilemmas, and concerns that they have been assiduously trying to avoid for many years.

The young adult from a Mission-Impossible family, like her counterparts in Centripetal and Centrifugal families, suffers great turmoil when she attempts to separate, because the mission she is asked to take on makes great demands on her and may be completely incompatible with what her faculties and proficiencies lead her to actually be capable of. She is essentially called upon to either help reconcile and resolve the *individual* conflicts that one or both of her parents experience or help reconcile the *interpersonal* conflicts between the two of them. She may tackle this herculean task with ingenuity, skill, and boundless determination, but she will always do so at the expense of her own liberation and constantly feel derelict in her duties.

I often witness this when parents, crushed by the weight of their own disappointments, find themselves face to face with their own midlife limitations and disillusionment and turn to their child for psychological salvation. She must embody all that the parents feel lacking or wanting in themselves, fulfill abandoned parental aspirations, and become extraordinary in a desperate effort to shore up their caregiver's sagging ego. Particularly when the child, like most of us, is *not* unprecedentedly talented, brilliant, or virtuosic, it is natural for him to finally give up trying, knowing that he's never going to scale the dizzying heights of acclaim and recognition that he is being asked to. I am reminded of the headline for an opinion piece from the satiric newspaper *The Onion*, which states, "As Long as My Child Does Something That Makes Him Happy and Wins the National Book Critics' Circle Award for Fiction, I'll Be Proud."

Still, the young adult from the Mission-Impossible family will try in vain to tackle the unenviable task of becoming his parents' narcissistic ambassador to the world, the Second Coming of their best, most idealized selves. To do so, he must make good on the promises that one or both parents made to themselves but defaulted on; or he must repair their broken dreams.

In other families, the impossible mission results from the young adult's two parents being unable to integrate their ideas and directives for how she is to leave—perhaps one parent provides permission and support for separation while the other one doesn't, or the two parents have radically different definitions of what a healthy separation entails, definitions that are so disparate that the young adult cannot figure out how to attune them.

So the young adult in a Mission-Impossible family is understandably confused as adolescence comes to a close, not at all certain whether being a good son involves staying put or heading out, seeking satisfaction and salvation *within* the family or *outside* of the family, becoming successful according to his *own* definition of success or according to one or both of his *parents'* definitions of success.

The child in this situation is, in essence, the parents' delegate—and what she is delegated to do is to carry the burden of, and somehow resolve and alleviate, her parents' ambivalence about their own lives, and about her separation. Young adults will often take on this task with great hope, energy, and initiative, but they invariably do so at the expense of their own growth and individuation. It is not their job to resolve their parents' internal or marital conflict, but out of their deep love and loyalty, they may try to do so anyway. Interestingly, the word *delegate* derives from the Latin root *de-legare*, which means to leave, and yet, paradoxically, this complicated form of parent–child delegation makes leaving home almost impossible.

In the Mission-Impossible family, as in the Centripetal family, one or more family members exploit the young adult's conscious or subconscious loyalty, but the process usually tends to be somewhat more nuanced and lower profile, since strong centrifugal forces are at work as well. Yet as subtle as this exploitation is, it still can be perversely effective at keeping him stuck, because his mission is dictated more by his parents' needs than by his own—he remains incarcerated in an Alcatraz of unachievable expectations.

Another typical impossible mission occurs when the parents' marriage is unsatisfying. When a husband and wife have lost the capacity or the desire to turn to each other when life is difficult, or when they have fallen into a hostile or sullen stalemate, it is natural for them to turn to the people who, it appears, have been designated to ameliorate their unhappiness—namely, one or more of their children. In these situations, the young adult is essentially a pawn in her parents' battles, maneuvered back and forth at will and, as a result, forced to forgo her own independence.

Some of the other undertakings that struggling young adults might be burdened with include:

- Living out or calling attention to internal conflicts that one or both parents have not resolved
- Living out or calling attention to aspects of the parent's personality that he or she has disowned and projected onto the young adult
- Providing his parents with experiences that they missed when *they* were young adults
- Fighting a battle for one parent against another parent
- Diverting one parent's anger away from the other parent

- Attempting to bring embattled parents together by attempting to be either absolutely perfect or an unsolvable problem
- Vigilantly guarding a fearful family secret for one or more family members
- Fulfilling dire parental prophecies for how things will ultimately play out
- Sticking around until they have lit a fire under their family and can trust that *their* growth as young adults will ultimately result in continued growth for the rest of the family

It must be emphasized that it is not always the number or intensity of expectations that are foisted onto young adults but *the extent to which these expectations conflict with each other* that can tear them asunder and impede their development.

For example, in one family I was treating, Celine, a 19-year-old college student, was delegated by her father to be an academic superachiever in college, which wasn't unrealistic, as she was quite bright. At the same time, however, she was delegated by her mother to go off to college and vicariously provide her with the social and sexual excitement that her mother had never experienced, which also wasn't unrealistic, as Celine was quite charming and attractive. Obviously, the two missions eventually became incongruent, prompting Celine to temporarily resolve the conflict by engaging in a long and dangerous semester of promiscuous behavior, culminating in her getting drunk and being date-raped at a fraternity party.

The lack of judgment on this otherwise thoughtful young woman's part appeared to be her way of trying to get both of her parents to back off from their irreconcilable aspirations. Because of how frightening this episode was, her father became less inclined to push her to become an academic star, and her mother became less inclined to push her to be a social star. Both, instead, shifted their focus to helping her to cultivate more maturity and self-respect when it came to her relationships with young men, and their unity freed her to proceed with her college career with better sense and more autonomy.

The missions that many young adults struggle to execute may be impossible because they involve conflicts of loyalty. We might remember that Hamlet was commissioned to remain faithful to his dead father and to destroy his own mother, which embroiled him in a tragic loyalty bind that brought him to the brink of a breakdown. Young adults from Mission-Impossible families may battle mixed loyalties toward their family versus toward themselves, or mixed loyalties toward individual family members, all of which can break them down. For example, he may feel most loyal to the parent or family member whom he perceives as the strongest, hoping to absorb, benefit from, and be protected by that strength, or he may feel most loyal to the parent or family member whom he perceives as the weakest, out of a commitment to supporting and bolstering the vulnerable underdog.

While young adults in Mission-Impossible families are often better able to lay the groundwork for leaving home than are young adults from Centripetal or Centrifugal families, they will still often find themselves laboring to be true to themselves as they make their way forward, because they are, in essence, doing battle for one or both of their parents.

Donald was a 23-year-old who had recently been expelled from medical school due to poor grades and unprofessional behavior with patients. I learned from him that his mother had always been angry at his father for having been such a disappointment as a provider and that his parents' marriage had been hostile and stifling for years.

As he told his story, it seemed to me that Donald had been recruited by his mother to show up his father and soften her disappointment with her marriage—a successful son might make up for how disenchanted she was with her under-functioning husband. So Donald was bathed in maternal approval, encouraged to study hard and move on with his life as a way of both surpassing and defeating his father and as a way of vicariously living out his mother's fantasy of leaving his father behind.

This he had, in fact, done by decamping from home for a fine college and suc-ceeding at a high enough level there to have been admitted to medical school on his first try. But, as he confessed to me, his heart was never in it, and he gradually realized that he had no idea why he was actually there, which most likely ac-counted for his academic underachievement and his graceless interactions in the hospital.

So while Donald was able to make strides toward a successful departure, the departure eventually ran out of steam because it was not driven by his own initia-tive and desire—a medical career was instead simply an assignment that he was taking on and playing out for someone else. As he became increasingly aware that he was being maneuvered into living out his mother's fantasy and, in the pro-cess, devaluing his own father—his same-sex role model—the loyalty bind that he found himself in made carrying out that mission truly impossible.

An additional facet of the Mission-Impossible family that is often difficult to detect is that the impossible mission is often delegated *covertly* rather than overtly. Parents will consistently and confidently assure me that they have no desire other than "wanting him to be happy" or "wanting her to be successful." Yet as I slowly peel back the sometimes obtuse and obscure layers of family history and com-munication, it often becomes abundantly clear that there is a teeming cluster of confusing and conflicted expectations that is being conveyed by the parents, sometimes with astonishing tact and subtlety.

This often is occurring when young adults are getting into the deepest trouble, because the most dangerous and potentially destructive mission that a child is generally called upon by her parents to shoulder is to embody the qualities and characteristics that they are least comfortable with and most conflicted about within themselves. In other words, when parents are unable to tolerate the pres-ence of their own forbidden wishes and impulses, they sometimes project them onto one of their children, surreptitiously convincing her to act out these very wishes and impulses, thus enabling them to self-righteously scold and punish her for behaving so poorly and, in the process, feel better about themselves.

It is when parents attempt to contain, neutralize, and annihilate rather than understand, and embrace the aspects of themselves that they most fear and are most troubled by that they may entrust their child to enact those very aspects. This temporarily relieves them of the discomfort of inhabiting a guilty or hostile inner world but puts the child in the position of having to live it out for them and grow into the very person that they don't want to be but fear that they inherently are, or might still become.

Because it is a subconscious process, parents are often not aware that they are actually (albeit invisibly) goading their child into engaging in activities such as sexual mischief, substance abuse, flouting authority, or acting with wanton disregard for the rights of others. In fact, they understandably appear flustered that they—who may, at this point in their lives, be forthright paragons of propriety and virtue—have raised a young adult who can behave so callously and reprehensibly. Yet it is precisely because of their unwillingness or inability to come to terms with their feet of clay that they entrust one or more of their children with the mission of a doomed, clay-footed march that may never conclude with autonomy.

For example, Darius never forgave himself for the period during his late teens when he was dealing drugs, an enterprise that resulted in the police coming to his house and arresting him, profoundly embarrassing his parents. From that point on, he committed himself to becoming a good Christian and leading an unblemished life of ethical rectitude, telling no one—not even his wife—about his adolescent misdeeds. Naturally, he was both horrified and incensed when he learned that his 16-year-old son, Javon, had been apprehended trying to establish himself in the same disreputable business. His initial reaction was to heap scorn on his son, as if he had never behaved similarly 30 years before.

What Darius didn't understand is that the shame that he still felt about his young adult transgressions, and his ongoing effort to simply erase them rather than make sense of them, set the stage for his young adult son to repeat them. In our sessions, he courageously summoned the willingness to own up to his dishonorable past, which then gave him the opportunity to speak more candidly with Javon rather than simply sitting in supercilious judgment of him. This brought father and son closer together and served to more fruitfully steer Javon away from further trouble.

Interestingly, this process does not always have to play out problematically (despite the fact that it often does). For example, family theorist Helm Stierlin observed that many non-Jewish German students in the post-Holocaust era went to work in Israel and acknowledged that they felt that they were doing so to help atone for Nazi crimes against the Jews, which their parents and grandparents were often working very hard not to recognize or admit to. In this case, the younger generation was somehow induced to step in and perform the redemptive work necessary to ease the guilt that their progenitors carried but were unwilling to acknowledge and atone for on their own.

It should again be emphasized that all families have centripetal, centrifugal, and mission-impossible tendencies—parenting inevitably is a complicated mixture of binding, expelling, and delegating. These tendencies become worrisome, stultifying, and possibly damaging when they are:

1   Inappropriately timed, from a developmental standpoint (too much centrifugality early in development, too much centripetality later in development);
2   Blended in problematic ratios (far too much of one than the other); or
3   Excessively intense.

It is also worth being reminded that some families simply don't fit neatly into any particular category; they are a chaotic mixture of all three tendencies and have, as a result, constructed a thwarting apparatus that reliably restricts growth on everyone's part.

But one way or another, the prospect of leaving home throws into bold relief the brisk interplay between the family's centripetal, centrifugal, and mission-impossible energies. Crises emerge when these energies cannot be creatively reconciled—through careful readjustment and reconfiguration—in the face of the young adult's need to individuate and separate and the parents' need to relinquish their identity as hands-on, day-to-day caregivers.

LGBTQ Issues

Tolerance of lesbian, gay, bisexual, transgender, and queer (LGBTQ) young adults and same-sex relationships continues to expand in many locations and cultures in the United States, although certainly not everywhere. For example, beginning with Massachusetts in 2004, same-sex marriage has been legalized in four other states, and the District of Columbia also now recognizes gay marriages. The Gay, Lesbian and Straight Education Network reports that in 1997, there were approximately 100 gay-straight alliances in U.S. high schools, and now there are more than 4,000.

Savin-Williams (2001) has observed that the contemporary generation of gay youth is less prone to suicidal thinking and behavior, less ostracized by society in general, and even less likely to define themselves based on their sexual orientation. Related to this, research exploring the mean age of gays coming out to others has concluded that this has decreased from age 23 in 2001 to ages 16 to 18 (D'Augelli, 2006). The fact that most 16- to 18-year-olds are still living at home strongly suggests that there is less fear on the part of gay youth regarding not only societal disapproval, but also family disapproval. A cartoon deftly chronicled this shift, portraying a father complaining to his young adult son: "If you don't hurry up, you're not going to be the first openly gay *anything*."

On the other hand, our society remains heterocentric and homophobic in many ways. Bullying against gays and antigay hate crimes have not decreased over the past decade. Many gays do grow up in families that are disapproving or rejecting of them, which results in a higher likelihood of drug use, depression, and suicide.

COMING OUT

The process of coming out to one's family is invariably a pivotal experience in the lives of LGBTQ young adults. Some eventually choose to come out, some are found out in an accidental way by a family member, and some never do decide to come out. It is not absolutely clear that coming out to one's family is a necessary precursor to healthy young adult development—while there are certainly advantages to doing so, particularly if there is a positive response among family members, there are many LGBTQ adults who never came out to their families and whose lives are nevertheless characterized by success and positive self-regard.

The risk of coming out is related to the fact that many LGBTQ young adults may still be psychologically and financially dependent on their families for support. So if their parents disapprove, there is much for them to lose, and their self-esteem is jeopardized. This is one of the many ways in which sexual minorities differ from racial or religious minorities—in general, the latter groups do not exist as minorities *within their own families*, but the former usually do.

Parents who do learn of their child's LGBTQ status—however they learn of it—will have a range of emotional responses. Some of these are both typical and predictable, such as feeling guilty or responsible for having "caused" their child to be LGBTQ, feeling anxious about the challenges that await their sexual minority child as he or she enters a heterocentric world, and/or grieving for what they imagine will be the comprehensive loss or devastating demise of their hopes and dreams for their child. All parents naturally long to protect their children from pain and disappointment, and the journey of the LGBTQ young adult is one that has a higher likelihood of pain and disappointment because it will be littered with the potential for rejection, marginalization, and ostracism by individuals, groups, and society at large.

Other responses vary depending on the parent's own personality, identity, and experience. For example, some parents I have taken care of interpret their child's coming out as a rejection of them, while others see it as having no impact at all on their relationship with their child. I have worked with parents whose main concern is that their LGTBQ child might be more likely to acquire a sexually transmitted disease, while other parents worry more about whether their LGBTQ child will ever find a suitable intimate partner.

But all parents who are placed in this situation will not only be forced to encounter and manage their own heterocentric thoughts, attitudes, beliefs, and values; they will also be forced to come to terms with and manage the heterocentrism, and possible homophobia, of their extended families, their communities, and the religious, cultural, and ethnic groups with which they are closely connected. One or both of these endeavors will likely present a significant psychological challenge to the parents and, at least temporarily, raise the odds of heightened levels of marital tension and nuclear- and extended-family conflict.

LGBTQ youth face many types of adversity. For example, some of the bisexual young adults whom I have treated struggle because they feel ostracized by both ends of the spectrum. They express frustration with not being accepted or trusted in a gay relationship or in a straight relationship and are shut down from a possible romantic relationship because prospective partners fear that they will suddenly "switch teams."

As noted above, LGBTQ young adults who are members of ethnic minorities often find themselves in a complicated position both inside and outside of their families. On the one hand, they may get solid family support when it comes to dealing with bias and discrimination for race-related reasons; on the other hand, they may not be the beneficiaries of similar support for sexual identity issues. Their minority status takes place on multiple levels, and they can be on the receiving end of rejection, disapproval, and unflattering stereotypes at home or in the community at large. LGBTQ young adults who have physical or mental disabilities are often in the same position—embraced in one way by family but spurned in another.

TREATMENT ISSUES

Having treated numerous families in which LGBTQ youth have come out, or have been outed, my main priority is to help parents to release themselves from the belief that they can or should attempt to influence their child's sexuality and to help them to examine whatever heterosexist myths and biases still reside within them. No matter how sensitive, open-minded, and intelligent they may be, most parents still need to be educated to some extent regarding issues related to sexual identity and the often rutted path toward coming out.

All mothers and fathers want their offspring to live rich, satisfying, and meaningful lives, and it is difficult for young adults to live that kind of life if they feel that they must be imposters, if they have to keep such an important aspect of their identity a secret from their own family—the individuals who should be counted on to love and support them unconditionally. When parents and their LGBTQ young adult children are able to make their way through the matrix of complicated feelings and conflicts associated with coming out and collaboratively experience and embrace their fears, worries, and irrevocably altered expectations, they generally find that they wind up feeling closer to and more connected with each other, much more trusting of the resilient bonds of family love.

As with any significant young adult identity issue, the family's capacity to adjust is an ongoing, reciprocal process. Parents often find it helpful to find the support of other parents, preferably nonjudgmental ones, whose child is also gay. They might initially respond to their child's coming out with disappointment, anger, reproach, or denunciation but feel more positive when they see that their son or daughter is feeling more positive as a result of having unlocked him- or herself from leading a life of concealment.

I often begin to address this issue by meeting with the parents and the young adult separately. It is important to allow the parents to voice their mixed feelings without having to worry about upsetting their child and for the young adult to speak freely without having to worry about parental censure or chastisement. The therapist must increase both generations' sense of safety, enlarge their access to supportive community resources, and enhance their capacity to confront and transcend whatever heterocentric stigma, bias, and discrimination they are facing or are likely to face. Two parents may differ in their readiness to accept a child's sexual identity or orientation, so marital conflict may arise as this process unfolds.

In one family, Omar had led what he felt was a "wicked" life up until his mid-30s, when he got involved with a church and began the process of redeeming and forgiving himself—he found the priest, and many of the new friends he made there, to be surpassingly supportive and understanding as he revisited, and endeavored to come to terms with, his painful past. About 10 years later, Omar's 19-year-old son, Adammi, announced that he was gay. This became a source of anguish for Omar, because the priest, as well as many of the fellow congregants whom he had grown close to in the past decade, frowned upon homosexuality and saw it as a sin against God. In fact, during one sermon, the priest asked the congregation to collectively pray that an amendment in the state assembly supporting gay marriage would be swiftly defeated.

It took us several individual sessions, as well as a session that included his priest, to reconcile the two forces that were at war within him: the part of Omar that loved the church (and loved who he had become as a result of attending) and the part of him that loved his son. Eventually, after much soul searching, Omar decided that it was not a betrayal of his son if he continued attending the church and that he could focus on what was best about its *spiritual* orientation without having to incorporate or believe in its *heterocentric* orientation.

In another family, Erin, the mother of a 22-year-old lesbian, met with me because she felt guilty about her inability to take delight in her daughter's coming out. I encouraged her to be patient and to accept herself for where she was rather than push herself toward a fraudulent state of jaunty optimism. I reminded her that she wouldn't be doing her daughter any favors by attempting to convey a counterfeit embrace of her daughter's sexual orientation and that Erin's willingness to accept herself was an important step in learning to accept her daughter.

The therapist must also help the LGBTQ young adult (and, if possible, use the family as a resource) to resolve any residual trauma resulting from his or her history with victimization or living in the closet and to address the negative attitudes toward nonheterosexuality that have most likely been internalized to some extent during the young adult's childhood and adolescence. For example, I have taken care of many LGBTQ young adults who are convinced that their parents or other important family members or friends will no longer love or care for them once they come out, but this sometimes appears to be the projection of an interior homophobia that has not been aired and examined rather than an accurate assessment of how others will actually respond.

The challenges for LGBTQ youth and their families are always significant ones in a heterocentric society, but the fact that young adults are free to move outside of the confines of the family at this stage of their life can reduce tension and increase the likelihood of their finding like-minded friendship, support, and romance among their peer group.

Chapter 6

Getting Unstuck at the Launching Stage

Too long a sacrifice can make a stone of the heart
O when may it suffice?

W. B. Yeats, *Easter, 1916*

One of my biology professors in college joked that "a chicken is an egg's way of making more eggs." The circularity of the chicken-egg dilemma has relevance when we think about young adults who are struggling to move forward, as does another piece of avian-related humor, in which a man visits a psychologist, complaining, "Doctor, my brother thinks he's a chicken." When the psychologist asks him why he doesn't just tell his brother that he's not a chicken, the man matter-of-factly replies, "Because we need the eggs."

In a previous chapter, we explored the dynamics of the family system that can forbid or interdict growth during the launching phase. The inherent reciprocity embedded in family dilemmas prompts us as clinicians to torment ourselves with complicated conundrums, such as:

Did Jonah become a drug abuser as a result of the frustration born of his parents' request that he stay close to home and sacrifice his future so that he could help them take care of his younger sister with Down syndrome as they got older? Or did they select Jonah (rather than either his older sister or brother) to be the sibling who would stay close to home and take care of his younger sister since it was clear he was not going to ever achieve much as a result of abusing drugs; that he was *already* sacrificing his future, so why not ask him to continue to do so?

Did Lakela become clinically depressed because she experienced her mother's silent but overpowering need to keep her close so that her mother didn't plummet into a serious depression (as she had just prior to conceiving Lakela), or did Lakela's mother choose her (rather than her older sister) to be the dutiful, stay-at-home daughter, because Lakela was unlikely to attract a partner and move out as a result of her clinical depression.

Does Hilton refuse to take advantage of tutoring to overcome his dyslexia because he understands that he dare not gain admittance to a four-year college and abandon his long-standing role as his warring parents' marital mediator, or was Hilton (rather than his younger sister) recruited by his warring parents to sabotage his career plans and continue to function as their marital mediator because he was dyslexic and likely to have a difficult time at a four-year college anyway?

The ties that bind parent and child will never broken—the question is the extent to which they allow the child to develop enough self-possession such that she no longer feels possessed by her parents and such that her parents no longer feel that she is their sole possession.

The bond during the launching phase is different from childhood and adolescence because the child—now an adult, with adult capacities, talents, and rights—has more say in the nature of the bond than she did when she was younger. If she chooses to utilize them, she has at her disposal both the interior resources and the societal sanctions to emancipate herself and become her own person, a psychological and legal adult.

As we know, many young adults take advantage of their maturity, slickly maneuvering their way through the challenges of young adulthood with the agility of an NBA point guard slicing through ponderous defenders. Confident as continents, they marshal their strengths, overcome their weaknesses, and make it unmistakably clear that nothing is going to stand in their way—that family, community, school, or societal dynamics, no matter how debilitating or constricting, are not going to mute their voices or truncate their development. Even if their family is as thick and sludgy as the La Brea Tar Pits, they will do anything required to extricate themselves and to ruggedly confirm and enlarge their presence on the larger stage of life and take on a significant role in the drama of their own biography. Psychologically, they sing along with Van Morrison in "Tupelo Honey": "You can't stop us on the road to freedom, you can't keep us, 'cause our eyes can see."

But for struggling young adults, the journey is more toilsome. There appears to be no yearning to grow, or the growth that is achieved feels more obligatory than urgent, more dutiful than driven. There appears to be no destination, or, if there is a destination, it seems to be oblivion—as Neil Young once sang, "Everybody knows this is Nowhere." It is as if they are living two-dimensional lives, and autonomy resides in some invisible, undiscovered, and even unimaginable third dimension.

Hopes are raised and dashed, or perhaps not even raised at all, leaving him (and perhaps his family) feeling ineluctably defeated. He may be buoyed by a small success one day, and then be dragged down by his ankles into a deep swamp of frustration and desolation the next.

Child development seems to perversely conform to one of Zeno's paradoxes, the one that postulates that if an individual proceeds half the distance to his destination in a finite period of time, and continues to do so, he will never arrive, because there will always be another "half the distance" to travel.

With these young adults, there is no sense of the inexhaustible possibilities of life—life, instead, simply feels exhausting as a result of the tremendous effort that even the smallest steps of growth seem to entail. Like how the Grand Canyon was created, a steady drip-drip-drip over millennia led to a massive erosion, but in this case the erosion is psychological rather than geological.

Every young adult that I have ever worked with who is not moving ahead with her life has, consciously or subconsciously, arrived at a self-defeating conclusion that keeps her stuck. She is stranded on a philosophical platform that precludes separation and individuation—one that has been carefully engineered, most likely for many years, and that she keeps securely in place at all costs.

The platform is usually built upon the bedrock of some well-thought-out but most likely subconscious premise, such as "It is better to fail to start than to start and fail," or "It is better for me to stagnate than to grow and trigger changes that may be hard for my family or me to deal with," or "I need to stay here and man the pumps rather than leap out of this sinking ship of a family and take my chances on the open seas." In my experience, it is the need to protect oneself and/or one's family that keeps young adults restrained, unable to take risks, rock themselves out of their self- or other-imposed ruts, and gain any developmental traction. They wave the flag of fear rather than courage, as they make mincing steps through the minefield that life appears to be, or simply sit down altogether and refuse to move in an effort to avoid getting blown up.

We often use the metaphor of a sloth to pejoratively describe someone who's not very productive, who does not contribute much, who is not moving very well or quickly. But what's important to keep in mind is that sloths survive precisely *because* they move so slowly, because they are able to maintain a camouflage that blends perfectly with their background, especially when they don't move very much. In other words, their very slothfulness is what keeps them from being noticed by their predators. Many of the young adults whom I work with have highly developed slothlike tendencies because they feel the need to safeguard themselves against that which they are afraid of, against that which might engulf them.

When I listen to these patients, they are rarely able, at least initially, to articulate their fears about becoming successful or independent with much exactitude, although sometimes their insight has the brilliance and focus of a laser beam. For example, a 23-year-old patient of mine who was chronically late for appointments showed up at the appointed hour for the first time ever. When I asked her what it was like to get in the car and drive to my office knowing that she was on time and didn't have to rush or worry about being late, she responded that she felt an intensely uncomfortable sense of pressure rather than relief, pride, or pleasure. When I asked into the origin of the pressure, she said, "The problem is that I feel like if I can be on time once, I should *always* be able to be on time. But I know I won't always be on time, so if I can't continue to be on time, why bother being on time at all? It's pointless."

Not every young adult has this kind of self-awareness or the ability to articulate it. But after having worked with hundreds of young adults over the years, I have inferred that these fears generally fall into one or more of the following categories:

- A fear that she'll disappoint herself by not meeting expectations for herself
- A fear that he'll disappoint *others*, such as his parents, by not meeting their expectations for him
- A fear that she'll indeed become successful but that she may not be able to consistently meet the raised expectations that accompany her success
- A fear that his success means that he'll be obligated to share it with others in ways that he won't be happy with
- A fear that she's abandoning, betraying, or inappropriately usurping someone important by becoming successful and moving ahead with her life
- A fear that he will no longer be taken care of, or feel entitled to be taken care of, if he becomes successful, separate, and autonomous
- A fear that, if she is successful, she will have no other way of expressing anger at or exacting revenge on her parents, who will feel unfairly (from her perspective) entitled to take pride in the success that resulted from their successful parenting

The old song goes, "You can't keep 'em down on the farm, now that they've seen Paree," but what happens not only when they're not allowed to see Paree (as discussed previously) but, in these cases, when they don't allow *themselves* to see Paree? The unhappy reality, of course, is that, quite often, they simply stay down on the farm.

We have seen how Fluid Family Therapy allows the focus to glide back and forth between the young adult and the family. With this in mind, let's look at a few situations in which individual sessions with a struggling young adult elicited family-related themes that were still unduly hindering them, and ultimately resulted in their finding a psychological escape hatch.

Usually when struggling young adults are given the chance to discuss the basis for their struggles, they begin to map out the territory that they have become mired in, which enables them to find their way out. It is my belief that these struggles generally emerge from or resonate to an unresolved issue or problem in the family—usually originating with the parents—and in some of the cases that follow, the young adult and I were able to disinter this issue or problem. I am always fascinated to observe the ways in which a child unerringly re-creates a dilemma or quandary that troubled or tormented one of his parents, most likely one that the parent has not fully acknowledged or resolved.

While such a clear linkage cannot always be established, sometimes just opening up the windows in the suffocating dungeon that the young adult has been living in is enough to give her a few gulps of air, which in turn provides the prospect of an eventual release.

Rafela was a 20-year-old who was making little headway in her life. She'd completed a random handful of classes at community college and had a decidedly unsatisfying part-time job shampooing dogs and cats at a pet store. A diabetic, she did not take particularly good care of herself—she smoked half a pack of cigarettes a day, ate irregularly and poorly, would often get drunk with her friends, and had been hospitalized several times for going into diabetic shock. During our first conversation, she used the word *flawed* to describe herself, so I thought it might be useful to spend some time exploring this conviction with her.

Rafela related that the deep-seated belief that she was flawed had been reinforced in a couple of tangible ways throughout her childhood. First, of course, was being diagnosed with diabetes at the age of seven. Her complexion had also started to become problematic beginning in third grade, "way before anyone else had a bad complexion," she pointed out. Then, after displaying poor academic performance in middle school, she was tested by an educational psychologist and found to be dyslexic. So by the time she was hitting adolescence, "I already felt like everything was wrong with me."

With this in mind, when Rafela's eighth-grade English teacher read some of the poems that Rafela had written for an assignment and told her how extraordinary they were and how she could "go far with this," Rafela remembered thinking, "I can't, I can't." When I asked her why that was, she started to cry: "I don't know; I just felt like I couldn't become a star at anything. I just felt like there was no way that I was going to amount to anything."

"Even when your teacher was suggesting that you might, in fact, amount to something?"

"I remember just going into a panic and thinking, 'I can't do this, I can't really be good at something.'"

"What's your concern with the possibility of amounting to something, of being good at something?"

"I don't know. It's like I'm not allowed."

"And why are you not allowed?"

"I don't know."

"What are you afraid would happen should you amount to something?"

She paused, then responded, slowly, "I think it would be lonely. I think I'd feel all alone." Her eyes brimmed with tears.

"Who would you be leaving behind, or who would you feel left by?"

"I'm not even sure. I think I'd be leaving myself behind." She paused again. "That's weird." She grew quiet, then repeated it as a question: "I'd be leaving myself behind?"

"It's difficult to imagine being successful and still being yourself?"

"I guess so . . . I guess I never thought about this until we started talking about it."

"What's it like to imagine leaving yourself behind?"

"I don't know . . . how can a person leave herself behind?"

"We could do that in lots of ways, I suppose . . . we can be loyal to other people, but we can also be loyal to ourselves, or at least a part of ourselves. And if that's the case, then I guess we can be disloyal to ourselves, as well."

"So what am I supposed to do?"

"I guess you're trying to figure out if you're allowed to leave the 'flawed' part of yourself behind."

"I'd *love* to!"

"Well, not so fast . . . it sounds like you would and you wouldn't. I can believe that you're tired of feeling flawed, and tired of holding yourself back. But you might not want to abandon 'little Rafela' quite so quickly—maybe you feel like you need to stay back and take care of her."

"Stay back and take care of myself?"

"Sure . . . people do it all the time . . . we all have parts of ourselves that we believe are vulnerable or need to be protected . . . sometimes we find ourselves staying put rather than running away from them."

"So maybe that's what I'm doing?"

"Could be . . . that's what I want you to think about between now and the next time we meet."

"Okay, okay . . . I will."

Rafela returned for her next session with some additional thoughts. "You know, it never occurred to me that maybe I wasn't flawed, that maybe I was holding on to being flawed, or that I was afraid to not be flawed. That was a different way of looking at things, kind of weird, really."

"I'm glad you gave this matter some reflection."

"And another weird thing happened. The other day I was at work, and I was shampooing this dog, a little one. I was staring into his eyes, and he looked so frightened, it was his first time there, and he didn't know what was happening. And I felt so bad for him, all wet and quivering and not knowing what was happening. And I started to cry. I was just hugging him and crying, it was the strangest thing."

"What's your understanding of what that was about?"

"I guess it goes back to that 'little Rafela' thing that you said. You know, that I was trying to take care of little Rafela, that I didn't want to leave myself behind."

I recalled, at that moment, that *she* was the one who had first observed that she didn't want to leave herself behind, not me, but I held on to that thought until later, not wanting to disrupt her flow.

"So what happened then?"

"Well, I got myself together—I certainly didn't want anyone at work to see me crying!—and then I went home, and I was telling my dad about this."

"What did he have to say?"

"Well, we were talking about a bunch of things, and then he told me something that I had honestly never heard before. He told me that he felt guilty about my having diabetes because he felt that it was his fault—because there are diabetics on his side of the family."

"What did you think?"

"I couldn't believe it. I mean I knew that his sister was diabetic—she was actually a big help to me when I was little—but I didn't know that his grandmother was diabetic, too. But mostly, I didn't know that he felt guilty about 'giving' it to me."

"I guess he feels almost as flawed as you do."

"Wow . . . that's something to think about."

"Do you think he should feel as flawed as he does?"

"No, I think it's ridiculous—he didn't mean to give me diabetes, I know that."

"But you still think that *you* should feel as flawed as you do, right?"

"Uh-oh . . . you're trying to trap me, right?"

"Answer my question," I suggested with a smile.

"I guess not . . . I mean, it's easy for me to say that my dad shouldn't feel like there's something wrong with him for carrying diabetes in his genes—there's a lot more to him than that."

"So maybe there's also more to *you* than being flawed."

"Maybe there is."

Gently exploring the history behind Rafela's sense of feeling flawed, and linking her feelings about herself with her father's feelings about himself, broke some new ground for her and got her thinking differently about what she was capable of.

Gabriel, a talented 21-year-old who aspired to be a professional hip-hop DJ, had painted himself into a corner because he was constantly afraid of being seen as a sellout. He had gradually stopped playing shows and dances and spent most of his time holed up in the small studio that he had built in his parents' basement. He recorded frequently but rarely made his music public. He did not release his material on CDs, on MP3 files, or on the Internet—everything stayed in his personal archives.

Of course, at this stage in his career, he wasn't close enough to musical success to even be *able* to "sell out" to anyone. But he told me that he was worried about that outcome nevertheless and spent much of his initial session with me discussing his favorite hip-hop artist whom, he felt, had "sold out and now is too pop, too mainstream . . . and now I don't even like to listen to him."

Clearly, this was an important theme for Gabriel and the loss of integrity and autonomy that he associated with selling out was on his mind. Taking some time to explore it turned out to be very revealing for him.

"What do you see as the definition of selling out?" I asked.

"I guess it means doing what your fans want you to do, what your record company wants you to do, what your manager wants you to do, rather than what you want to do."

"So why do you think someone sells out?"

"For the money! Why else would someone sell out?"

"What do you think it's like for someone to sell out?"

"It's probably cool to get all that bank. But inside, you probably hate yourself."

"How can you tell the difference between someone who has sold out and someone who is doing what he or she wants to do, and it just happens to become popular and make him rich?"

"I don't know . . . how would that happen?"

"Well, sometimes it does . . . do you believe that *every* musical superstar has sold out?"

"Well, maybe not . . . I mean some artists get to have it both ways. They're real popular but they're still making their own music, doing what they want to do."

"So it *is* possible to be popular and still be true to yourself, right? *Rare*, but still possible."

"Yeah, I guess so . . . but it's not easy."

"I'm sure it's not. I'm sure the temptation to sell out is a significant one for any artist. After all of that hard work, after maybe having been poor and struggling for a long time, why not succumb to the wealth, to the fame, to the adoration of millions of people, right?"

"Right. And that's what I'm afraid of. That I'll make it, and then I won't do my own thing anymore. I'll just get too caught up in the adulation and lose track of the music, the reason that I do it."

"But what indication do you have that that's what would happen if you allowed yourself to become successful? Are there other ways in which you have sold out, not been true to yourself?"

"I don't know; that's a good question. I'm down there in my basement studio, working away at my beats, working, working, working . . . and I'm lost in it, and I just don't want to lose that feeling."

"Well, no one is saying that you have to. You can certainly stay down in your studio and keep your music private. You could become a truly great, but truly unknown, artist. Maybe not to be discovered until long after you're dead. Maybe not to be discovered at all. That's okay, too, you know."

"It is?"

"Sure it is . . . no one's holding a gun to your head saying that you have put your music out there so that people can love it."

"Yeah, I know, I know . . . but that's the thing, I *want* people to hear my music! I love that feeling of people dancing to my music, people grooving to my music . . . it's the greatest feeling in the world!"

"Then you have a complicated decision to make, Gabriel. You can ensure that you never become a sellout by not selling at all, or you could begin to sell—make your music more available, do more dances, more shows—and see if you can figure out a way to sell without selling out. And that's not an easy decision."

"You're right. I mean, I don't really want to live in my parents' basement my whole life."

"If that's the case, then you might have to take the risk of selling a bit while making sure that you don't ambush yourself into selling out. Not easy, but certainly doable."

"I hear you, dude . . . I hear you."

"I'm also curious . . . when did this fear of being a sellout first occur to you?"

"I'm not sure, really . . . I never thought about that."

"Just wondering—is there any history in your family of someone selling out?"

"Well . . ." Gabriel paused before proceeding. "I guess now that I think about it, my dad sold out, in a way."

"How so?"

"He wanted to be a writer; that was his main goal in life."

"And what happened?"

"He supposedly went to college saying he was going to major in writing, but I'm not sure what happened. Now he's an engineer. Pretty big switch, huh?"

"So do you think he sold out by becoming an engineer rather than a writer?"

"Sure . . . that's *exactly* what he did."

"Have you ever talked with him about this?"

"No, not really—I mean, it was actually my mom who told me he was going to be a writer. My dad and I, we don't really talk in that way."

"Do you imagine you could have a conversation with him about this?"

"Not really . . . he gets pretty awkward."

"Perhaps we could talk about it in here together?"

"Yeah, I guess that would be a little better."

We scheduled the next session with Gabriel and his father, Amari. As it turns out, despite Gabriel's concerns, Amari was more than happy to discuss the career crossroads that he faced at the end of college.

"I really did hope that I was going to become a writer, you know, the next great novelist. But college was kind of a humbling experience for me, and I couldn't believe how many good writers there were. And a couple of my professors made it clear that it wasn't going to be easy making a living as a writer, which I kind of knew, but they really rammed it home."

"So how did you become an engineer?"

"I was always very good at science and math, and I really liked the engineering classes that I took. And while I didn't grow up poor—there was always food on the table, we were always clothed—we certainly didn't have a lot of money, and life got kind of rough at times. My dad was a bus driver, and my mom really couldn't work, she had lupus, so I wasn't particularly excited about continuing to live on the edge. So I eventually made the decision to pursue engineering, and it worked out fine."

"Gabriel, do you have any questions for your dad?"

"Yeah . . . how come you don't write anymore?"

"That's a good question, Gabriel . . . I don't know. I guess I got to a place where I wasn't going to get any better at it. When I left college, it's like I left behind my dream of becoming a writer. I wasn't sure what the point of continuing to write was if I wasn't going to be 'real writer,' a writer who made a living doing just that."

"Do you miss it?"

Amari sighed. "Oh, I'm not sure I even let myself think about that anymore, Gabriel. It's like my writing days are part of my youth, the youth I left behind."

Gabriel continued: "So does it make you sad?"

"I'm very happy being an engineer, Gabriel, you know that. And I'm happy that your life has been a lot better than my life was when I was growing up. I do a lot of neat stuff; being an engineer is like being an architect of the world."

Gabriel persisted, re-asking the question that I was going to follow up on if he hadn't done so. "But does it make you *sad*?"

"Of course it does, son. Of course it does."

"So why did you give it up?"

"Because those are the difficult decisions that sometimes have to be made."

Father and son are now embarking on the conversation that should have been entered into years ago but that it is never too late to begin. Amari continued to map out for his son the path that he chose to follow when he was Gabriel's age, which in turn freed Gabriel to view his own dilemma from a different vantage point.

We scheduled a follow-up, and I learned that the two of them had sustained their dialogue, and that Gabriel had for the first time begun sharing with Amari his concerns about selling out as a musician. Amari had surprised Gabriel by being very understanding of this conflict. One of the things that I added to their discussion was that Gabriel seemed to be intuitively blending both of his father's interests—creativity (in his case, music rather than writing) and engineering (in his case, making music that relied on modern computer technology).

With a new perspective in mind, and with his father's support, Gabriel renewed his commitment to trying to make a living at his musical career. In addition to making some new connections with club owners whom he might DJ for, he also started hiring himself out as a producer for musical friends and colleagues in his home studio. Meanwhile, his father, inspired by his son's initiative, enrolled in a creative writing class at a community college, and began to revisit, if only as an enjoyable hobby, his original calling.

Many of the struggling young adults I have worked with appear to be struggling because they simply don't feel entitled to succeed. It is as if their dysfunction or inertia is a form of ongoing penance, designed to help them expiate the oppressive guilt that they carry with them for crimes that they may be fully, or only dimly, aware of.

Betsy was considered the golden child in her family, particularly in comparison with her older sister. The girls' parents, the McClellands, explained that their first-born, Helen, had been difficult from day one—colicky as an infant, "allergic to everything" as a toddler, and diagnosed with sensory integration dysfunction (now more commonly known as sensory processing disorder) in second grade, which significantly limited her academic achievement through school. Helen was now 26 years old and had graduated from college and was living away from home, but her trajectory remained a bumpy one. She had yet to hold onto a job more than one year, and her boyfriend, Andreas, was an alcoholic who would usually become verbally abusive with her when he got drunk.

Betsy, meanwhile, had always flowered nicely in school and was now thriving academically in college, hoping to become an occupational therapist. Despite her solid success, the parents contacted me because Betsy had been arrested for shoplifting at a local mall. This surprised them because Betsy actually had been working as a nanny part-time for several years, and was paid well, and in cash. That, combined with the fact that the girls had grown up comfortably middle class, left the McClellands grasping at straws when it came to explaining what would have prompted their youngest daughter to shoplift.

In getting to know Betsy, it became clear that being the "preferred child" was an onerous burden for her. She shared with me the tremendous guilt that she felt as she constantly outshone her sister over the years, and the many ways in which she attempted to "trim her sails" so as not to leave her older sister behind. Clearly the ancient laws of primogeniture still had applicability when it came to the McClelland family

"You don't know what it's been like for me—I've always been treated as Helen's older sister, even though she clearly looked older than me when we were growing up. It's just that I was seen as more mature, and I *was* more mature. But I felt horrible about it. Like when we would go out as a family, I would check out what Helen was wearing first and make sure that I didn't outdo her. I used to get these excellent report cards, and I would dread my parents praising me about it at dinner, right in front of Helen—I'm not even sure she cared, but I know that *I* did.

"And it's like Helen will turn to me for advice—she's always asking me how to handle her wacko boyfriend—but I feel bad because I know that I would never ask *her* for advice . . . I just wouldn't value anything she had to say."

"Are there other ways in which you worry about outshining her?"

"Oh, God, yes, I think about it all the time . . . I mean, here's a weird one—I'm already dreading the day that I get married."

"Why?"

"Because I'm afraid that I'll get married before she does, and I'll just feel awful about that. I get a sinking feeling in the pit of my stomach when I think about my wedding day, especially if she's not married, or if she *is* married, but to someone like that creep Andreas that she's seeing."

"This has weighed heavily on you for some time, hasn't it?"

"That's for sure."

"Anything else you do in an effort to not surpass her?"

"Oh . . . I don't know . . . that's a good question . . . how else do I do that?" she mused, almost to herself. "Well, one thing I do is to make sure that I don't take too much pride in what I do. I mean, I've done very well in school, and I got very involved with a group of health care students, so now I'm the vice president of that group. But it's like I don't really believe in myself. I can't figure out why people take me so seriously."

"What happens when people do take you seriously?"

"I don't know . . . I just get down on myself . . . I figure that they just don't know me, they just don't see me, they just don't *get* me."

"So you're sort of an imposter? A fraud?"

"Exactly! It's like I'm not real, like I'm faking everybody out. Like nobody really knows."

"So how do you understand your decision to shoplift, with all of this in mind?"

"Well, here's the thing . . . I've actually been shoplifting for quite a few years now. And I have no idea why I do it. It's not like I really need any of the things that I shoplift. It's not like I don't have a decent supply of money. So I do it, but I'm just not sure *why* I do it."

"I can understand why you're confused. Although often when we do something out of character, it's because we're busy trying to protect someone *else's* character."

"Oh, wait a minute, *I* see where you're going with this . . . so do you think that I shoplift because of Helen?"

"It's occurring to me, that's for sure. Let's face it, what a wonderful way to ensure that you don't sail too far ahead of her, that you remind her, your parents, and yourself that you're not so special after all, and that you don't better her. After all, has *she* ever been arrested for anything?"

"No . . . one thing about Helen is that she's very honest . . . almost too honest, she used to tell our parents everything about what she did."

"So you have selected a wonderful way to lower yourself in everyone's estimation, by committing an illegal act and doing so until you got caught. Now, at least, Helen can outshine *you* for a while. You know, that was very generous of you."

Betsy grinned. "Thanks . . . I guess."

Our subsequent discussions with Betsy and her parents involved bringing this issue more out into the open so that Betsy didn't feel like she constantly had to sabotage her progress for fear of eclipsing her older sister.

As we discussed in the chapter on assessment, it is helpful, in situations like this, for the therapist to excavate the young adult's maladaptive motivation to protect a family member by asking questions such as:

- How long do you imagine that you've been sacrificing yourself for this individual?
- When did it first occur to you that you were doing so?
- Were you recruited for this position, or did you volunteer, or was it some of both?

- How long do you anticipate that you'll need to continue sacrificing yourself for this individual?
- What are you afraid will happen should you discontinue your self-sacrifice on his or her behalf? Who will be most disappointed, angry, or upset with you?
- How will you forgive yourself if you do, in fact, terminate your self-sacrificial acts?
- Is there some other way in which you're likely to continue to feel the need to make a sacrifice? If so, are there ways to do so without it working to your disadvantage?

Regarding this last question, Betsy acknowledged that she'd probably always feel bad about outpacing her sister, but she also acknowledged that the work that she was heading into—occupational therapy—might be a way to continue to "support" her sister symbolically (occupational therapists are often a significant part of the treatment team for children and adults with sensory integration difficulties).

Twenty-two-year-old Jorden was living at home with his parents. He had left home for college after high school but was not successful, and since he had returned home, he had bounced like a pinball from job to job and from community college course to community college course. He generally did well at the jobs he had and generally succeeded at the courses he took, but it was impossible to detect whether there was any overall progress or direction.

During one of our initial family sessions, Jorden's father observed that "Jorden's main problem is that he finds the cloud behind every silver lining—he's the most negative person I've ever met." When I asked Jorden if there was any truth to that observation, he replied, frostily, "Well, this is kind of lose-lose, isn't it? I mean, if I agree with my dad, that means I am, indeed, negative. But if I disagree, that looks like I'm being negative, too."

I commended him for pointing out the bind that he was in and then asked his parents to have a seat in the waiting room. As he and I explored his negativity, he at one point noted that he felt the need to "punish" himself. When I asked why he needed to be punished, he paused, as if debating a plunge into white, raging rapids, and then asked me, "Do you want to know my deepest, darkest secret?"

"Do you want to tell me?"

He took a deep breath, puffed out his cheeks, then blew it out, and proceeded:

"I killed kittens when I was little." He sat there, stony-faced, looking like he was awaiting the swift chop of a guillotine.

"Tell me about it."

Apparently relieved that I had not instantly evicted him from my office, he went on: "I was four or five, and I was over at my neighbor's house, and he was showing me a litter of kittens that his cat had had. And then I was on the floor playing with them and I don't know what happened, but I killed some of them,

I just busted their necks. I'm not sure if I meant to, but I was playing with them, and I snapped some of their necks. And then I realized that some were dead. And then I said, 'Oh, no.' And then I ran home."

"Did anyone find out?"

"I don't know . . . I never heard anything about it after that . . . no one ever said anything about it. I eventually figured that they must have assumed that some had just died, maybe they thought some of the kittens were asleep and then realized that they were dead. I don't know if anyone knows I killed them. I never told anyone. I just did for the first time."

"What is it like to talk about this?"

"It's horrible. I can't believe I did this."

"That's quite a secret to have kept to yourself all of these years."

"How could I tell anyone? I felt horrible! I still feel horrible! And then when I was in high school I was taking a psychology class, and I read that people who torture animals are really sick, really disturbed people. And all I could think about was, 'That's me, that's me!' I mean, I knew I was a horrible person, but now I knew that I was sick, too." He added, in a voice tinged with unmistakable sorrow, "Not that I didn't know that before."

"So what other data supports your conclusion that you are a horrible person?"

"That's not enough?" he marveled.

"Well, I'd be a little hesitant to leap to conclusions about an individual's character based on a transgression he committed when he was four years old. Surely a bright person like you must have accumulated some other evidence."

He shook his head. "I was pretty mean in middle school, too. There was this kid, Willy, who I was sort of friends with, but I also teased him. Anyway, it turns out that he tried to kill himself at one point, we all heard about it, this was in eighth grade. He missed a bunch of school, and then we heard that he was coming back, and our teacher had a meeting with the class the day before he returned and talked to us about the importance of being nice to Willy and not making him feel uncomfortable. Well, I was sure she was talking to me, and me alone. I was sure that Willy had told people that the reason that he had killed himself was because I was always teasing him and he couldn't stand it. I never bothered him again. I just stayed away from him once he got back. But I always felt like I had driven him to suicide."

"Single-handedly?"

"Who knows? I knew that I could be mean."

"Anything else that comes to mind as you're sharing your deep, dark secrets?"

"I knocked a kid out once."

"How?"

"Playing football. We were out at recess—this was middle school, too—and I clotheslined him. We weren't supposed to be playing tackle, but we did it when the teachers weren't looking—and I remember him lying there on the ground, not moving, and I thought I'd killed him."

"What happened?"

"Well, I didn't personally get in trouble, since we all did. We all lost recess for a week. And he was back in a couple of days, but I still felt terrible."

It was, of course, impossible for me to know the extent to which Jorden had been mean to Willy or whether he had intentionally hurt his football opponent. But in touching base with his parents, I learned that there were no indications of worrisome or sociopathic behavior throughout his childhood and adolescence (they knew about the football injury that his friend had incurred but didn't know about the kittens or about the role that Jorden believed that he played when it came to Willy's suicide attempt). With this in mind, it certainly was possible that his teasing of Willy and his football opponent's loss of consciousness were re-shaped in Jorden's mind so that they were congruent with the elemental self-concept that he had formed, built on the premise he was some sort of sociopathic executioner.

We continued to explore these memories and eventually brought our discussion back to his belief that he deserved to be punished. I suggested that perhaps the best way to excoriate himself for the sins that he committed in the past was to deprive himself of enjoying a successful life in the present.

"After all," I suggested, "you can't turn back the clock and bring kittens back to life, be a better friend to Willy in eighth grade, and prevent a football injury. But you *can* make sure that you don't achieve anything and remain unhappy."

Jorden deliberated this for a few moments and acknowledged that this was a possibility. "You know, I've always wondered why I didn't succeed at college. I mean, I was very happy there, I had made some friends, and I liked my classes. But it was like I was hell-bent on blowing it. And I did—*boy*, did I blow it. And it's like I've never recovered."

"It could be, though, that just as you were hell-bent on blowing your college experience, that you're equally hell-bent on making sure that you don't recover, either, and that you don't forge ahead on some new pathways. After all, what right does a kitten murderer have to a successful life?"

Jorden chuckled wryly. "I see where you're going here."

It was brave of Jorden to invite me into the psychological ghetto that he had sequestered himself in for almost 20 years, but once he did so, it allowed him to consider departing and leaving that dungeon behind.

Interestingly, while he and I never obtained (or needed) a more longitudinal context for his guilt, Jorden's mother, Denise, consulted with me several years later around a separate issue. During our initial interview, I learned that Denise had given birth to a stillborn child two years before Jorden was born, something that she had not told Jorden about. Apparently, the fetus had never developed a functional spinal cord, and Denise still carried tremendous guilt about having cre-ated and carried a deformed baby for nine months. It was, of course, striking for me to think back to two of Jorden's perceived crimes—breaking the kittens' necks and clotheslining a fellow student, resulting in a loss of consciousness—and how these events almost physically pointed to the location of his unknown older brother's underdevelopment. As I noted earlier, we do not always need to know the details of the emotional dramas that sluice back and forth across the generational membranes—we just have to believe that they do so.

We have been examining situations in which family-centered individual consultations with young adults have enabled them to get unstuck and grow. Now let's rotate back to the parent generation and take a look at how we can help them to support their young adult's growth.

Chapter 7

Consulting with Parents at the Launching Stage

Families are always more than the sum of their parts. To be of assistance, clinicians must attend to the individual developmental tasks of each child, of each parent, of each generation, and of the intergenerational family as a whole. The convergence of these various, intersecting developmental trajectories is what makes treating families so fascinating, but also so difficult—the patterns are molten, complex, and ever-shifting.

Every developmental stage carries with it a mixture of possibilities—the potential to become emotionally enriched or impoverished, the potential to become relationally connected or detached, the potential to be renewed and revivified or to be stifled and stunted. The nature of human growth is that there is a part of us that is born or reborn with every new stage, and there is necessarily a part of us that dies.

In this chapter, I will be focusing on the important developmental tasks that parents need to undertake for the successful negotiation of the emptying family nest and the treatment strategies that can bolster this process.

Ideally, the launching of children into their own, autonomous orbits brings with it a sense of liberation for the parents, an upsurge of energy, hope, and initiative as the ties that bind begin to be unbound and the chains of bondage begin to loosen. We often use the word *crisis* alongside *midlife*, and with this in mind, it is worth noting that the word *crisis* derives from the Greek word *krinein*, which means to sift—when we are in a crisis, we have the opportunity to sift through different possibilities and arrive at those that are worth preserving or pursuing.

For many parents, the gradual departure of their children allows them to reclaim the parts of their lives that were lost to the tensions and pressures of work and child rearing, or perhaps allows them to claim a life that was never lived at all. An emptying nest allows for a springtime of potential to arise, for a glimpse of the ignored, deferred, or hidden possibilities that have been lurking patiently or restlessly beneath the surface of a parent's life.

But for this to happen, much needs to be accomplished. The major tasks of the launching parent include coming to terms with the loss of youth and the awareness of mortality, making the adjustment to the beginning of life without children, and shouldering more of a filial role in relation to one's parents and in-laws. Sometimes these agendas intercross in complicated ways. In one poignant example, a father whom I was working with was in the position of having to fight to take car keys away from both his 20-year-old son (who had acquired his third speeding ticket in one year) and his 85-year-old mother (who was experiencing unexplained fainting episodes) all in the same week.

Parents at midlife need to discover sources of growth and fulfillment other than their children. They have to discover new stars, or rediscover old stars, in their slowly cooling universe. But a parent's concern about his children makes him feel important, so if children are not there to be concerned about, he may feel less important. One father described this feeling to me in a poignant way: "It's like my son stole my soul and now he's going to go off to spend it somewhere else."

There is a beautiful lyric by singer-songwriter Schuyler Fisk, from her song, "What Good Is Love?" in which she plaintively sings, "What good is love . . . without you?"

All parents have to figure out how to answer that question—when the children whom they love so dearly are no longer around to love in the same way, what good is love, and can it be extended to other endeavors, other people, or expanded within themselves and their important relationships, such as with spouses, extended family, and friends?

For some parents, the preparation for an empty nest has been gradual, and the prospect of a child's leave-taking is not particularly urgent or dramatic. For others who have not been attending to the transition as it has been approaching, it feels more like an upheaval. Either way, however, it is likely that the parents will experience a surge of complicated emotions—regret, desire, sorrow, creativity—that will prompt them to glimpse and possess certain aspects of their identity.

With all of these changes in mind, here are some of the common challenges that therapists may have to help launching parents meet.

RELATIONSHIP WITH GRANDPARENTS

The prospect of preparing to finish up parenthood will generally shine the spotlight on unresolved issues between parents and their own parents. How the parents feel about their own parents as parents and grandparents, and how the grandparents feel about their children as parents and about their grandchildren, will be reinvoked and reanimated at this stage of development. With this in mind, clinicians must look carefully at the multigenerational realities of the family.

Grandparents can provide important bolstering and perspective for parents and their young adult grandchildren during the launching phase, particularly if the relationship between the three generations has been mostly positive over the years. They can lightly or playfully remind the parents of their own glacial or lurching steps toward autonomy years before, which can help the parents to maintain their hope and equanimity in the face of a young adult separation that may not be going all that smoothly. Grandparents, who generally have a much less ambivalent and conditional relationship with the young adult than her parents do with her, can also provide wisdom, nurturance, and guidance to their grandchild, and do so in ways that the young adult grandchild may be better able to receive.

On the other hand, the unaddressed fault lines and fractures between parent and grandparent can become magnified during the launching phase, resulting in even more strife between the generations. Some parents may have felt that their grandparents were too detached or rejecting of their young adult child and blame the young adult's difficulties on the absence of a wished-for and idealized grandparental nurturance. Some grandparents will respond to a stalled-out young adult by criticizing the parent, adopting a gloating or hostile "I told you so" attitude that only adds to the parents' frustration.

When I invite grandparents into family therapy sessions, I will often hear these thinly (or not so thinly) veiled critiques of their children's approach to parenting the young adult, either spoken directly to the parents, or indirectly, through me:

> "I've been saying for years that they were too strict with her, and now they're paying the price—they basically broke her spirit; no wonder she has no get-up-and-go."
> "This is the kind of situation that the two of you can expect when you're both so busy with your careers and not attentive to the children."
> "I told you years ago you were too lenient with the kids. They've been taking advantage of you for years, and they're still doing it."
> "I never thought that they should have divorced; I said that over and over again, and now my daughter's been trying to finish raising my grandson without a father in the picture, so it's not surprising that he's drinking and drugging all the time. They should've stuck it out; that's what her father and I did, that's what everyone did in my day."

Of course, in these situations, the grandparents often feel just as worried and frustrated as the parents, but their inability to manage their own anxiety exacerbates, rather than solves, the problem.

And because one or more grandparents are often aging, ailing, or recently deceased at this stage of life, issues and conflicts that inhabit the parent–grandparent relationship will be stirred up to the surface with even more intensity, which will in turn affect the parent–young adult relationship.

The deterioration or death of a grandparent does not inevitably have to result in difficulties between the parent and young adult. Sometimes, for example, the departure of the grandparent is a sorrowful but unifying experience that brings the entire family closer together, particularly if the grandparent has had a good relationship with her children and grandchildren. Family members connect with each other around the shared sense of loss, and there is a determined, collective commitment to honor the deceased and what she lived and stood for, and to do so in constructive and creative ways.

Sometimes a grandparent's death is a source of liberation, perhaps because his demise has been a long and draining one (such as when death results after a long illness) or because he was such a difficult and demanding individual. In these situations, there is a palpable sense of relief among children and grandchildren, an overall sense of gain rather than loss.

Generally, however, some aspects of unfinished business linger between the parent and grandparent that will be resurrected as the older generation passes on, and it is imperative for the therapist to take note of how this business is or is not addressed. As one father of a 20-year-old confessed to me, "Both of my parents died when I was a teenager, so they left me before I could leave them—which means that I really have no idea how to say good-bye to my son and no idea how he should say goodbye to me."

For example, parents will often take on the qualities of their own missing parent in a desire to stay connected with the parent, and those qualities may or may not sponsor the young adult's growth. In other situations, parents will shift aspects of their relationship with their own parent over to their relationship with their young adult child, usually with mixed results.

One patient of mine, Cynthia, had devoted much of her time and energy over the past several years to caring for her mother, who was suffering from and eventually died with Alzheimer's disease. Cynthia then became increasingly clingy with and critical of her own daughter, Caitlyn, in the months after her mother died. The timing of the grandmother's death occurred at the beginning of Caitlyn's senior year of college, and tension in the family was rising quickly as Caitlyn was struggling to make plans for life after graduation and not feeling that her parents were supportive of the possibilities.

"No matter what I come up with, Mom's unhappy, and Dad doesn't say a thing. I was thinking of moving to where my boyfriend is in graduate school, but she said that would make me too dependent on him. I was thinking of going abroad, maybe to teach—a friend of mine is doing that—but she said that was too far away."

"Is there anything that she *has* been supportive of?" I asked.

"Yeah, anything that brings me closer to home," Caitlyn said, with an acid chortle. "All my grand ideas aren't worth a cent in her eyes, but then she comes up with the idea of coming home, getting my old job back at the restaurant where I worked in high school, and saving my money so that I can eventually go to graduate school. I'm not saying that graduate school isn't on the horizon for me, but why would I want to live at home and work at that stupid restaurant? I mean, I haven't even walked *into* that place since I quit. I *hated* it; it's the last place I'd want to go. How can she think that would be a good idea after having been away at college for four years?"

"What's your dad have to say?"

"He says what he always says when Mom's on a rant—*nothing*. He basically just backs her up, doesn't want to get into it with her, he knows he'll get an earful. So I'm between a rock and a hard place here."

In my discussions with Cynthia and her husband, Frank, it seemed that she was shifting her focus from her mother to her daughter, and perhaps attempting to keep the latter close to her now that the former had left her. Bringing this to light, and helping Cynthia to complete the mourning process for her mom, eventually helped to thin the viscosity of her relationship with her daughter.

EMPATHIC DETACHMENT

The level-headed receptionist at an in-the-trenches mental health clinic I used to work at had a sign on her desk that I've never forgotten: "*Your* emergency is not *my* emergency."

Much psychological research confirms the hypothesis that exposure to manageable levels of adversity has a positive impact on child and adolescent development, including an increased coping capacity, an enhanced ability to tap into others for support, a sense of mastery resulting from having survived and surmounted challenges, greater self-assuredness and efficacy when it comes to anticipating and managing future challenges, and an overall sense of psychophysiologically- based strength and resilience.

While there are certainly countless young adults who have been exposed to overwhelming levels of adversity, many have parents who have assiduously worked to protect them from adversity to the extent that they are ill equipped to handle it when it comes their way, as it inevitably will.

In this regard, the issue of allowing for manageable adversity is somewhat akin to chicken pox—when children get chicken pox at a young age, it tends to be a relatively harmless (albeit uncomfortable) experience, and one that generally immunizes them for life. Children who don't get chicken pox at a young age (and who don't get the vaccine) are at risk for being infected as adults, and adult chicken pox is a more serious, and even potentially fatal, illness. In other words, there are significant physical and psychological advantages to being exposed to adversity at certain ages, and obtaining the immunity that results.

One of the family therapist's central objectives is to help parents create a loving detachment from young adults and allow them to more fully experience the consequences of their actions, or inactions, and, as a result, to put them in the position to solve their own problems. As the Chinese proverb states, "The gem cannot be polished without friction, nor man perfected without trials." Or, put more gastronomically. "The difference between cookie dough and cookies is heat." Despite the despair that might tug at the worried parent's heartstrings, they must learn to stand back and allow the heat of life to do its baking.

There is a Hebrew word with a playful sound, *tzimtzum*, loosely translated as "contraction," which captures this concept. Some Jewish mystics teach that God began the process of creation by shrinking heavenly omnipotence and infinite presence in order to allow for the existence of an independent world. Only through the withdrawal of divine energy and essence could a space for imperfect humanity, and for human growth, become possible. Likewise, parents of young adults must contract themselves, condense their presence, so that their child has space and room in which to grow and think more independently.

All parents want to be better parents, and family therapists can help parents to redefine effective parenting by reminding them that they will be an even better parent by learning how to hold back, and by being able to give young adults the freedom to make decisions as well as their inevitable and attendant mistakes.

Countless patients have told me that they have a difficult time holding back, because their son or daughter is going to regret the decision that he or she has made:

> "I tell you, you're going to regret changing your major one day when you graduate and can't get a job."
> "You will regret it when you wake up in your thirties and realize that you spent your early twenties in a druggy stupor and everyone else has moved on."
> "You're going to regret it if you keep this relationship going—it's time to move on, she's not right for you."

What I say in response to these concerns is that one cannot and should not live without regret, that the experience of regret is a significant psychological achievement—without regret, one regresses. Rather than trying to buffer children from making decisions that they will regret, it's better to help them learn to distinguish between experiencing regret and indicting themselves for their shortcomings. Regret can easily shade into self-loathing (which might be better spelled "self *low-thing*"), and, when it does, it loses its capacity to instruct us, to inspire us. The scale of our failures may at times intimidate us, but our job is to right-size those failures so that they can be understood, appreciated, and learned from.

One of my favorite songs by Sly and the Family Stone is "Thank You Falettinme Be Mice Elf" (Thank you for letting me be myself). Children always experience deep gratitude when they are allowed to become their own person. Many individuals have shared with me, either personally or professionally, how difficult it was to lose a parent during childhood, adolescence, or early adulthood, and yet how that loss led to developmental gains and propelled them to achieve a state of self-reliance and mastery that might not have been reached should their parent have remained alive. I have heard this story not only when the parent has been an oppressive or suffocating one but even when the parent–child relationship has been a satisfying and developmentally appropriate one.

Popular myths and stories such as the Harry Potter series and *The Wizard of Oz* maintain such relevance for young people because these are stories of protagonists who are forced to encounter the world without the protection of their parents—and they find, over time, that they can actually survive, despite the feelings of fear, loss, and grief.

For various reasons, children are not given enough credit for their resilience, and they continue to be seen as fragile and brittle, unlikely or unable to survive and thrive without the guidance of their parents. It would obviously be unwise to underestimate the value of enduringly positive parenting behaviors, but it would be unwise to overestimate them, as well.

One of the reasons that empathic detachment can be so difficult for parents is that it requires a recognition of their limitations, the reality that they cannot enduringly protect their child (or themselves) from misfortune or discomfort. I often remind parents that the most important lessons in life are not lessons that can be taught—they have to be learned. When parents come to terms with their limits as parents, it becomes easier for them to take a few steps backward, giving their young adult more room to grow.

I'll also use phrases that may help parents to make the distinction between helpful and unhelpful support, such as the difference between being *responsive to* the young adult rather than *responsible for* him, or discouraging the parents from continuing to build and feather the family *nest* and encouraging them instead to build and spread out a *net* that lies below the nest, so that the young adult has a safe place to land if her first flights are not entirely successful ones.

LIMIT-SETTING

A patient of mine began a recent session by telling me that she had been rear-ended by a car at a traffic light, resulting in light damage to her bumper. She and the other driver got out of their respective cars, exchanged insurance information, and then returned to their vehicles and drove on. Less than half a mile later, at another traffic light, she was rear-ended again—by the same driver! When I asked her what she said to him this time, she responded, "I just asked him a question—'Hey, Mister, how do you stop when I'm not here?'"

Many parents of young adults feel like they are in the same situation as my beleaguered patient—constantly having to stop their child from continuing on into harm's way, but wondering exactly how long they're going to have to play this role, and how many thumps and bumps they're going to have to absorb until he develops the capacity to use his own brakes to slow down and, when necessary, to stop.

Sometimes this means encouraging the parent to simply say no and sliding the puck of responsibility back onto the young adult's home ice. The mother of 24-year-old Giuliana told me that Giuliana asked her for money so that she could get braces. What was interesting is that Giuliana had had braces as a teenager but chose not to wear her retainer for an additional year after her braces were off, as the orthodontist had suggested—naturally, her teeth had moved back into their original, crooked positions.

Nevertheless, Giuliana's mom was initially prepared to agree to this request because, "I want my daughter to look good, and it's hard to look good unless you smile—Giuliana won't smile anymore because her teeth have gotten crooked." It was difficult for this parent to grasp the idea that it might be better for Giuliana to experience the consequences of her actions, and that if she became more responsible as a result, that sense of mastery might lead her to smile more, as well.

Sometimes parents must do this by asking more of their young adult child. We all have surely worked with young adults who are so comfortable in their own homes that there's little motivation for them to move out. We all boil at different temperatures, so the family water may have to be heated to different levels for a reluctant young adult to take the leap out of the pot.

One mother complained that her 19-year-old son continued to barge into his parents' bedroom any time he had a request. When I suggested locking the bedroom door, she said, "Oh, I can't do that; he'll pound on it until we open it." When I asked her how many nights she thought he'd do that before he got the message, she said, "Oh, he'll do it forever." I asked them to give it a try, and within one night of their not responding to his door-banging, he had stopped. (Should that not have worked, I was going to suggest that the parents sleep naked, but things never got that far.)

A family asked me for advice on how they might promote more responsibility on the part of their 19-year-old, Aceline, and I suggested that they might start by having her take over her own laundry. Yet even that small shift was deftly met with resistance. The mother instantly stated that she was "fine" with doing laundry, that she was doing her own anyway and it wasn't any trouble to throw in Aceline's. When I asked the father what he thought, he countered with the ecological efficiency of doing all of their wash together. "It's really not very 'green' for her to do her own wash when we're doing wash every week, anyway." Then they sat back and waited for me to come up with another suggestion (which they were surely preparing to refute). Instead, I asked them to give it some thought between sessions and let me know what they came up with, hoping that they might internalize that approach and begin applying it to their relationship with their daughter.

Twenty-three-year-old Audie had been dating 32-year-old Ewing for several months, but their relationship was a volatile one. He had been in prison twice during his 20s, once for drug dealing and once for resisting arrest. Since their relationship began, he had already threatened to kill her dog once and had put his hands around her neck during a fight; she called the police and pressed charges against him, then decided to drop the charges. During a brief peaceful phase in their relationship, Audie asked her mother, Venus, whether Ewing would be invited to the family's Thanksgiving dinner.

Venus was well aware of Ewing's aggressive behavior and the fact that he had been in prison and discussed with me her ambivalence about having him in her house: "This is a guy who almost strangled my daughter, who threatened to kill her dog—I mean, I've got a dog! He's probably got a rap sheet two pages long; why would I want him in my house?"

"Maybe you don't. You can always say no."

"But I want to support Audie's relationship. I've always been a supportive mom. I always support my kids one hundred percent!"

"Not everything or everyone is worth supporting one hundred percent, however."

"I know, I know. But Audie will feel very hurt if I don't invite Ewing along. She may not come herself."

"She might not, and it's her right not to. But it's also your right to not have Ewing in your house when you don't feel that he can be trusted."

"What kind of mother won't invite her daughter's boyfriend over for Thanksgiving?"

"The kind of mother who wants to be safe . . . and the kind of mother who wants to model effective limit-setting for her daughter so that her daughter doesn't get taken advantage of."

"Oh . . . "

Parents don't have the same influence over their children during young adulthood as they do during childhood or adolescence, but they still have some, and it's important for them to be able to exert that influence to whatever extent possible.

BALANCED SUPPORT REGARDING REMAINING CHALLENGES

Many parents are trying to launch young adult children who have minor or severe limitations, be they physical, emotional, or behavioral. In these situations, the parents have to find a balance between remaining supportive and allowing their child to learn to accept, live with, and compensate for these limitations.

For example, when it comes to academic issues, even parents who have for many years been supportive of children who struggle with learning disabilities, attentional deficits, Asperger's syndrome, autism, and other forms of neuropsychological unevenness will at times succumb to the belief that academic problems are the result of the child being unmotivated or lazy. And no matter how understanding and tolerant they have been, most parents would simply like to be liberated from the responsibilities and worries associated with playing a supportive role in a child's education by the time compulsory schooling has been completed.

The reality is that continuing to play a supportive role can make the difference between the young adult who acquires a marketable degree or certification that serves him well in the job market and the one who does not. So one of the challenges becomes finding a way to gradually cede more autonomy to the young adult while still maintaining an encouraging and helpful presence.

Staying with this example, parents of students with learning issues may also have to adjust their expectations and realize that, for example, an elite four-year college may not be the most conducive environment for their son or daughter despite their long-standing wishes. Instead, a smaller, less prestigious college, or one that is designed specifically to help students with learning problems, or a training program designed to provide the young adult with sought after skills in a trade or technical area (computers, automotive repair, plumbing, etc.) might be the best bet. Just because a young adult has turned 18 and finished high school doesn't mean that she is automatically ready to flourish independently according to parental ideals.

Of course, while at times parents have to remain involved, sometimes the best thing they can do is to do nothing. Many young adults I take care of are so inflamed by the end of high school from constantly dealing with various academic and clinical interventions that the inflammation has to be given a chance to subside before the possibility of anything different can be introduced.

If a young adult with an uneven learning profile wants to try to make a go of it at college without going to the writing center for editing help or without touching base with the school's learning specialist, for example, I encourage parents to respect that wish. If things work out, that's great—if not, then it's likely that the young adult will realize how valuable or necessary those resources are and will be more likely to energetically take advantage of them.

ACCEPTANCE

> *Do not be angry with the rain; it simply does not know how to fall upwards.*
> Vladimir Nabokov

All parents dream that their child will carry forth into the world their shining strengths, negate their glaring weaknesses, and finally enable them to achieve, through proxy, breathtaking heights of eminence and immortality.

But there is a breach of trust that occurs in every parent–child relationship. In some of my previous books, I have written that every child experiences three births in her parent's mind: her birth as a fantasy child, her birth as an actual child, and her birth as a "good-enough" child. Parents have to make the journey from raising the child of their dreams to raising a flesh-and-blood child, one who is doomed to disappoint and disillusion them, and integrate the fantasy and the reality into the good-enough child, one who is worthwhile and lovable simply for being who she is rather than for being whom the parents want her to be.

That journey is a long and complex one, and the launching stage demands that the parents complete that integration and come to see not only their offspring but also themselves as good enough rather than perfect. Many parents struggle with this, though, and remain so clotted with disapproval and disappointment that everything that they think about or say to their child gushes forth in a fierce torrent of anger and criticism.

When I think about acceptance, I always return to Friedrich Nietzsche's discussion of *amor fati*, a Latin phrase that can be translated as an abiding love of fate. In Nietzsche's words: "My formula for greatness in a human being is *amor fati*: that one wants nothing to be different, not forward, not backward, not in all eternity. Not merely bear what is necessary, still less conceal it . . . but *love* it." I'm also reminded of the final line of Robert Frost's poem, "Hyla Brooke": "We love the things we love for what they are." If this line were translated specifically for parents, it might read, "We love the children we love for *who* they are."

ACKNOWLEDGING THEIR STRENGTHS AS WELL AS THEIR WEAKNESSES

During a family session, Sammy, a 22-year-old struggling with depression, was talking about how difficult his life had been during his primary school years, when his mother, Yolanda, suffered through a long depression. She sat patiently as he described what it was like to wake up and get himself off to school while she remained in bed, or to come home from school and find her still lying in bed, not having moved for the entire day. She continued to listen as he shared with us how worried he was about her, how he would try to entertain and distract his younger brother, and how upset he would get when his father would angrily lay into her at night for being immobilized, not understanding the severity of her illness.

It had been years since Yolanda had recovered, with the help of medication and therapy, but Sammy spoke about those years as if they had just happened yesterday. And Yolanda felt as if his words had sent her back in time. I could see her growing increasingly upset and asked Sammy to have a seat in the waiting room while I met with her alone.

Without her son in the room, she burst into tears, filled with guilt and shame for all the years that she had been overwhelmed and unable to function in the way that she desperately wanted to.

"He's correct; I was worthless during those years. I was no help to anyone at all. He basically raised himself and his brother, my husband was busy trying to keep us afloat financially. I listen to him, and I can't tell you how awful I feel."

"It surely is painful for you to have to revisit such a nightmare, one that, thankfully, now lies in the past. But that is essentially what Sammy is telling you, that it is far enough removed that it can now be discussed. His capacity to talk with you honestly about this, and your capacity to *listen* to him as he talks about it, is a tremendous accomplishment on both of your parts. It means that, in his eyes, you have recovered and that you can hear the words that he didn't believe you were strong enough to hear years ago. And it means that you taught him something about persisting in the face of adversity—you eventually found the will to seek help and get past your depression, and that is exactly what he's doing here now."

Parents must acknowledge the ways in which they disappointed their children (and themselves), but we may have to remind them of what they *were* able to supply their children with, despite their flaws and imperfections as caregivers and humans.

In other families, however, taking full ownership of inappropriate parenting is just as important. One father was describing for me his role in the family, and he made an interesting slip of the tongue—he meant to say how critical he felt he was *to* the functioning of everyone in the family, but he wound up saying that he was critical *of* the functioning of everyone in the family, which was, in fact, how he came across—almost quivering with anger, he constantly distributed looks of unalloyed contempt to his 22-year-old twin sons and his wife, as if spearing them on a spit and turning them over and over again in the flaming oven of his disappointment.

Parents of young adults must find a way to acknowledge, understand, and apologize for the hurt that they have caused over the years, for the ways in which they have, despite their deep love and best efforts, let their child(ren) down.

In one session, 23-year-old Parker and her mother, Carol, were discussing Parker's memories of her childhood. Parker recalled that her mother was prone to suddenly erupting in a cascade of resounding anger, but then her rage would pass, like it had been a brief thunderburst. Within moments, it was as if the sun had come out, and her mother would become pleasant, friendly, and bright. The fact that these eruptions had lasting repercussions for Parker, however, seemed to be completely lost on Carol.

"Mom, you terrified me—when you got angry it was awful."

"But, honey, I didn't get angry very often, and I never stayed angry. It's not like I would hold a grudge or anything. I said what I had to say, and that was it."

"Well, you might not have stayed *angry*, but I certainly stayed *scared*. And the worst part was, we never knew when you were going to hit the ceiling. You're right, you didn't hold a grudge, but when you blew, you really blew, and we never knew when it was coming."

"Look, Parker, I did the best I could. I know I have a temper, but I never hit any of you, not like my mother used to hit me."

"Mom, you're not getting it. I'm not saying you weren't an improvement over your mom, and I know that you didn't hit us, and I'm *glad* you didn't hit us. But you don't realize how terrifying you were."

"One day when you have children, you'll see how hard it is to always keep your cool! You'll see what it's like when you're at the end of your rope and then that one more last thing goes wrong! You'll see it's not so easy!"

"Oh, Mom, that's not what I meant. I'm not saying I don't understand. I just want *you* to understand that even though you got over your anger quickly, it wasn't so quick for me. That's all I'm saying. Can't you just hear that? Can't you just acknowledge it?"

It was at this point that I stepped in.

"Carol, what is it that you think your daughter is asking you for right now?"

"I think she wants me to apologize for having had a bad temper."

"And what goes through your head when you consider her request?"

"What goes through my head is that I don't have anything to apologize for. I said this already, I say it over and over again—I did the best I could. If I exploded from time to time, so be it. What, was I supposed to be on good behavior all the time, like a saint or something?"

"Having raised three children of my own, Carol, I can promise you that none of us are saints when it comes to being a parent. But I want you to take a moment—silently—to just consider your daughter's request. I'm not asking you to agree to it or to rule it out. I'm not pushing you to apologize for losing your temper or to defend yourself. I'm just asking you to sit quietly for a few moments right now and consider it, with an open mind."

Carol agreed, and slowly closed her eyes. After about a minute, tears began to squeeze out. She opened her eyes, looking tremendously sad. Parker visibly relaxed in response.

"What're you thinking?" I asked.

"I'm just imagining what it must've been like for the kids when I lost it. I remember my own mother, how her face used to just get bent out of shape with anger, how her eyes would blaze and how scary it was. And if I was anything like that, if I looked *anything* like my mother looked . . . well then I feel so bad for my children, I just feel so bad for them."

Parker reached out and touched her mom's forearm lightly. "That's all I wanted to hear," she said softly. "I just wanted to know that you knew what it was like for us. That's all I needed to hear."

Carol spent the remainder of the session talking about her own memories of childhood, and how scared and vulnerable she felt, while Parker listened attentively. Carol's capacity to identify with her daughter, rather than to defend herself, got the two of them past their stalemate and into a different form of relatedness.

RECLAIMING (OR CLAIMING) IMAGINATION

A 55-year-old patient whose three children were now grown admitted to me, "The problem is, I really don't ever seem to have gotten the hang of living my own life. It's like I've been a passenger on a train all these years, watching the cities go by, but without any control of where it's going. I don't know how I got on this train, and I don't know how to get off of this train—I just keep sitting here."

Many adults, as they approach midlife and move through this phase, appear to have experienced only the slightest, most glancing relationship with themselves. They may or may not have marched through their lives with an ambitious checklist of milestones and accomplishments, and they may or may not have checked many of those milestones and accomplishments off of the list. Nevertheless, they still feel at sea, as if they have not really been living, or have been living someone else's life rather than living their own. These feelings invariably intensify as parents consider the emptiness of their lives in the context of the emptiness of their nest.

We will often be in the position of working with parents to help them put their imaginations to work and forge a path forward that does not depend exclusively on child rearing for definition and direction, one that enlarges the hitherto stunted dimensions of the life that they have been living and helps them to relocate their lost selves.

PROMOTING PATIENCE AND COMPOSURE

Sometimes I feel that my main job as a clinician is preventing anxiety from becoming dread. Doubt can so easily settle into the family, much like a psychological gangrene that takes root and slowly rots everything inside. Numerous parents have to be regularly reminded that youth is a rough draft of a life and can and should be revised many times.

As discussed in the introduction, the time frame within which young adults become independent is a very different one than it was for the parents. There are many more developmental highways and byways, scenic routes filled with twists and turns. Sometimes a young adult will take life by storm, directly attacking and besieging its fortresses, and sometimes she will be steadily preparing a guerilla resistance movement in the mountains, providing not the slightest indication that she is intent on one day coming down to conquer life and extend her former frontiers.

We frequently use the phrase "suddenly dawned on him," but dawn is not a sudden process; it's a snail-like, incremental process, and this may be the case with young adult development, as well. As clinicians, we have to help parents to distinguish between a young adult's stability, stasis, and stagnation, because they are all different. As poet T. R. Smith writes in "Waking before Dawn": "The river, even/when frozen, arrives at the right place."

DIMINISH THE FOCUS ON HAPPINESS
AS LIFE'S ULTIMATE OBJECTIVE

Many struggling young adults have developed a genius for self-pity that is partially calculated to blunt their parents' legitimate anger and frustration and the changes that would come about should that anger and frustration be channeled into intervention. Twenty-three-year-old Chaz was a patient of mine who exploited his mother mercilessly, insisting on being taken care of by her while giving back almost nothing in return. Yet whenever she seemed to finally be at the end of her rope, he would somehow find it within himself to launch into a tearful monologue about how much he hated himself, a command performance that reflexively drew out his mother's sorrow and instantly discouraged whatever motivation she might have had to finally put her foot down and refuse to comply with his incessant demands.

Parents make themselves unnecessarily vulnerable when they decide that they want their child to be happy—happiness for most of us is a by-product of living a productive and responsible life, not a commodity that can be single-mindedly sought and grabbed. It is the belief that happiness is paramount that prompts many young adults to inappropriately rely on recreational or prescription drug abuse—"There must be something wrong with me if I'm not happy, so I must do what I can to achieve that state." Other young adults conclude that if their parents' primary wish is for them to be happy, then their parents should grant their every request, since that would, ostensibly, make them happy.

I often find myself in the position of discouraging parents from just wanting their child to be happy and helping him to see the value in becoming acquainted and comfortable with other states of emotional being. If nothing else, this can turn out to be a source of creativity and courage. In his biography of David Ben-Gurion, Shimon Peres writes, "The Jews' greatest contribution to history is dissatisfaction . . . we're a nation born to be discontented. Whatever exists we believe can be changed for the better." Where would we be without the efforts of the many individuals who fostered positive social change or created great art that was born of their unhappiness?

A young adult who repeatedly sings the melodies of discontent over and over again, like a troubling fugue, can become tiresome for others to listen to, but by the time he's reached adulthood, it remains entirely up to him if he wants to continue to do so, and it is no longer his parents' responsibility to change it.

FINDING BALANCE AND OBJECTIVITY

All parents will have a tendency to either exaggerate their children's strengths or magnify their weaknesses. We want to help parents to come up with as balanced and objective an assessment as possible so that they know when and when not to get involved.

There was a song by The Carpenter's that I listened to back in high school, entitled "Yesterday Once More," about the yearning to go back to the past. The song title, and its theme, comes to my mind when I'm working with the parents of struggling young adults who insist on remaining focused on their child's early achievements while ignoring the disturbing realities of her current life. When a young adult is not making her parents proud in the present, it is, of course, natural for them to reflect back to when she made them proud in the past. So we will often hear parents share comments such as:

"She was always the fastest kid in her class, boy or girl—her elementary school gym teacher told us she was definitely going to be a great athlete."

"He was incredibly gifted from an early age—I remember when he was still in kindergarten and he took apart his grandfather's alarm clock and put it back together—he didn't even know how to read!"

"Her middle school science teacher told us that he'd never had a student ask such sophisticated questions."

"I should bring you the story that she wrote when she was in fifth grade—it read like a novel, nobody could believe that a fifth-grader had written it. The teacher showed it to everybody in the county."

Comments like these have value in that they keep everyone in the family from getting too demoralized by the current state of stressful affairs. But they can also keep the young adult, and the family as a whole, imprisoned in psychological amber, so focused on what happened long ago that nobody has to fully acknowledge what is *not* happening right now. The desire for everyone to rest on their previous laurels is a tempting one, but also one that is best resisted.

So the clinician must skillfully join with the family in acknowledging the young adult's strengths but resist calling forth heraldic trumpets because of that which took place in the past that, for whatever reasons, is not being built upon in the present.

On the flip side, some parents truly undersell their young adult's resourcefulness and see him as much less capable than he really is. The therapist must help to affirm and accentuate the young adult's strengths, which helps prevent parents from constantly rushing in to protect or rescue him. One father whom I was working with prepared his 19-year-old "directionally challenged" son for local driving trips as if he was traveling to the moon, programming his GPS, printing out directions from Mapquest, and going over the route verbally before he headed out. Yet one day, this same young man rescued his neighbor's dog, who had been hit by a car, and drove the injured canine to an emergency veterinary hospital more than half an hour away, somehow without the benefit of any paternal or technological support.

AWARENESS OF ANNIVERSARIES

As discussed in chapter 4 ("Family Assessment at the Launching Stage"), we want to be alert to what was going on in the parents' lives when they were the age that their son or daughter is now. Fara recalled that she had great difficulty organizing herself as a young adult, which might have been what was accounting for how anxiously she was inserting herself into her daughter's life as Delia was finishing up college.

"I keep telling Delia that she's got to make plans, she's got to have something in place, but she keeps telling me not to worry, not to worry."

"What are her plans at this point?" I asked.

"Nothing firm. She talks about maybe going to graduate school one day, but not now. She wants to live in a different city for a while. She applied to a couple of programs like Teach for America, in which they send you somewhere to be a teacher. She says she's prepared to just get any old job she can so that she can support herself, if necessary."

"So it sounds like she's got some ideas to work with."

"Yes, but, like I said, nothing firm, nothing firm. It's making me crazy; that's why I'm such a loon right now, I'm calling or texting her every day with questions, with ideas, and she's getting sick of me, and I don't blame her."

"What were things like for you when you were preparing to graduate?" I inquired.

"Awful. I was so lost, I didn't know what I was doing. I was in this miserable relationship, and it just got worse and worse. I had nothing else to focus on. I spent a couple of years basically just gaining weight and getting high. Those were lost years, completely lost, and I just don't want Delia to have to go through the same thing."

"I can understand why you're worried, but it's not abundantly clear to me that she's destined to follow the same pathways."

"If she doesn't make any plans for herself, she probably will. That was my problem; I didn't have any plans."

"But you pointed out that she *is* making plans."

"I guess . . . they just don't seem like very *good* plans."

With this family, it was important for me to help Fara distinguish her daughter from herself. It was scary for her to anticipate that Delia was guaranteed to hit the same turbulence that Fara hit when *she* graduated from college, but as we spoke, we were able to find several ways in which she and her daughter were different, both in terms of their personality as well as their experience in college.

Keeping in mind those differences helped Fara to back off a bit and give Delia a chance to map out her future without too much maternal interference.

IDENTIFY WITH THE YOUNG ADULT'S STUCKNESS

Family therapy sometimes involves elucidating one generation's confounding behavior for the other generation. Dad, for example, doesn't understand why his daughter won't prepare for her SAT exam when she says that she wants to go to college. But it was easy for me to see how it was a win-win situation for her to desist from studying. After all, if she didn't prepare and performed as well as she wanted to, that was one less onerous responsibility she had to take on. And if she didn't prepare and didn't do as well as she'd like to, then she could save face and attribute that (perhaps accurately) to not having studied.

One father complained that his son, David, wasn't creating any "vision" for his life. "He doesn't work hard because he doesn't know what he wants to achieve. If he knew where he was going, he'd be better able to put in the time and effort necessary to get there." But I pointed out that David might be hesitant to create a vision when he didn't have much confidence in his ability to make that vision a reality. If this was the case, he might feel that he was better off not establishing goals since he didn't believe he'd ever attain them anyway.

When parents learn that there's a logic to the apparently illogical behavior of their child, they tend to be somewhat more tolerant and less critical of it.

MAINTAINING CONGRUENCE

The developmental trajectory of shared parenthood is always one of a kind. Parents always come from different backgrounds, so their parental style of engagement will always differ as well. One of the advantages of having two parents is that a child observes and experiences a range of ways to engage and adjust.

These parental differences will show up with varying degrees of salience at different developmental stages, often depending on the parents' experience at those stages.

In one family that I treated, the parents, Mel and Nina, worked well together for many years until their children reached early adolescence. It had been at that point in Mel's development when his parents, who were U.S. diplomats stationed in India, had sent him back to the United States to complete his secondary education. So from the age of 12 on, Mel had had only infrequent face-to-face contact with his parents, confined to the two or three yearly vacations that they shared. Since he hadn't experienced much parenting from his own mother and father once he left childhood behind, he was a blank slate when it came to how to interact with adolescent or young adult children.

Meanwhile, Nina had completed her high school and college years living at home. So her experience was the opposite—she had had abundant contact with her parents through adolescence and early adulthood.

Not surprisingly, Mel and Nina were often at odds with each other as their children rambled through middle school, high school and beyond. Mel hung back and added little to the family, while Nina assiduously tried to fill in the gaps—a not atypical polarization occurred, in which the more Nina inserted herself into the children's lives, the more Mel pulled away, and the more Mel pulled away, the more Nina felt compelled to insert herself into the children's lives.

This laid the groundwork for difficulties with their 20-year-old daughter, Deanne, who was going through a phase of heavy drug use. Nina kept pushing her husband to "do something," while Mel kept pushing his wife to "stay out of it and let her solve her own problems." Either approach might have worked were they to unify themselves into a cohesive team. But because they continued to neutralize each other and cancel each other's efforts out, Deanne continued to slip through the widening cracks of the family and continued her dangerous behavior.

The clinical objective with this family was to tighten up the parenting team so that they were articulating a consistent message regarding Deanne's worrisome behavior.

RAISING THE PARENT'S ANXIETY

I have frequently made reference to the importance of reducing parents' anxiety when it comes to launching young adults, but sometimes our job is to *raise* their anxiety—they have become too passive, too resigned, too accepting of the current state of affairs, and they have to be firmly nudged off center. Our job sometimes is to keep, or even increase, the tension on the line.

Ernie was a 23-year-old who lived at home with his single mother, Bernadette. He had graduated from high school and been a heroin addict for the last four years, which obviously had hindered his efforts to train for a career and learn how to support himself.

His father had asked for a divorce about 10 years before, then remarried and moved to another state with his new wife. Ernie had two older siblings in their late 20s, both of whom were married, living on their own, and raising small children. Ernie did not work but regularly stole money from his mother, a teacher, so that he could purchase his drugs. Bernadette was aware that Ernie was using drugs and that he was stealing from her, but because Ernie had threatened to hurt her if she told his brother or sister, or anyone else, she agreed to keep it under wraps, essentially underwriting his addiction. Bernadette had contacted me at the encouragement of her minister, whom she had finally confided in after Ernie had shoved her against a wall when he couldn't find any money at home one evening, bruising her shoulder. Not surprisingly, Ernie refused to join his mother for our session.

When I asked Bernadette why she hadn't told her other two children what was happening, she said that she didn't think she should bother them, that they were both busy with their own families and didn't need to be bothered with these difficulties. When I asked her why she hadn't told Ernie's father, she said that she hadn't been in touch with him for years and didn't think he would care anyway. She also believed that hearing how poorly Ernie was doing would provide further validation for her former husband that he was wise to have left her, married someone "better," and moved on.

When I asked her why she hadn't called the police to have Ernie arrested for stealing and for abuse, she looked shocked and offended.

"Call the police on my own son?"

"Well, let's face it, he has been breaking quite a few laws."

"But he's my son! I love him!"

"Of course he's your son, and of course you love him, and you always will. But right now, your son is basically living like a bum. He's not working, he's addicted to drugs, and he's stealing from his own mother, whom he threatens and whom he shoved into the wall and injured."

"It was just a bruise . . . I'm really okay now."

"You're okay this time, but, as you know, it could happen again, and your son is probably bigger and stronger than you are, so you might get more seriously hurt the next time."

"I know, I know. I have tried to talk with him about this, and we've actually had some good conversations recently. He has said that he doesn't want to be an addict his whole life."

"When does he plan on giving up heroin?"

"He says once he gets a job, he'll stop."

"What is he doing to get a job?"

"I see him on the computer, looking at Craigslist, looking at websites. I know he's trying."

"Is he out in the community filling out and turning in applications?"

"Not that I'm aware of."

"Do you hear him on the phone making employment inquiries?"

"Well, he might when I'm at work, but not that I'm aware of."

"So it's okay for him to continue using drugs, stealing from you, threatening you, and occasionally abusing you, as long as he *says* that he's looking for a job?"

"Well . . . "

"What do you think would happen if you called the police and reported your son for drug use and violence?"

"I'm afraid they'd put him away."

"And if they did?"

"He'd never forgive me . . . putting my own son in jail? How could a mother ever do that?"

"*You* wouldn't be the one putting him in jail."

"I know that, but I'd still feel responsible—he'd never forgive me."

"You wonder if he would ever forgive you, but when he eventually overdoses on heroin, or gets murdered during one of his drug purchases, will you be able to forgive *yourself*? Will you feel as if you had done everything possible to stand in the way of his habit? Because he will no longer be around to forgive you at that time."

"I pray that that won't happen. I pray every day that that won't happen."

"It is good that you pray, but will you be able to forgive yourself?"

"I don't know, I just don't know. Heroin is such a tough habit to break, I have read about it. Receptors in the brain, it's very complicated."

"You are right, it's a highly addictive substance. But nevertheless there are heroin addicts who do break their habit. It takes great courage and great strength, but they do it. And sometimes they do it only when they are *forced* to do it, forced by someone or something outside of themselves. It is possible that Ernie needs some of those outside forces helping him. It is even possible that Ernie is actually *asking* for some of those outside forces, although doing so silently."

"How can I help him, then?"

"By rallying those outside forces on his behalf."

"You mean call the police?"

"That would be one way."

"Oh, I just don't know if I can do that."

"I don't know if you can do it, either. And of course, you don't have to do it. You do have choices here. You could, if you'd like, continue doing what you're doing, living like a hostage in your own home, blackmailed and sometimes injured by your own son until he dies what is likely to be a premature and ugly death."

"You really think it's okay to call the police on your own son?"

"Believe me, Bernadette, I am not suggesting this lightly. You are living a nightmare, and the nightmare hasn't yet come to its end. It's a horrible thing to contemplate, and it will take great courage and strength on your part to make that call—as much courage and strength as it will take him to break this terrible habit. But perhaps if you can summon that courage and strength, he will see that, and it will inspire him to start getting his life together."

"Oh, I think he'll just be so angry with me, so angry and hurt."

"He probably will. But at least there's a chance that he'll be alive to *feel* that anger and hurt. And, believe me, the anger and hurt will pass if he beats his addiction and begins to realize how courageous and strong you were."

"Calling the police on my own son," she mused, quietly. "I just never thought . . ."

She remained silent for a moment, and then asked, "Isn't there another alternative?"

"Sure, some others come to mind. For example, you could let your two older children know what's happening."

"But they'd just feel awful. They're both so tied up with their own children. And I promised Ernie that I wouldn't tell them; he's very embarrassed about this, you know. He always felt like he didn't measure up to his brother and sister. They had the benefit of a father for their whole lives, while he didn't—his father left me when Ernie was just becoming a teenager, it was devastating for him, I still feel terrible. So I promised him I wouldn't tell them."

"How do you think they'll react if you did?"

"Honestly? I think they'd kill him," she admitted with a chuckle, the first time I had seen any lightness in her bearing.

"Really?"

"No, not really. But I think they'd be incredibly angry with him."

"And what might they do?"

"After they killed him?" she joked.

"Honestly . . . what might they do?"

"I don't know, really. I know they would be angry with me for putting up with this and not telling them."

"But would they be more angry with *him* or more angry with *you?*"

"Oh, him, definitely. They'd be furious with him."

"So it sounds like you have three legitimate alternatives right now, Bernadette. You can do nothing different and continue laying the groundwork for his tragic and untimely death, and/or yours, if he loses control again. You could call the police. Or you could tell your older children. We could also consider your getting in touch with his father, if you'd like, to see if he would step in."

"I'll tell you this, I'm definitely *not* going to contact his dad. He doesn't care, and I haven't talked to him in years and I don't want to invite him back into our lives. I've got enough on my hands without announcing to him that I'm a bad mother."

"I'm not sure I'd agree that that's what he'd be seeing, but I can understand your hesitancy. Ultimately, it's your decision. You don't have to decide now, but I do want you to make a decision, even if your decision is not to do anything different, even if your decision is to decide that you are not yet ready to solve this problem. So why don't you give it some thought and get back to me? How much time do you think you'll need to arrive at a decision?"

Bernadette sighed with relief at being temporarily let off the hook and suggested we follow up in a week. At that time, she arrived for her session and told me that she had given it careful thought and decided that she couldn't call the police on her own son but that, with some reluctance, she had told her two older children what was happening. Not surprisingly, they were appalled when they learned what had been going on—so appalled that they both came over and called the police to have Ernie arrested and taken from the home in handcuffs that day.

Given the choice of prison or a drug rehabilitation program by the court, Ernie chose the latter and departed for a three-month stint. This was the first step in beginning the difficult process of straightening his life out and his mother being released from her captive status.

In this family, it quickly became apparent Bernadette had become hesitant to ask anything of her son, so much pity did she feel for him as a fatherless teenager, and so much guilt did she feel for not having been able to keep his primary male role model in place for him.

So, as I came to find out in some subsequent sessions, she never held him accountable when he began to get into trouble in middle school, constantly endeavoring to affirm his innocence and shield him from paying the price for his misbehavior. With the rule of Protect Ernie At All Cost in place, it wasn't a surprise that his initial experimentation with pot back in eighth grade was never grown out of, but instead eventually grew into a much more dangerous addiction, stunting his emotional growth.

Over time, Bernadette's unwavering commitment to following this rule prevented her from behaving differently and helping to solve the problem. However, once she was open to seeing this, she was able to modify the rules, which resulted almost instantly in a modification of Ernie's behavior and a much greater possibility for recovery and change.

One of the strategies that I have used to good effect when attempting to raise parents' anxiety level in an effort to mobilize them is to read to the parents a progress note that I have written after having met with them. Quoting aloud from what sounds like an official clinical record (although it is basically just my opinion and an effort to convey the seriousness of my concerns) often has great impact on parents who do not seem to be grasping the seriousness of a situation.

Here's a section from a note that I read aloud at the beginning of my third session with two parents who seemed to regularly cancel each other out when it came to setting limits with their increasingly antisocial 21-year-old son (he had thus far refused to come for treatment, so I used my note to speculate regarding his motivations).

Antonio appears to be confident in his ability to play his parents off of one another. He most likely believes that his father's "boys will be boys" perspective means that just about anything he does short of armed robbery will be accepted by his dad with a wink and a nod, even though he is no longer a boy.

He believes that his mother's enduring faith in his inherent goodness means that he can basically get away with anything that he does as long as he displays sporadic, intermittent periods of kindness, and as long as she can continue to recall pleasant examples of this from the past, like when he volunteered at a senior center in middle school. Antonio has probably concluded that he can essentially buy her off at a very small price.

He may not see his parents as capable of ever becoming truly unified in thought, deed, and word, and most likely finds it rewarding to be able to split them, and exploit the differences to his advantage. He doesn't really see his parents following through on any one consequence because he knows that if he is patient enough, he can just wait them out and count on them to neutralize and undermine each other, if not right away, then at some point. Nothing packs much of a wallop because he knows he can just hang in there and emerge unscathed.

What is particularly worrisome is that Antonio seems to be bringing this same set of beliefs into the world outside of his family as he prepares to venture forth. Just as he has grown confident in his ability to outwit his parents, he is now becoming convinced that he can outwit the legal system. He is more and more solidly coming to the conclusion that the rules that apply to others simply don't apply to him. He continues to skirt the laws in the community, but his arrogance has grown to the extent that he feels almost no anxiety that a hammer will ever be lowered—which is how he feels at home—or if it is lowered, he'll simply ride it out.

Meanwhile, he continues to believe that ultimately he need not ever work hard and that he will always be taken care of by his generous parents in a comfortable way. This sense that there is a deep cushion against any distress further fuels his conviction that he is above the law and need not perform according to the dictates of anyone other than himself. That is one of the reasons that his relationship with his girlfriend is so unstable—everything is fine as long as everything goes Antonio's way, but if people, or the world, don't conform to his dearly held beliefs, then he gets upset and destructive.

Antonio remains tremendously insecure, and, ironically, his belief that he can pull the wool over everyone's eyes is feeding that sense of insecurity. He still knows, at some level, that he is not taking care of business in a way that will lead to his becoming successful and self-sufficient. But rather than confront that fear directly and working to overcome it, he has taken the tack of avoiding it and counting on being perpetually taken care of, no matter what he does.

Antonio doesn't want to have to transcend adversity; he wants to sidestep it and truly believes that with his family's enduring and indulging support, he can. Despite short periods of parental distress, anger, and disapproval, he seems to have incorporated the belief that he's really okay and that things are going to be just fine, putting him on a path toward a narcissistic, self-involved existence, or one that may turn out to be sociopathic in direction. In other words, he is well on his way to becoming a derelict.

The parents were stunned by this report and silent for some time as they took it in, but it seemed to get the point across and compel them to yoke together more completely in the face of Antonio's intransigence.

BEING IMPERFECT

While having an underfunctioning parent does not make the transition into adulthood easy for a child, having an overfunctioning parent presents its own challenges. When parents appear perpetually confident and perfectly competent in every area of their lives, their children are likely to believe that they will always suffer in comparison to their parents. Not only that, they will come to doubt that they will ever have the opportunity to play a meaningful or significant role when it comes to taking care of their parents, which will prompt them to feel that they will never be in the position of being able to give what they have received.

It is certainly difficult to become an adult when you have not had a sufficient childhood, but it is also difficult to become an adult when you believe that you will forever feel like a child because your parents appear to be so completely self-sufficient, precluding the possibility that you will ever be able to become the adult in the relationship and treat them, in the best sense of the word, as a child.

I will usually look for opportunities in treatment for solidly functioning parents to disclose their vulnerabilities to their young adult son or daughter—it minimizes the yawning chasm that seems to separate them and makes it seem perhaps a little more likely that the child can one day measure up to the parent.

We have been discussing some of the developmental tasks and related therapeutic objectives related to the parents of young adults. Now let's do the same thing with the young adults themselves.

Chapter 8

Consulting with Young Adults

The important thing is this: To be able at any moment to sacrifice what we are for what we could become.

Charles du Bos, *Approximations*

The history of a family begins, and its true nature reveals itself, when a child dares to leave home. I have heard many young adult patients say the words, "I'm dying to leave." This phrase connotes the urgent, life-and-death struggle that is sometimes associated with the child's separation and differentiation from the family. This chapter will address some of these struggles and how therapists can help young adults to resolve them, with and without the presence of their family.

THE ENTERPRISE OF YOUNG ADULT IDENTITY

In the 1987 movie *Moonstruck*, Cosmo Castorini admits, "I don't know where I've been and I don't know where I'm going." As clinicians working with young adults, our foremost job is to enable them to answer the former so that they are better able to determine the latter.

Along these lines, a young adult recently confessed to me, "I never feel like myself . . . I can't remember the last time I felt like myself." These extraordinarily revealing words left me transfixed. What choice does one have other than to be oneself? What is it like to not feel like yourself? And if you can't remember feeling like yourself, then is it possible that the self that you are seeking is not the self that you truly are anymore?

The construction of young adult identity is an unavoidably clumsy affair. She must hack off a piece of herself here, suture a gaping split there, try to splice together several disparate parts of herself to see how it looks and feels. She must *renounce* certain parts of her identity without *denouncing* herself, and simultaneously welcome back other parts that have been exiled for years. She will behave in ways that she longs to believe are out of character and then have to contemplate the possibility that these behaviors are, indeed, crucial and inescapable components that lie *within* her character. She will suddenly descend into vast regions of psychological terra incognita and stagger through them, hoping she doesn't get lost or ambushed. She will constantly feel like a fraud, an imposter who is bound to one day be unmasked. As the band Neutral Milk Hotel sings in "Planes in the Sky," "How strange it is to be someone."

Successful young adulthood requires the creation and elaboration of a personal philosophy, a way of life that is acceptable to her regardless of whether it is acceptable to her family and her peers. She needs to nurture and safeguard her emerging self, to make explicit both her discovered self and her still-being-discovered self. She needs to ask, Who was I, Who am I, Who am I becoming, and What am I here for? She has to determine what kind of ecology best nurtures her growth, and believe in the dignity of the life she has chosen to live within that ecology. It is not about "occupying Wall Street" as it is about more fundamentally "occupying herself."

She must understand that much of her identity takes root in the solitary confinement of the self and that learning to bear an unbearable loneliness is one of life's great victories, one that can be sustaining through many challenges and disappointments. She has to prove that she can stand up to life's pressures, stresses, disappointments, and even tragedies, and emerge with her personal banner, tattered as it may be, still held proudly aloft. She must learn to see what she endures as important and meaningful and find ways to wrest something positive and nourishing out of the personal events and psychological experiences that may diminish and defeat her. She has to find ways to consolidate her new position and progress, to maintain the ground gained in the necessary fight against despair, absurdity, and meaninglessness.

She has to welcome the humble, bruised truths that arise from her encounters with life, its humiliations and comedies, its blessings and indignities. She has to allow the uninvited squalls of suffering to do their work and strengthen the inner fiber of her soul, and recognize and release new dimensions of her being, enlarging her life. She must realize again and again that it is through adversity that we define and recognize ourselves, that it is how we behold our suffering, not how much we suffer, that determines the extent to which we will be transfigured.

PROMOTING SELF-AWARENESS

There is a Chasidic tale about a man trying to get to the other side of the river and not finding any bridge that will carry him across. He sees a person on the opposite bank and shouts over the raging waters, "How do you get to the other side?" which elicits the response, "You already *are* on the other side!" The therapist may have to remind the young adult that she is already making it to the other side, which means helping her to fillet her self-image from the image of her that has been groomed by her parents.

Recently, a 19-year-old patient of mine complained that her parents underestimated her strengths. "They don't think that I persist; they don't think I stick with anything."

"Is that how *you* see yourself?"

"No, they're wrong. I think I persist. I think I've survived a lot. They don't even *know* how much I've survived."

"So *you* see yourself as persistent."

"Right. But how come they don't?"

"I don't know. But how long will you decide that what *they* think about you is as important as what *you* think about you?"

"But why don't they see my persistence?"

"I'm going to ask you the same question I asked you a moment ago. How long will you decide that what *they* think about you is as important as what *you* think about you?"

"But I want them to see me differently."

"You're entitled to want them to see you differently. But how long are you going to let it bother you if they don't?"

"But it's important to me that *they* see me the way *I* see me."

"I understand that it's important, and it's nice when everyone is in agreement. But I am still curious about your willingness to place *their* evaluation of you over *your* evaluation of you, and how long you intend to do this."

"I guess I didn't realize that that's what I was doing."

"Well, that's what it *sounds* like you're doing. I don't have the sense that you would place *their* evaluation of the music that you listen to over *your* evaluation of the music you listen to, right?"

"Of course not," she agreed, laughing.

"Then why would their evaluation of something far more significant than the music you listen to—in other words, their evaluation of *you*—be more important than your evaluation?"

"I see what you're getting at."

"So go back to my question. How long do you plan on believing that their evaluation of you is more important than your evaluation of you?"

"I guess I'd better think about that, huh?"

As I tell many patients, if you don't *distinguish* yourself, you *extinguish* yourself.

An important component of self-awareness is being aware of the survival strategies that you have been using and determining whether they are still relevant. A 20-year-old patient of mine who was extremely passive in his relationships with his family, his girlfriend, and his employer enjoyed playing chess and decided to join the chess club at his college. He acknowledged that the basic game plan that he had originally learned from his first teacher was to "burn moves while waiting for my opponent to make a mistake," but now that he was playing against more skilled adversaries, he realized that maintaining a wait-and-see approach was resulting in slaughter after slaughter on the chessboard.

"I'm going to have to adopt a more aggressive strategy," he allowed, "or I won't win a single game."

We then attempted to extrapolate from the chessboard and worked at finding ways for him to deploy a more assertive game plan in the rest of his life.

Many young adults have been engorged and engulfed with so many possibilities and options while they were growing up that everything eventually began to feel like an imposition rather than an opportunity, something to spurn and repudiate rather than consider and embrace. This strategy, too, may need to be reevaluated as they encounter ordeals and challenges that exceed what they have faced during childhood and adolescence. They must learn to become more permeable to outside influence, to focus on building a foundation for themselves rather than a citadel against others, to allow for others to airlift emotional supplies into what was previously designated as their psychological no-fly zone.

There is a shock to having to adjust to new ideas and new strategies that are different from the dearly held ideas and strategies that have been their standbys in the preceding years—the ones that may have legitimately kept them afloat up until now—but it is a necessary shock for them to encounter.

RESOLVING LOYALTY BINDS

An essential component of healthy separation and differentiation is finding the right balance between loyalty to oneself and loyalty to others. When we are overly loyal to ourselves, we run the risk of becoming self-absorbed, but when we are overly loyal to others, we run the risk of becoming self-sacrificial. Particularly in Centripetal and Mission-Impossible families, young adults often run aground because they are unable to find a workable symmetry between their fidelity to their wishes for themselves and their parents' wishes for them, and the latter winds up overwhelming the former, severely compromising the possibility of growth.

Twenty-two-year-old Suchin was finally making some professional headway after having attended and withdrawn from two different colleges, being without a job for more than a year, and having made a serious suicide attempt that resulted in a two-week hospitalization. Her parents' marriage was shaky, and her mother had recently confided in her that she was considering separating from her father. Meanwhile, her shiftless 26-year-old brother was still living at home as well, marginally employed from time to time as a plumber's helper and harboring no apparent desire to move on or move out.

Once she was discharged from the hospital, Suchin had finally decided to forego obtaining a college education for the time being but, upon the recommendation of a friend, decided to enroll in a class that focused on becoming a personal trainer. She took to it instantly and was already experiencing some success, having quickly obtained a part-time job at a local athletic club and getting excellent feedback on her skills.

However, just as this was coming together, her mother was diagnosed with multiple sclerosis, and, shortly thereafter, Suchin made another suicide attempt, resulting in a second hospitalization. Once she was discharged, Suchin and her family began working with me.

It became clear through our initial conversations that Suchin was struggling to make a decision regarding whom she was going to primarily be faithful to, her family or herself.

"What's your understanding of the basis for your most recent suicide attempt?" I began.

"I don't know . . . it's funny, because I had just finished a one-day class on doing personal training with individuals with physical disabilities, and it had gone really well; my instructor was really impressed with my approach. So I was feeling great about that, and then I went home, and everything felt so bleak—my mom was having a bad day, lots of pain, my brother was sitting around, as always, my father was nowhere to be found. And it's like all of a sudden I felt this gloom settle over me, and everything started to feel pointless. Like why bother moving ahead with my life when I'm going to have to take care of my mother for the rest of my life?"

"What about your father and your brother? Can't they be a support to your mother?"

"Hah! That's a good one! My brother can't even take care of himself, let alone my mom, and my dad just gets annoyed whenever anyone in the family needs anything. Nope, it's really just me. My mom's always been there for me, so I guess it's time for me to be there for her." She sighed sorrowfully and looked up—her eyes were swimming in tears.

"In a way, you are right, your mom does need your support right now. But there's a difference between supporting her and sacrificing your life for her."

"How can I not be worried about her? She's in an unhappy marriage and now she's gotta deal with MS."

"I'm not asking you to not be worried about her—that would be unrealistic. I'm suggesting that perhaps we should think of the best way to be present for her during a difficult time. And you certainly don't want to *add* to her worries about you by becoming self-destructive."

She paused. "I know, when she came to the hospital, she told me how devastated she would be if anything happened to me. That's one of the things that always kept me from killing myself in the past, knowing what it would be like for her."

"I guess at certain difficult junctures you must conclude that you're more valuable to her dead than alive," I surmised.

"Yeah . . . which makes no sense, really . . . I want to be there for her, and two times now I have almost made sure that I'm not there for her at all. I don't even know what I'm doing anymore."

I invited Suchin's mom, Somsri, in to join us for a session. Somsri shared with me how unsettled and distressed she was upon learning of her neurological diagnosis, but she had clearly not lost hope.

"At least now I know what I'm dealing with. I joined a support group, and I've got a good doctor, and I'm going to handle this the best way I know how."

"And what is it that you would like from your daughter at this point in your life?"

"I'd like her to move on with her life. I'm so pleased that she's finally making progress, and I hate to see it derailed."

"But, Mom, I don't see how I can be there for you if I'm starting to pick up more hours training at the club—I'll be busier with my clients than with you!"

"But, honey, don't you see that's what I want? Don't you see that I don't want you stopping your life just because I've gotten sick? Don't you see that?"

"But who is going to take care of you if I don't?"

"I don't have a good answer for you, Suchin, but I'm going to figure that out. That's one of the reasons that I joined this support group, so that I can talk to other people who have MS. It's not a death sentence, you know—I'm not happy about this, but I'm beginning to come to terms with it."

"What about your plans to leave Dad?"

"I don't know about that either, Suchin. Certainly, this throws a crimp in my plans to move out. But that's really not for you to worry about. That's for me and your dad to figure out, not you . . . and we've begun to do that a little bit."

My subsequent work with Suchin involved helping her to realize that the best way to be there for her mother was in fact to *not* be there. This did not mean absenting herself through death (which may have been part of her original motivation for making suicide attempts), but through forging ahead with her own, independent life. As we worked to discover the psychological algorithm that would best solve this complex problem, Suchin began to create a more harmonious blend between being dutiful to herself and dutiful to her family.

RESOLVING THE PAST

Every family has experienced traumas, conflicts, ordeals, crises, and other complicated issues that may have been resolved, partially resolved, or left unresolved altogether over the years. Many of these settle like sediment to the family's ocean floor but will get agitated back up to the surface when a leave-taking is embarked upon, at which point they will need to be revisited and, hopefully, more fully resolved.

Dennis's parents separated when he was five years old and divorced when he was seven. They remained amicable and continued joining each other and the children for holiday dinners and birthdays. Dennis and his younger siblings adjusted reasonably well to the separation, rotating between their parents' two homes and developing a positive relationship with their stepmother, who married Dennis's father when Dennis was nine.

Dennis engaged in some not atypical misbehavior during high school but graduated on time and left home for a four-year college after his senior year. However, he didn't manage his time well there and began drinking heavily, partially as a result of his pledging a fraternity. After two semesters of withdrawing from or failing most of his classes, Dennis, now 19, returned home for summer break, and he and his parents consulted with me to help them make a decision regarding whether he should return to college in the fall.

During our initial session, when I was spending some time alone with Dennis, I asked him about the impact that his parents' divorce had had on him. He spoke about how difficult it had been for him but how he had tried to put his feelings aside and be there for his younger sister and brother.

"My sister was very upset, and I was always trying to cheer her up. I was a pretty good artist, so I'd make up little cartoon books for her, and I'd leave funny drawings in her bed for her at night. And I'd always try to distract my little brother, he was the youngest, by having pillow fights with him when he was getting sad. I felt so bad for both of them."

"Do you remember much about what it was like for *you*, separate from your desire to make things easier for *them*?"

Dennis paused, and stared at the floor for quite a while. "You know, I don't even know. I mean, I guess I was sad, but that's sort of in retrospect. We were watching home movies last year over the Thanksgiving break, and there was one of my birthday, this was a couple of years after the divorce. And I just looked so out of it, like I wasn't even there for my own party, everything was swirling around me and I had this sort of zoned-out look. It was weird."

"You are to be commended for having been such a devoted and caring older brother while the family adjusted to this transition . . . but it's certainly possible that you never gave yourself a chance to make sense of and grieve for the end of your parents' marriage, the end of this stage in the family's life."

"Yeah . . . I mean, I know that my parents felt bad, too, and it was like I was trying to keep everything together, I didn't want anyone to be upset, my siblings, my parents, *anyone*."

"So it wouldn't be surprising that as you began your own process of separating, it stirred up some old feelings about your parents' separation."

"I really didn't think of going away to college as a separation. I mean, everyone does it, all my friends were doing it . . . I remember I never wanted to go away to camp or anything during the summers, we were always home. And I was a little jealous of my friends who would go away, but I really didn't want to . . . even in high school, there was this summer art program that my teacher recommended to my parents, but it would've meant living away from home on a college campus for a month, and I just didn't want to do it."

"Perhaps, because of your parents' separation, you had the sense that separations weren't such good things, even ones that took place for positive reasons."

"It's funny, though, because it's not like I got very homesick at college. Lots of kids seemed like they really missed being home, but it wasn't that; I was kind of happy living away from home."

"Having been released from the pressure of keeping everybody happy and well adjusted, I would imagine that there would actually be some relief to leaving home."

Dennis chuckled. "Yeah, I guess . . . but I sure didn't make the best of it, did I?"

"Maybe you didn't feel that you deserved the opportunity to go off and focus on your own future, rather than the future of your siblings. Maybe you felt a little guilty and that's why you didn't take advantage of the opportunity as much as you would've liked."

Dennis grew silent again. "There was some guilt," he admitted quietly. "I'd be having some fun times but then all of a sudden I'd get the image of my sister and brother at home, and it would make me kinda sad, like I didn't belong here, like how dare I enjoy myself when they're home by themselves."

"It's hard to make a successful experience out of something that you don't feel that you deserve to succeed at."

After pursuing this train of thought with Dennis a while longer, I invited his parents into the office to join us, and, with Dennis's permission, shared some of our discussion with them. Both were completely taken aback by the possibility that their divorce had had any bearing on Dennis's functioning at school.

"Our divorce was *years* ago, Dr. Sachs, I mean Dennis was in second grade! And he did fine with it. I mean nobody was very happy, of course, but we've all adjusted and done better than most, I believe," declared Ms. Dinizio defensively.

Mr. Dinizio chimed in: "We always got together for birthdays and holidays. Everyone thought we were the model divorced couple because we got along so well with each other, because we put the kids first and put our differences to the side. And the kids really like their stepmother; she's become very important to them."

"I'm certainly not questioning how conscientiously the two of you went about the complicated process of separating and divorcing, and how well you handled it . . . but that doesn't mean that it wasn't a painful experience for Dennis."

"But why is he in pain *now*, now that he's almost a man?" Ms. Dinizio asked. "Why wasn't he in more pain when this first happened, when he was a little boy?"

"I believe that he was, but that he chose to focus on making sure that his brother and sister got through it. And once he left home for college, and didn't have them to focus on anymore, some of that pain—the pain that he had shoved under the carpet—reared its head and asked to be recognized."

I encouraged Dennis and his parents to spend some time revisiting, with more depth and candor, their memories of the divorce. Because I sensed Mr. and Ms. Dinizio's defensiveness regarding the possibility that the divorce had been more challenging for the family than they had allowed themselves to believe, I scheduled a meeting with the two of them, without Dennis, to discuss this. I also scheduled a couple of conjoint sessions with all five family members to explore the same topic.

By the end of the summer, Dennis no longer felt as if leaving home was a betrayal or abandonment of his family and was ready to recommit to college.

His parents agreed to allow him to try one more semester, at their expense. He checked in with me during Thanksgiving break to tell me that he was doing well, and I received an e-mail from his mother in December telling me that he had passed all four of his classes and would be continuing.

Helping young adults to make the connection between what is old and what is contemporary often enables them to resolve vexing problems. When we are stranded in the past, the vistas of the future are greatly narrowed. Twenty-three-year-old Gavin had lost one job due to being "insolent" with his boss, and had just been placed on probation by his current boss. Both bosses were women.

We spent some time exploring his reactivity to women employers, and he found himself talking about his mother, who had been physically and verbally abusive with him when he was a child until his father had fought to gain custody of him, which restricted the amount of time he had to spend with her.

When he realized how evocative and provocative it was for him to be told what to do by a woman, he was better able to mitigate his surly behavior and keep his job.

EMPOWERING THE YOUNG ADULT

Many young adults have lost traction because they have lost their sense of efficacy, of the power to author their own lives.

Eighteen-year-old Amrita complained to me that her parents did not envision her as capable of independence and were not willing to pay for her to go to college. This was particularly galling for her because her two older sisters were both away at college. Her parents, the Maliks, were hesitant when it came to Amrita, however, because she had displayed disordered eating and dieting for several years, at times becoming so thin that her doctor had asked the family to consider hospitalizing her.

"We are not saying that she can't go away to college; we are saying that we don't think she's *ready* to go away to college," Ms. Malik explained in our initial session, which took place almost halfway through Amrita's senior year of high school.

"But you decided that my brother and sister were ready when *they* finished high school," countered Amrita.

"Well, Amrita, they were more ready than you. That doesn't mean that we don't see you as ready one day. It means that we don't see you as ready right now. You still have not gained enough weight, and you haven't shown us that you can maintain a weight. We can't send you away to college until we see that you can do this."

Amrita turned to me: "See, this is the problem; they have a double standard. My brother and sister were getting into all kinds of trouble in high school, but they get to go away to college, so why can't I? It's so unfair."

We batted this around as a family for a few more moments, as Mr. and Ms. Malik clarified that, while their older son and daughter had not been "perfect angels" in high school, they had not displayed problems of the sort that Amrita had. They also observed that, in general, she did not take very good care of herself when it came to personal hygiene. "She will sometimes go a week without showering, and her hair is a mess—is this the kind of girl I can send to college?" Mr. Malik asked, perplexed. At this point I asked for some time with Amrita alone, and we had the following conversation:

"Amrita, when do you turn 18?"

"This coming June—in six months."

"And when do you graduate?"

"Right around then, in May."

"So in six months you will have graduated from high school and be a legal adult, correct?"

"Yes, and I can't wait."

"Your excitement is understandable, because in six months you won't really need your parents' permission to go away to college, if that's what you want to do."

"But you heard them—they don't think I'm ready."

"I did hear them. But what I'm saying is that within a few more months, it won't really matter so much whether *they* think you're ready; it'll matter more if *you* think you're ready."

"But what am I supposed to do? They haven't even let me apply to colleges. The only thing they're allowing me to do is go to community college, and I don't want to do that."

"But that is my point, Amrita . . . I'm saying that they don't have to let you apply to college; you can do it on your own."

"I can?"

"Sure, people do it all the time. Do you think that *everyone* who is in college has parents who gave them permission to go?"

"But I haven't even applied anywhere."

"At some point we should figure out why you didn't. But in the meantime, while it's getting late to apply, it's not too late for every college. I'm sure there are some colleges that are still accepting applications."

"I doubt that . . . all of my friends who are going to college have already applied."

"Well, let's take a look." I brought my laptop over, and Amrita and I went on-line and discovered numerous colleges that were still accepting applications.

"Okay, but how am I going to pay for it?"

"That will be a challenge if your parents don't agree to do so, but it's still possible." We then spent a few minutes looking up student scholarship and loan information. Amrita seemed stunned.

"So you're telling me that I can apply to college even if my parents don't think I'm ready?"

"Yes, Amrita, that is exactly what I'm telling you. There are many students whose families are not supportive of them going to college, or who come from families that are unable or unwilling to support them at all, but who still find a way to go to college. This is *entirely* in your hands."

The thought that going away to college was something that Amrita had some say over was a revolutionary one for her. I suggested that she meet with the guidance counselor in her school to begin looking into the possibility of getting some applications in.

I was aware, of course, that Amrita had her own ambivalence about going away to college, or else she would have done more to make this a possibility than grumble about her parents' objections to this possibility. But empowering her by reminding her of her autonomy changed the hopelessly subjective argument between her and her parents regarding whether she was ready and placed this issue more squarely where it belonged—in Amrita's lap.

I met with the parents separately to explain what Amrita and I were working on. I made it clear to them that I understood their concerns about sending her away and that by supporting this idea with her, I was not disagreeing with their hesitancy, nor even necessarily believing that it was a good idea for her to go away to college at this point. All I was saying, I emphasized, was that this conflict had to be cleaned up by disentangling the two of them from Amrita.

"Remember," I reminded them, "it may be enough for her to know that she is *entitled* to apply to colleges—that will be a tremendous boost to her self-confidence. Applying doesn't mean that she's going to be admitted, and being admitted doesn't mean that she's going to want to go, or be able to arrange the financing to go." The Maliks reluctantly agreed to sit back and let the process play out.

When the family returned, Amrita excitedly told me that she had met with her guidance counselor and they had quickly come up with a list of several small colleges (she had been advised to start with a small school) that were still accepting applications. The discussion between her and her parents had a very different tone to it, as they sorted out who should pay for these applications. Amrita surprised them by suggesting that she should pay for some of the cost, "because this is *my* idea, not yours," and they eventually agreed that they would split the cost of the applications.

Amrita did go ahead and complete her applications and was admitted to one of the three schools that she applied to, which provided another upgrade for her self-regard. She eventually decided, though, that she was better off staying put for a year and going to community college. However, the process seemed to have grown Amrita up—her parents observed that she was taking better care of herself and her personal hygiene. Also, her eating habits had normalized—she still ate irregularly, but her weight had remained stable for several months.

Amrita experienced a solid first year of community college while living at home, and toward the end of that year, she decided to remain there for another two semesters and earn her associate's degree.

One of the most elemental aspects of empowering young adult patients involves helping them to find ways to balance autonomy and heteronomy. Heteronomy is the condition of being influenced, dominated, or under the sway of another. Autonomy is the opposite—the state of self-governance, of independence and freedom. Every adult life requires autonomy and heteronomy to be yoked together and experienced in some form of creative tension. True maturity requires finding a way to both challenge and submit to the rules and expectations of others, and of society.

A 19-year-old patient once explained to me that he was going to stop drinking "even though my parents want me to." Another patient promised me that, "I'm going to give up drugs, although definitely *not* because my parents want me to." Despite how boldly these two young adults pronounced these striking comments, their words revealed how little autonomy they felt, and the extent to which they remained disempowered when it came to their relationships with their parents.

STRATEGICALLY ADDRESSING THE YOUNG ADULT'S LACK OF RESPONSIBILITY

In their song, "Consequence Free," the band Great Big Sea sings, "I want to be consequence-free, I want to be where nothing seems to matter." Whatever the source of a young adult's immature reasoning and his belief that consequences should not ever have to be faced, it is the therapist's job to find ways to nonjudgmentally spur maturation.

Every day I will hear at least one young adult blurt out an irrational but firmly held conviction that startles me with (and, often, makes me want to laugh at) its absurdity. Today, for example, a 20-year-old young woman whose parents were upset with her for "not contributing anything but carbon dioxide" to the house complained, "I don't *want* to be here at home with you guys, so why should I have to help you out?"

Later, in the afternoon, 22-year-old Barrie professed surprise when her employer was upset with her for coming late. She felt that it was unfair that her oversleeping had been presented to her coworkers in an unnecessarily negative light: "My boss told the rest of the staff that I wasn't at work because I was 'still in bed'—she could have said it in a nicer way, like 'Barrie accidentally overslept.' I mean, does she really think that I *intentionally* slept in? And then I had to deal with all of these dirty looks and snarky comments when I showed up later that day, because there had been a big project and a couple of people had to fill in for me. I felt terrible, but it wasn't my fault. It's not like I went to sleep last night *planning* on sleeping in!"

I recently came across a cartoon showing a bird arriving at a nest with several worms protruding from its mouth, getting ready to feed the baby birds. In the caption, one of them chirped, "Is there a vegan option?"

Many young adults—particularly those from middle- and upper-class families—have been raised to believe that the world will accommodate them and make the necessary adjustments to keep them happy. But while the world may be a somewhat more flexible place now than it was in previous decades, it is certainly not always going to provide the options—dietary or otherwise—that neatly fall in with an individual's personal preferences.

Nineteen-year-old Gerain had finished high school but did not want to go to college and had not been diligent about finding a job. After several months of indecision and heavy drinking, he and his mother, Javina, met with me a couple of times, and he eventually came up with the idea of moving to Atlanta to stay with his favorite uncle and aunt and see what he could figure out from a launching pad in a different state. "It might be a good idea to get away from some of my drinking bro's," he noted.

During a session that included Javina's brother and sister-in-law participating by telephone from Atlanta, everyone agreed to this plan on the condition that Gerain earn the money for the plane ticket to Atlanta and that he submit at least five online job applications to stores or restaurants near his uncle and aunt's home.

Two months later, Javina told me that Gerain still had not earned any of the money necessary to purchase his plane ticket and that he had not applied to any jobs in Atlanta—his plans to move remained on hold. Gerain tried mightily to break the contract that his family had established, but his mom held firm.

"Why don't you just buy me the plane ticket, Mom? I'll pay you back when I get a job in Atlanta."

"But the deal is that you need to buy the ticket."

"But what's the point of getting a job here to earn money to go to Atlanta when I'm just going to leave that job?" he asked. "This is a stupid plan."

"But that's the plan we've all agreed to, Gerain," his mom reminded him.

"You're trapping me here! That's what you're trying to do. You don't want me to leave!"

"I'd be happy for you to leave, Gerain, but you've got to do it the right way."

"The right way is for you to send me to Atlanta, just like we agreed."

"But that's *not* what we agreed to, Gerain."

"I can't stand living here! I can't stand you! You're so . . . so . . . you just won't let go!"

"I'm willing to let go, Gerain, but you've got to uphold your end of the bargain."

"Why won't you just let me go?! Why won't you just let me go?!"

Gerain stood up and was literally stamping his feet. Concerned about the escalation, I asked Javina to have a seat in the waiting room while I spoke with him alone.

"Do you see why it's impossible? Do you see why I want to leave?" he shrieked, still on his feet.

"I certainly can understand why you want to leave, but I don't understand why it's impossible for you to do so."

"Because she won't let me go!"

"She has said that she's willing to let you go. But your mother has also said that you need to earn the money for the ticket yourself, and your aunt and uncle have said that they don't want you down there until you've completed some applications."

"She doesn't want me to be independent; *that's* what the problem is!" he shouted.

"She may or may not *want* you to be independent, Gerain, but, according to the plan that has been established, you're going to have to show her, and your aunt and uncle, that you're independent before they agree to this trip."

"I'll be independent when I'm down there! Why don't they trust me? I can be independent; I'm just not independent *now*!"

"And apparently, that's the problem—until you show them that you're independent here, you're not going to have the opportunity to show them that you're independent down there."

"Why do I have to prove myself? Why can't they just let me go?"

"Because proving yourself is how they will know that this plan has a good chance of being successful. Your mother doesn't want you to go down to Atlanta and continue your unemployment. This *plan* isn't going to work if *you're* not going to work."

"Why doesn't anyone believe me?"

"What is it that you want everyone to believe?"

"I want them to believe in me! I want them to believe that I'm independent!"

"That's a good sign . . . and you have a way of doing that."

"How?"

"By earning money up *here*, and by applying for jobs down *there*."

"You're not getting it!"

"What is it that I'm not getting?"

"I just want to go to Atlanta, that's all I want! I just want my chance!"

"Gerain, I feel like we're talking in circles here. What is it that I'm not getting?"

"You're not getting how trapped I feel!"

"So tell me more about feeling trapped."

"I'm stuck, I'm stuck, I'm stuck! I've got to get out of here! Don't you see, all I do is sit around all day and drink all night! I've got to get out of here!"

When these kinds of stuckpoints are arrived at—and all therapists have arrived at plenty of them—I generally find it useful to travel back in time for a bit and see what the origins of the stuckpoint might be. I had learned during my initial interview with the family that Gerain's father, Josiah, had died a tragic death at the age of 27, shot and killed by a police officer in the midst of what appeared to have been a violently psychotic episode when Gerain was six.

Javina told me that Josiah, whom she had separated from when Gerain was four, was schizophrenic and functioned well when adhering to treatment but that he went through numerous periods of not attending therapy sessions and refusing to take his medication, resulting in his quickly becoming symptomatic again. I had assumed this matter would come up at some point in my work with Gerain, and this seemed like a good opportunity to address it.

"Gerain, you're telling me about feeling trapped, and you're frustrated that I'm not getting it, and I apologize for not getting it. Maybe it would help me to get it if you told me about some other times when you have felt trapped."

"I don't know, I can't think of anything."

"Well, just take a moment. Can you remember the *first* time you felt trapped in any way?"

"Hmmm . . .yeah, I guess . . . I remember I used to visit my dad after he and my mom split up. And those were pretty strange visits."

"In what way?"

"My dad could get very weird. He could get very strange. Like one time, he basically barricaded us into his apartment for the whole weekend. He shut all the shades and he locked the door and he told me that we had to hide in the closet. At first I thought this was kind of a cool game, but after a while I started to get scared. I started to think that I would never get out, and it was like all fucked up."

"So what happened?"

"What happened was that we were there for I don't know how long, it seemed like forever, sitting there in the dark with him, and him telling me that we had to lay low, lay low. And then there was this loud knocking on the door and it was the police, and then I got really fucking scared, like maybe he had been right, maybe there was a reason that we were hiding."

"And then?"

"And then the police knocked down the door and my mother was with them, and she was freaking out and she grabbed me and they grabbed my dad and it was all so fucked up . . . and I think that was the last time I saw my dad."

Gerain let out a skimpy laugh, then grew quiet for a time.

"Trapped, huh?" I offered, after some silence.

"Trapped . . . yeah, trapped, all right," he dismally agreed, his voice quivering with sadness.

We spent a little more time talking about his memories of his father and some of the many other disturbing recollections that bubbled to the surface as he opened up that vent into the past. In our subsequent sessions, we began talking about his own fears that he was going to become psychotic and the difficulty he had distinguishing his own thinking—which was at times irrational—from delusional thinking of the sort that suggested an actual disorder.

These were complicated discussions, but exploring the genesis behind Gerain's insistence on keeping himself stuck did help him to get unstuck. He obtained a part-time job in the kitchen at a friend's family's restaurant with the understanding that it was only going to be for several months, until he earned the money to go to Atlanta. He also began the process of applying to jobs in the Atlanta area and spoke to his uncle about the process by telephone a couple of times. When the family finished up their work with me, Gerain had earned the money for his plane ticket, and he had a couple of job interviews scheduled in Atlanta upon his arrival.

ESTABLISHING REASONABLE EXPECTATIONS FOR SELF

A patient of mine who was giving college the old college try once told me, "My problem is not that I'm a perfectionist—it's that I'm an *imperfect* perfectionist." His paradoxical comment described the thin ice that many young adults walk on because they are experiencing difficulty establishing reasonable expectations for themselves. One of the main reasons that this can become problematic is because they have spent so much of their lives fending off or protecting themselves from the reckonings of others that they have never taken the time to establish what they reckon for themselves.

As part of the process of helping patients who are in this situation, I will ask them to give thought to some of the following questions, either in a session or on their own:

1 What is it like when you believe that others' expectations of you are unrealistic, overwhelming, or oppressive?

2 What is it like when you believe that others' expectations of you are too low?

3 What is it like when you believe that others' expectations of you are higher than your own expectations for yourself?

4 What is it like when you believe that others' expectations of you are lower than your own expectations for yourself?

5 What are the relative advantages and disadvantages of self-sabotage (anything self-destructive) and ensuring that you don't come close to meeting the expectations of others?

6 When did you first realize that you were focused more on others' expectations of you than your own expectations of you?

7 How can you become less focused on others' expectations of you and more focused on your expectations of yourself?

8 What are the dangers of expectations that are set too high? That are set too low?

9 What is the worst possible outcome of not meeting others' expectations for you?

10 What is the worst possible outcome of not meeting your own expectations for yourself?

11 Is it possible to have and meet high expectations and still be seen as normal, as a regular person?

12 Are there disadvantages associated with meeting the expectations of others? Of meeting your own expectations?

The value of this kind of inquiry tends to be not so much in the actual answers but in stimulating the young adult's awareness that he may have become entrenched in measuring himself against standards set by others rather than having embarked on the crucial process of setting his own standards by which to measure himself.

ESTABLISHING REASONABLE EXPECTATIONS FOR ONE'S PARENTS

A young adult patient once complained to me that he was sick of dealing with his parents' "idiot-syncracies." He didn't catch or acknowledge the slip (perhaps that's actually what he thought the word was), but it said a lot about where he was developmentally. When young adults become locked into thinking that their parents are "idiots," they are precluding their own growth. This loops back to the quote that is attributed to Mark Twain but that may or may not have originated with him: "When I was a boy of fourteen, my father was so ignorant I could hardly stand to have the old man around. But when I got to be twenty-one, I was astonished at how much the old man had learned in seven years."

Coming to terms with one's parents' strengths, as well as their weaknesses, is a hallmark of maturity. A young adult is not a true adult if she is still organizing her life around the belief that she was wronged by her parents or if she is making decisions mostly based on her opposition to her parents or to make a point to her parents.

But many young adults collect, polish, and house their resentments as if they were erecting a museum devoted to enumerating the ways in which they have been cheated and mistreated. Their fierce notions of idealized love and justice have been severely violated by the ways in which their defective (as seen by them) family actually behaved. As one young woman groused to me, "Why can't I just have the mother that I *want* to have?"

It is important to help young adults conceive of a new and different acceptance and understanding of their parents that is free of the star-crossed wish that their parents should have been, or must still try to be, different than they are. This kind of mature acceptance and understanding requires them to consent with the reality that one's life is one's own responsibility and no one else's.

I discourage my young adult patients (indeed, all of my patients) from making their happiness dependent on someone else changing his or her behavior—it's a vulnerable and helpless position to operate from. Jean-Paul Sartre defined freedom as "what you do with what's been done to you." To become self-reliant, young adults have to develop the ability to allow the chips on their shoulder to fuel their growth and achievement. They have to learn to swim strongly against the currents of a childhood that may have been anything from mildly disappointing to inexplicably traumatic.

One 26-year-old patient of mine who was a long-time drug addict described his mother to me in the following words: "She overmothers, she's such an enabler, she's been giving me money all these years, knowing that I was using drugs. What did she think I was spending the money on?"

While he was asking a good question, and astutely taking note of his mother's enabling tendencies, he was also shirking responsibility for his own behavior—in this case, the chronic unemployment that left him in the position of needing financial support from his mother and his decision to use that money to support his drug habit. He was expecting his mother to rescue and protect him from something that he needed to learn to rescue and protect himself from.

Another patient, 22 years old and chronically underemployed, explained his lack of discipline as being the result of his parents not *teaching* him self-discipline: "My father grew up on a farm, and that's how *he* learned to work hard, to follow through—how come he didn't teach *me* the same things that his father taught *him*? My life would be *so* different if he had just done his job." Our ensuing conversation involved my asking him to think about how long he would be waiting around for his father to finish this job, and at what point he might consider taking on this job—and, as a result, getting a better job—himself.

While we will often have to help young adults adjust their expectations of their parents downward, at other times, we may have to encourage them to *raise* their expectations—some young adults look at their parents through too soft, rather than too harsh, a lens.

For example, 20-year-old Janae frequently pursued relationships with guys who were unavailable—usually because they already were in a committed relationship. She was able to get them to sleep with her but not to commit to her. During one of our initial sessions, I took note of the great effort she expended to justify her father's emotional neglect of her, which I speculated had to do with her unswerving pursuit of other neglectful males.

Janae's father had separated from her mom and remarried 7 years ago and seemed to have trimmed back his relationship with Janae since then to focus on his three younger stepchildren, rarely making contact with her or going out of his way to see her. When I asked into this, she defended him vigilantly: "He works very hard, and I know he's busy with his new wife and her children."

"But you mentioned that he didn't make any time to get together with you for your birthday. It's one thing to be a hard worker and to be busy with your stepchildren; it's another thing to not celebrate your birthday with you."

"But *his* parents were never divorced. So how can I expect him to know what this is like for *me*?"

"I don't think you have to have divorced parents to know that your daughter would like you to spend some time with her on her birthday, Janae."

"Yeah, I guess. But he wouldn't understand even if I tried to tell him."

"He might, he might not. But it sounds like it's hard for you to even *acknowledge* that he has let you down in some important ways."

"He's my father, though. I know he still loves me. He does the best he can."

"Did you remember him on his birthday?"

"Yes, I did. I sent him a card and got him a gift."

"So what's it like to recognize his birthday but not have him recognize yours?"

"Oh, he will, he will, I think. He was probably just busy with the kids around then."

Some of our subsequent work involved helping Janae to give voice to her legitimate feelings of hurt and anger as her father pulled far away from her to attend to his new family. This in turn spurred her to think differently about her dedicated commitment to pursuing relationships with men who were unlikely to ever commit.

The recognition of parental fallibility and limitation is a challenge for the young adult because it, of course, calls into question whether it is wise for him to continue to rely on his parents as much as he has. "If my parents are *this* inadequate, who can I depend on?" is one of the internal questions that begs to be asked. But, at the same time, this difficult recognition makes the young adult's separation more achievable as he realizes that his own fallibilities and limitations need not preclude the possibility of becoming more independent, or at least as independent as his insufficient parents have become.

FINDING (AND LOSING) A MENTOR

In addition to relationships with peers and romantic partners, many young adults need to establish a relationship with a mentor, an individual who can serve as a transitional adult support person while they are dissolving some of the bonds with their parents and working on their self-definition. This is even more necessary when a young adult has not benefited from having had one or more solid, reliable parents or a dependable same-sex role model during childhood.

The mentor may be a member of the extended family, such as a grandparent, aunt, or uncle, or someone from outside of the family, often one who is experienced in an area of the young person's interest, such as a coach, a teacher, a member of the clergy, or an officer in the armed services. For antisocial, mentally ill, or at-risk youth, the mentor may be a gang leader, a savvy street acquaintance, an older patient in a treatment center or hospital, or a senior inmate in a jail or detention center.

The bond with the mentor often has idealized and worshipful qualities—it is important for the young adult to be able to invest the mentor with superhuman talents and capacities, to imagine that there is, indeed, someone who has all the answers in a world that seems to be increasingly populated by perplexing questions. The mentor, at least for a time, functions as a perfect parent figure for the young adult who is trying to disentangle from his own parents and begin the process of parenting herself.

Many young adults remain in a comfortable, growth-promoting relationship with their mentor for years and are able to regularly turn to them for support and perspective through life's panoply of challenges and rites of passage. For example, one patient of mine, 28-year-old Kaneesha, had developed a very close relationship with the minister at her church, Reverend Donna, 10 years before. When I asked Kaneesha what she admired about Reverend Donna, she explained, "Reverend Donna preaches *for*, not against. Her sermons aren't *against* homosexuality or abortion; they're *for* being kind and warm. She's very inclusive." That sense of inclusiveness had been very important for Kaneesha, who was black and gay and, as a result, prone to feeling excluded as an adolescent and younger adult.

However, because of the idealization of the mentor and the young adult's level of immaturity and vulnerability, the mentor relationship can become a destructive one if engineered in an exploitive way. A 19-year-old patient of mine, Cedric, had been extremely close with his choral director, Mr. W., throughout high school. Mr. W. had recognized and nurtured Cedric's musical talent starting in ninth grade and strongly encouraged Cedric to take himself seriously and establish lofty goals for himself. Mr. W. became a father figure to Cedric, which was a vital role for him to play as Cedric's father had left the family many years before, and his mother was quite depressed and emotionally unavailable.

Cedric graduated and went off to college, which was mostly doable because he had earned a partial scholarship as a result of his academic and vocal abilities. He remained in touch with Mr. W. by e-mail during his first semester, and Mr. W. helped him through several of the common but complicated freshman dilemmas that Cedric ran into—a roommate conflict and a dictatorial choral director. Mr. W. essentially played the role that one of Cedric's parents would have played, were either of them up to the task.

Cedric excitedly contacted Mr. W. as soon as he finished his first-semester finals and returned home, asking if he could come by to visit him at after school. Mr. W., whose winter break hadn't begun yet, said that his afternoons were going to be busy with rehearsals but suggested as an alternative that Cedric come by his house one night that week.

The evening that Cedric visited him, Mr. W. offered him some wine, and, shortly afterward, began to sexually molest him. Cedric was paralyzed and did not know how to respond. "I couldn't believe this was happening. I couldn't believe that this was me in Mr. W.'s living room and we were having wine and he had his hands all over me. I wanted him to stop, but this was Mr. W.! He had been everything for me! And so what was I supposed to do? If I shoved his hands away and walked out the door, I would lose him forever! And I still needed him! So I just kind of tolerated it. But it was awful. It is a night I will never forget."

Cedric and I spent several sessions trying to make sense of what had happened and coming up with a game plan for how to proceed. He eventually decided that he could not continue his relationship with Mr. W., but this was an anguished decision for him to make, and it opened up a significant cavity in his life for some time, which he eventually began to fill with other students and professors at college.

Even if the young adult's relationship with a mentor does not come to some sort of sudden, traumatic end, this liaison will often dissolve over time as the young adult continues to mature and reluctantly realizes that the beloved mentor, like everyone else, is imperfect. The gradual disillusionment that young adults feel when they begin to see the mentor for who he or she is, rather than who they have wanted him or her to be, is painful but a necessary part of emotional development. It enables them to come to terms with the fact that hitching themselves to a "star" is not a good way for them to grow themselves up and that ultimately they need to take responsibility for their own growth rather than rely on someone else to advance it.

GRIEVING FOR LOSSES AND LOST OPPORTUNITIES

Many of the young adults we treat have suffered significant setbacks and reversals of fortune. The clinician has to help struggling young adults through these losses so that they realize that as one door closes, others open, and that many closed doors can be reopened at a later date.

Twenty-year-old Oonagh had dreams of going to college and becoming a doctor. She started off on the right foot, getting accepted to a college with a solid premedical program, one whose sports teams she had enthusiastically followed for years. But by the end of freshman year, she had become depressed and withdrew from college. She returned home, which was not a particularly pleasant place to be as her parents' marriage was a chilly one, and she also had an older brother who had remained at home after high school, unable to support himself, which produced additional tension on the home front.

For the next couple of years, Oonagh didn't do much of anything except hang around the house, just like her older brother. She didn't socialize with her peers because she was embarrassed about not being in college, and, as a result, she became increasingly isolated. Eventually, her depression worsened to the extent that she made a suicide attempt and needed to be hospitalized, and it was upon discharge that she and her family began working with me.

Oonagh admitted right away that one of the things that was making it difficult for her to move forward was that all she could think about was how close to graduation she would now be if she had been able to continue and how many of her high school friends were now excitedly preparing for *their* graduation. We agreed that she needed to mourn for that lost opportunity as a way of letting go and creating new opportunities.

I asked her to accumulate some items that were symbolic of the college that she had withdrawn from and bring them along with her to her next session. She returned with the letter of acceptance that she had received, the T-shirt emblazoned with the college's mascot that she had excitedly bought when she had first visited, her ID card from freshman year, and a poster advertising the college's football schedule.

We came up with a mock funeral for the deceased dream of graduating from the first college of her choice, and I encouraged her to write a eulogy as part of the funeral service, which went as follows:

> Here lie Oonagh's dreams of going to University of _____. These were dreams that were very important to her and to her family, and they lasted a

while, but, unfortunately, they died very prematurely. All deaths are premature, when you think about it. But I believe that there can be life after death. I don't know what form that life will take. But I do know that these dreams were very dear to her, and they deserve a fitting farewell. It is time to say good-bye to these dreams, sad as it is that they cannot survive. Maybe now some new dreams will arise in their place. Good-bye, dreams, good-bye. It was good to have you, but I need to say good-bye.

Oonagh completed the funeral at home with her family, and, as part of the ceremony, chose to bury her ID card in her back yard. This ritual of closure helped her to let go of her old dreams from the past and to start incubating new dreams for the future.

GROWING WITH SIBLINGS

We are often focusing on struggling young adults' relationships with their parents, but it is unwise to ignore the significance and impact of their relationships with their siblings as well. This phase of life provides an opportunity for the young adult to reconfigure and reconstruct relationships with brothers and sisters, often to everyone's benefit.

Donald, a 20-year-old patient of mine who was not moving ahead with his life, confessed to me that he still felt guilty about the fact that one of his boyfriends sexually abused his younger sister in his presence 9 years before, when his sister was 5. The guilt that he still carried was making it impossible for him to move ahead with his life, because he felt that he needed to stay around and keep an eye on her, that it would be yet another abandonment of her for him to leave home.

In another family, Jackie noted that there was a significant division of labor between her and her brother, Vaughn, a polarizing specialization of the sort that inevitably accompanies sibling rivalry. "Vaughn is the smart one, and I'm the social one," she casually disclose during our first session. As I got to know her, it became clear that this unbending belief seemed to be holding her back from moving on to college, since Vaughn was "the one with the brains," which apparently meant that she couldn't have any of her own. I invited Vaughn to join her for a session, and we discussed how they might relax the rigidity of this distribution, which allowed her to acquire more confidence in her intellect and him to begin resolving his friendlessness.

Sometimes parents have worked hard to keep siblings from becoming close, fostering their conflict or keeping them emotionally sequestered from each other as a way of disenfranchising them and preventing the possible sibling uprising that might threaten the family hierarchy. One patient of mine, Darnell, who was two years older than his sister, Preye, was telling me how distant he and his sister were and admitted that he did not know her birthday—and at this point, he was too embarrassed to ask. The siblings were both living away from home in college and, for various reasons, had kept themselves completely cut off from each other. I encouraged him to begin connecting with her, and their relationship began to blossom in the coming months as they each began to compare notes about their upbringing and bring to light some family secrets that had been lying under the surface.

Oni constantly found herself in relationships with "guys with issues, guys that I've got to take care of." We examined this in the context of her history with her autistic older brother, Carl, and the ways in which she had always been expected by their parents to be his watchdog and his source of emotional support. Several family sessions were devoted to disentangling Oni from her role as caretaker for vulnerable men and determining a more balanced and healthy foundation for an intimate relationship.

RECOGNIZING THE CONSEQUENCES OF SUCCESS AS WELL AS FAILURE

All parents want their young adults to be successful, but it is sometimes important to help a young adult understand that not all of the consequences of success are positive ones—options can evaporate not only when you fail but also when you succeed. I saw a cartoon in which one young adult commented to another, "I want to be so successful that it ruins my life." There is a wisdom to this, and it is not only extravagant success that can ruin one's life—*all* forms of success carry within them the seeds of joy and sorrow, uplift and disappointment.

One patient of mine soberly disclosed to me that, "I'm as vigilant about avoiding doing well as other people are vigilant about avoiding screwing up." In discussing this comment, she acknowledged that she felt torched by the fires of ambition much more than she felt flooded by the waters of failure and that when she was in the hottest pursuit of success, she felt most estranged from herself.

Along these lines, many of my patients who are in midlife or beyond observe that what they had believed at one point in their lives were their greatest successes actually said little about who they were but that, looking back, their failures spoke volumes and taught them more about who they really were than their successes ever had.

Sometimes when young adults experience success, they simultaneously experience regret that they weren't able to achieve success sooner. A 23-year-old patient of mine who was a chain smoker felt so good when he gave up smoking that he couldn't bear the thought that it had taken him so long to give up smoking, so he returned to smoking to distract himself from that sorrow. It took several tries before he was able to let go of this regret and appreciate the fact that he was free of cigarettes in the present even though he couldn't turn back the clock and eliminate them from his past.

I often see situations in which the success of a family member handicaps a young adult's quest. Twenty-one-year-old Carlos was mired in a terrible slump that had left him completely adrift, without a full-time job or a college degree, living with his parents without any observable light at the end of the tunnel. As we discussed his situation, he spoke admiringly of his father:

> My dad is really the true self-made man. I mean, he will tell you that he was in the right place at the right time, but what he has accomplished is amazing. His dad died of a heart attack when he was six, his mother had to go to work as a secretary, he had three brothers, and yet he figured out how to work his way through college, even though it took him about six years to do so.
>
> He'd always worked construction jobs, so he got involved in the industry after he finished college, and then the owner of the company he worked at kind of plucked him up and made him one of the sales managers—he was their first Latino sales manager—and then that company was bought out by another, bigger company and they promoted my dad and now he's one of the top dogs at one of the top five commercial real estate companies in the state. This was a guy who never had his own bed when he was growing up, he always had to share with one of his brothers, and now we have this nice home and even a condo at the beach. I've never even had to share a *room* with either of my brothers, let alone a *bed*—so tell me, how am I ever going to measure up to that? Here I've had this great life, and how can I ever accomplish what he accomplished?

Many of the struggling young adults I've worked with feel as if there's no point in even trying to climb the mountain of life if they are not likely to come close to gain purchase on the peaks that one or both of their parents have settled on. Or the prospect of doing so seems to become equated in their minds not with success but with unhappiness—they attribute their lack of motivation to having parents who have made it but who, in the process of making it, have made *themselves* very unhappy, at least in their children's eyes.

> "My father is a very successful salesman, but he's miserable—he drinks all the time, he and my mom never have any fun, he just comes home from work and then he gets in front of the computer and does more work. Why would I want to become like that? What kind of life is that?"
>
> "My mom was the first woman in her family to go to college, and then she became an accountant, but you should see her during tax season—she's a wreck! It seems like half of the year she's demented, and the other half of the year she's recovering from being demented. There's gotta be another way."
>
> "My parents started up their first restaurant on a shoestring, it was this little shack, but now they've got three of them and their lives have gotten harder, not easier. They want me to get involved and take over one day,

but that's the last place you'll see me working—I was a server there during high school, but I don't even like to go near the place now. I'm sure they'll die there one day, but I sure don't want to."

It is not always easy to discern the extent to which these kinds of rationalizations and complaints on the part of underachieving young adults function simply as justifications for not working hard—an easy out, so to speak. And, of course, sometimes the parents' success—however hard-won—has made the young adult's life a little too easy, such that he or she may have been protected from committing him- or herself to working hard over the years. I've worked with numerous parents who take pride in the fact that their child does not have to work as hard as they had to work, and sometimes this pride gets in the way of reasonable expectations of the child over the years.

Nevertheless, I have often sensed that there is a legitimacy to these kinds of concerns that creates a painful paradox in the family in which the parents' conscientiousness seems to have backfired and to have demotivated, rather than animated, their offspring.

When these matters can be discussed openly, including encouraging the parents to share more about their experience, it often makes it easier for young adults to resolve some of their ambivalence about achieving success.

THE ART OF GENTLE SELF-EXPLORATION

While a few of my young adult patients are a little too easy on themselves, most of them are too hard on themselves and benefit from approaching themselves and their dilemmas with a little less hostility and a little more benevolence. Clinicians can urge young adults to find ways to end, or to better fend off, the self-inflicted blows that have been deforming and contorting them.

Grady was in his fourth year of college but had earned less than two years of credits. The problem was procrastination—he put off everything until the night before it was due. While he had gotten through high school using this strategy, it was not successful in college. He failed or withdrew from as many classes as he passed, and those that he passed, he passed by the skin of his teeth.

Grady was a dour-looking 21-year-old who never appeared even close to smiling. He acknowledged that procrastination was at the root of his lack of academic progress but confessed that he was unable to subdue it.

"I have all of these plans to stay on top of my work, but within a few weeks, I start to fall behind. I know that if I put in the time ahead of time, I'll do okay, but it's like I can't force myself to do what I don't want to do."

"I'm assuming you've tried creating reminders for yourself, correct?"

He looked at me with barely restrained contempt. "I've tried *everything*. I make plenty of notes to remind myself, but then I ignore the note. My mom used to be the reminder when I was in high school, and I guess she stayed on top of me—that's how I graduated, that's how I finished my college applications—but my mom's not with me and I would ignore her plenty of times, too. I only wound up actually completing two college applications, even though I was planning on applying to seven or eight schools."

"Anything else you've tried?"

"My buddy told me about an app for my phone, but I haven't installed it yet. It rings when you're supposed to do something."

"Do you think you'll install it?"

"Honestly . . . no . . . and even if I did, I suspect I'd just ignore it when it rang. 'Oh, yeah, I'm supposed to do that,' I'll probably tell myself, and then go back to playing poker with my friends."

"So do you see this as a solvable problem?"

Grady paused. "You know, no one's ever asked me that. My parents made me see organizational tutors in high school. I had to go see a therapist. Everyone had all of these ideas, but the reality is that I'm just not going to implement them. So I guess, in a way, it isn't solvable . . . as long as I choose not to solve it."

"What's the worst part of procrastination?"

"The stress . . . I hate the stress . . . I just hate realizing that it's Sunday night and a paper is due or a test is coming up or a lab has to be written up, and there's just no way that I'm going to be able to get it done . . . certainly not get it done well."

"And then what happens?"

"Then I feel like a piece of shit. Then I feel like I'm never going to graduate, that I'm going to be stuck here in college forever, or eventually just drop out, and get some crap job."

"Do you remind yourself of the stress when you choose to avoid doing what needs to be done?"

"No, I don't even bother . . . that's what I hate about myself. That's why this is not a solvable problem. You can give me all the advice you want—if I don't follow it, it's obviously not going to help."

"So what do you wind up concluding about yourself?"

"Like I said . . . that I'm a piece of shit . . . that I'm doomed."

"A pretty harsh assessment of yourself, don't you think?"

"I've always been harsh with myself, that's just who I am."

"When did you first notice that?"

"I remember back in elementary school, the teacher asked us to grade ourselves, and I would always give myself a C even though the teacher would usually give me an A."

"So it's not unusual for you to be hard on yourself."

"No . . . but I don't think there's anything wrong with being humble."

"There's certainly nothing wrong with being humble—I wish that more people were—but there's a big difference between being humble and demeaning yourself."

"I don't see the difference."

"Maybe you should . . ."

"So I'm supposed to be happy about procrastinating and making a mess out of my college transcript?"

"I'm not saying procrastinating is something to celebrate, but I wouldn't conclude that just because you engage in it, you're a 'piece of shit' either. I actually find it interesting to hear you talk about it."

"*Interesting?* How?"

"It's such an intriguing apparatus that you've built. It's both logical and illogical, intuitive and counterintuitive, satisfying and dissatisfying. I don't understand it completely, but I do find myself curious about it—how it developed, what role it has played and does play in your life, what your life would be like without it. You've developed an enterprise that is both complex and mystifying but certainly interesting."

"I can't tell if you're complimenting me or making fun of me."

"Well, I do mean that as a compliment. I'm not saying that it doesn't have its disadvantages, but you've clearly taken much time to manufacture this complicated system, so there must be some value to it."

"That's funny . . . because I mostly hate myself for procrastinating."

"But that's what I'm saying; it's not that simple. You may hate yourself when you have to deal with the *results* of your procrastination—the last-minute stress, the low grade that you wind up with—but when you are in the act of choosing to procrastinate, you are, at some level, happy with your decision—like your decision to play poker with your friends, for example, instead of deciding to study. To me, that's a bargain that you're making with yourself, albeit one that may need to be reexamined as you think about your long-term goals."

"How do I stop?"

"I don't know that you have to stop, or that you should stop. We all procrastinate at different times in our life—for example, around April 14, you might start asking people if they've finished their taxes yet. The question to ask yourself is when it is and is not okay to procrastinate, and to approach it a little less aggressively. You don't have to eliminate it altogether, but you may want to modify it."

"Well, that's good to hear, because I'm never going to be the kind of guy who gets work done three weeks ahead of time, who reads ahead in the book."

"And you don't *have* to be that kind of guy to succeed. All you have to do is take a step back and see your procrastination as a project that you conceived of rather than a mortal enemy that you have to annihilate."

Grady sat silently for a moment. "Sometimes I have thought about just trying to get started on work two days before it's due rather than the night before it's due."

"And have you ever tried that?"

"No, I'm usually so disgusted with myself for having procrastinated in the first place that I get fed up and don't even give myself the chance."

"So perhaps your goal this week is to observe your procrastination tendencies through a more objective lens—not as something good or bad but as something that serves a purpose but that at times makes your life harder than you'd like it to be."

Grady returned for his next session feeling more optimistic.

"I thought about what we talked about, and I realized how hard I am on myself. Some people look at me and probably assume that I'm chill and laid-back, but they don't see how rough I am on myself."

"I'm glad you gave this some thought. Where did that realization take you?"

"It took me to thinking about my procrastination differently. Maybe there is a way to just do a little less of it, without giving it up entirely. If I didn't procrastinate at all, I wouldn't be me!"

"Most of us don't want to change to the extent that we don't recognize ourselves anymore," I acknowledged.

"So I decided to join a study group in my anthropology class, and I'm thinking maybe that'll keep me on track. I've never done that kind of thing before, but maybe if I'm with other students who are working on the same projects, it'll be harder for me to ignore what needs to be done."

The process of viewing his tendency with curiosity rather than criticism enabled Grady to soften up a bit, which in turn allowed for the possibility of change.

One of the interventions that can help young adults to create a less punishing inner world is to try to keep them from catastrophizing. For example, Terence did not achieve at a high enough level in high school to qualify for a four-year college, and even if he had done so, his parents were not enthusiastic about paying for it, based on his low levels of academic achievement. He bewailed his fate of having to go to community college, instead: "All of my friends are going to go away to college but me. I'll be the only one around; it's gonna be horrible. I've basically ruined my life."

It took a couple of conversations for him to begin thinking more realistically about going to community college. I encouraged him to touch base with the guidance counselor at his high school to get a sense of who else from his school would be attending community college. It turned out that one of his friends—not one of his best friends but someone who was more than an acquaintance—was going to a four-year school but was going to be living at home and commuting.

As he began to contemplate the possibility that he wasn't being abandoned by his cohort, he was able to start thinking more positively about the possibilities that awaited him and to become less harsh with himself. In fact, he eventually concluded, "Maybe I was doing the right thing by not doing too well in high school. Let's face it, I really wasn't ready to go away to college anyway."

We have been examining the developmental tasks of parents and young adults at the launching stage, but, as we have seen in much previous case material, it is also valuable to examine the role that the parents' marriage plays during this stage of life, which is what we will shortly turn our attention to.

Digital Media

I do a good deal of writing and lecturing about youth and digital media, but must confess that I'm usually hesitant to do so, because the virtual landscape transforms itself so quickly and so dramatically that I fear that whatever I conclude will be hopelessly outdated by the time it is in print. Nevertheless, it is impossible to discuss young adult development without discussing technology, so I will proceed, knowing that these words may quickly lose their relevance.

When I refer to digital media, I am including Internet use in general (including social networking), video gaming (both individual and online), MP3 players, smart phones, iPads, and related devices. Access to and use of digital media varies according to social class, gender, ethnicity, and the values of the individual young adult, along with those of his or her family and community. With this in mind, we must recognize the unevenness of the digital playing field as we explore this topic.

In general, U.S. culture vacillates between technophobia and technophilia, which appears to be our time-honored response to any significant changes in technology. We pivot between irrational fear and panic ("Digital culture represents a dangerous departure from existing standards for knowledge, literacy, and human engagement") and inflated appraisals and fantasies ("The digital generation is our best hope for the future").

So the technophobic response will insist that digital media are responsible for a litany of social ills, from obesity to academic underachievement to commercial exploitation, and that technology ultimately transforms us into unidimensional consumers who willingly sacrifice our privacy in return for settling for the illusion of human contact without any of the demands or benefits.

And the technophilic response insists that digital media have opened up an entirely new world, that they raise our intellect, strengthen our moral bonds, become a medium for social and political awakening, produce a higher level of civic responsibility, increase our respect for the environment, lay the groundwork for a more interactive and engaging world, and even lay down the neurological blueprint for more complex brain structures.

The reality, from my perspective, lies somewhere in between. Any form of technology, particularly communications-based technology, will change our rules of engagement and likely create the need or desire for us to revisit, redraw, and redefine the boundary between intimacy and solitude, between self and other, between depth and superficiality. We have always turned to technology for ways to both better connect with each other as well as to protect and prevent ourselves from connecting with each other.

For example, telephone answering machines were originally envisioned as a way for people to stay in better touch with each other—someone might not be available, but she would know that we were trying to reach her, and, as a result, she would be better able to respond. Eventually, however, telephone answering machines became a convenient way for many people to *avoid* staying in touch—we let the answering machine "pick up" rather than picking up ourselves and having to talk, or we are certain to make the call when we know that an individual is not around so that the answering machine will record our message and we don't have to talk directly to the other person.

As clinicians, we have to ask important questions having to do with digital media, especially because our young adult patients are digital natives and possess an intuitive, spontaneous, and natural relationship with technology. These questions are not always easily or entirely answerable, but they at least enable us to get both young adults and their parents thinking carefully about their (sometimes instructive and creative but sometimes mindless and problematic) travels through the virtual world. Some of these include:

> What impact does virtual connectivity have on how young adults see themselves?
>
> What impact does virtual connectivity have on how young adults experience friendship and intimacy?
>
> As young adults distribute and publicize themselves online, to what extent are they abandoning themselves? To what extent are they defining themselves?
>
> Does virtual engagement degrade or enhance the potential for actual, interpersonal engagement?
>
> Do digital media reduce or expand the relational expectations that parents and young adults have of each other?
>
> Does the Internet encourage true freedom of expression, or are young adults actually being regulated and constrained as they always have been, just in subtler ways?
>
> If we can always be in touch, do we retain the right to be alone?
>
> How does each generation define the rules of the virtual world, and how are these rules different between the generations? For example, how does each generation distinguish between private and public or between private and secret?

From a clinical standpoint, we also have to realize that one difference between the digital revolution and other technologically based revolutions is that the digital revolution has dramatically shifted the power relations between adults and youth. The power to control and utilize previous technologies generally remained in the hands of the adults—the ones who created, distributed, and marketed it. But that has changed dramatically—a college sophomore sitting in a cramped dorm room has as much power to create a life-changing technology as does a corporate giant, and will probably be a good deal more organizationally nimble as she's doing so.

But this same revolution, in other ways, essentially mimics previous revolutions. For example, most young adults who participate in social media do so to construct their identity. Online authorship of blogs, web pages, profiles, and avatars, and participation in online video games and other virtual endeavors, provide them with an important and endlessly imaginative opportunity for self-realization and self-reflection in which they can express and make sense of the conflicts and crises that characterize this stage in their lives.

When young adults participate in social networking, they are being given a chance to interact and affiliate, to assess the impact of their behavior on others, to ascertain behavioral and communal norms, and to negotiate the channels of life in an increasingly complex world. Our identity emerges not from a simple, singular, unified self but from being able to navigate adroitly between our many different selves without losing sight of any of them, even when they at times contradict each other.

So a constantly changing Facebook profile, for example, can be understood as nothing more than the normal way for a modern young adult to assemble and reassemble the building blocks of his identity on his way to integrating them into a coherent sense of self. This is simply *part* of an evolving statement about who he is, who he was, and who he is becoming, which is a rite of passage for young adults in *every* generation, not just the digital one. It is essentially no different from regularly changing his major in college, or toggling back and forth between different peer groups depending on what activity he is involved with, or interacting one way with his same-sex peers and another way with his opposite-sex peers or his romantic partner.

On the other hand, some aspects of constructing a sense of self through digital media are distinctly different from constructing a sense of self in other contexts, and are potentially more problematic. The challenge of finding ways to represent yourself to yourself and to others, for example, is not new a new one for young adults— but what *is* new is confronting this challenge in public, permanently, and for all to see.

Also, the complexity of this process of representation means that it is not going to conform well to the standards of typical online profile production, which is superficial in nature. Digital media encourage young adults to believe that a thought or feeling must be shared with and validated by others before it can be fully experienced and understood. Online life suppresses moral inhibitions, and young adults will find themselves doing things online or behind a screen that they would never do in person, such as stalking, spying, bullying, and hacking. The world of social networking also emphasizes tentative and temporary attachments that are likely to be abdicated as soon as something better comes down the pike.

Perhaps most significantly, the perpetual circuitry of electronic affiliations can annihilate the quiet, sacred space within which true self-awareness germinates—private thought and healthy introspection are vanquished by the power and easy availability of constant connectivity. The digital world provides many substitutes for real personal interchange, some of which may have value, but they cannot replace human contact. It is one thing to sit down and write a blog; it is another thing to sit down to lunch with a friend and converse face-to-face. It is one thing to see an emoticon of a sad face or a smiley face on your iPhone; it is another thing to be in the physical presence of an individual who is crying human tears or laughing human laughter (this reminds me of a cartoon I saw in which a minister is standing next to a coffin in front of almost completely empty pews, staring at his cell phone and commenting to the lone congregant, "There's been a huge outpouring of emoticons.")

Not surprisingly, many of these same issues infiltrate family life, as well. There is a sense with many families I work with that no one is fully *there* at any one time. They may be in physical proximity, but the ease with which they each become diverted or distracted by their smart phone or iPad or MP3 player is impossible to ignore. Numerous children, adolescents, and young adults have complained to me about their parents' infatuation with digital technology rather than the other way around. They are conscious of their mother's incessant texting or their father's inability to maintain eye contact because he is constantly checking the stock market or ESPN.

The electronic umbilical cord solves some family problems while inevitably creating others. For example, when parents give a teenager a cell phone, they may be more likely to allow her to go places or do things that they might not otherwise be comfortable with, because they know that they can reach her, or be reached *by* her. On the other hand, with the privilege of the phone comes the expectation that she will respond to her parents whenever they text or call. So while, on the one hand, she might be given *more* room to separate, on the other hand, she is being given *less* room to separate.

I have worked with many college students whose parents expect a text when they've gotten back to their dorm room, no matter what time it is. Clearly the concepts of leaving home and being on your own have been transfigured dramatically in response to technological innovation.

It doesn't appear that we are going to be able to turn back the clock on technology, so, as clinicians, we owe it to ourselves to galvanize a useful conversation with young adults and their families regarding how they will pilot through the digital world. The web can become a place where we find and discover ourselves and each other, or where we lose and abandon ourselves and each other. Technology by itself is neutral and does not present a risk—what presents a risk is our misguided belief that technology can and will solve all of our problems, relational and otherwise.

With this in mind, I don't encourage families to use the word *addicted* when they are referring to their young adult's use of technology, whether it's video games or texting or using Facebook. While there may be some neurobiological basis for how emotionally rewarding these activities may be, the addictions metaphor suggests that we have to give it up entirely, in the way that an alcoholic has to give up alcohol entirely, and that is not possible for most young adults—having a computer and being online in one form or another has become an unavoidable prerequisite for reaching important academic, professional, and social goals.

Instead, we want to encourage young adults and their families to think carefully about how to put technology in its place, and how to understand our vulnerability to it, so that it is subservient to us rather than the other way around.

Here's a segment from a therapy session with a withdrawn 21-year-old patient of mine named Sophia, who had been diagnosed with Social Anxiety Disorder and who was struggling to build a bridge from the world of video-game relationships to the world of human relationships. The conversation took place at the very end of our fourth consultation:

"We're running short on time for today—is there anything else you want to fill me in on or put on the table for next time?"

[Silence] "Well, there's one thing I've been wanting to say, but it's a little embarrassing."

"Take your time."

[Silence] "Well, I guess I should just tell you . . . I'm falling in love."

"Do you want to say more?"

[Silence]

"No hurry."

[Silence]

"Do you know what's making it hard for you to say more?"

"Yes . . . yes."

"Do you want to tell me?"

"I guess I should just tell you more about who I've fallen in love with."

"If you'd like."

[Long pause] "His name is Alistair."

"Do you want to tell me more about Alistair?"

"Alright, here's the thing . . . I've been playing this new video game nonstop for the last two weeks . . . it's one of those medieval ones that I love . . . and Alistair . . . Well, Alistair is a knight in the game . . . I have fallen in love with someone who does not exist . . . but I can't get him out of my mind."

"Tell me more about Alistair."

"You really want to know? I already told you that he's not *real.*"

"But *you* are . . . that's why I'm interested."

"Hmmm . . . okay . . . well, he's funny, he's kind, and he's *very* romantic."

"Anything else that draws you to him?"

"This feels silly . . . it's very embarrassing . . . Listen, I'm telling you Alistair is not real . . . he doesn't *exist.*"

"But remember that the feelings that you are experiencing about him *do* exist."

"But so what? What's the point of having these feelings if the person you have the feelings for is not real?"

"Well, maybe it's a way to get better acquainted with those feelings so that you're on better terms with them."

"And what's the point of *that*?"

"The point might be that this is how you're getting yourself ready for a relationship with a real person."

"But what if all I'm doing is avoiding a relationship with a real person by falling in love with a video game character?"

"Is that your fear?"

"Yeah, I guess . . . I mean, I go to all these websites with all these fan boys and fan girls, and they're talking about being in love with video-game people and it scares me."

"What scares you about them?"

"It's like they'll never be able to have a real relationship because a real person will never be as perfect as someone in a video game."

"Well, your awareness that a real lover will never measure up to a video lover is a sign that you may not fall into that trap."

"So you mean I don't have to worry about my love for Alistair?"

"Rather than worrying about it, I believe it would be better to get to know it better—to explore it and experience it and respect it."

"That's weird . . . *respect* it?"

"Why not? It's *your* heart that beats harder when you're with Alistair . . . doesn't your heart deserve to be respected?"

"I, I . . . I never thought of this as something serious."

"Well, I'd *like* you to think seriously about it . . . maybe your heart deserves a little more respect than it's getting."

"But what if I'm not ready for a *real* love affair?"

"Maybe you aren't . . . but there's no hurry . . . and, to my way of thinking, the love that you feel for Alistair is a step in the direction of loving an actual partner . . . messy as that love can sometimes be."

"Oh, I don't know if I can handle that."

"Well, I don't know either, and neither of us has a crystal ball . . . although, like I said, the fact that you have allowed your longing for Alistair to poke its head above the surface tells me that you may be a good deal more ready than you *think* you are."

"Oh, this is so hard, so hard . . . how am I ever going to deal with love?"

Helping Sophia to see her online relationship as a step in the direction of a *real* relationship made it possible for her to experience it differently, and to contemplate the possibility that her gaming did not have to be an end in itself but could also be an overpass that carried her above her isolated entrenchment in the cyberworld.

Chapter 9

Marital Issues at the Launching Stage

One of my professors in graduate school started off her course in couples treatment by observing that she had been married six times—which naturally triggered a barely audible groan among the students—"So *this* is who we have teaching us how to help couples? An individual so unskilled at relationships that she's been through six marriages!?"

With perfect timing, however, she then added, "Fortunately, all six marriages have been to the same man." Her point, which we came to grasp in the coming months, was that any enduring marriage has many divorces and remarriages built into it. The marriage endures precisely because the spouses are able to blossom and ripen together as a result of each of these nonlegal, growth-promoting divorces and subsequently find ways to reconnect with additional perspective and maturity.

Any couple that has started a family and raised their children to the point of young adulthood has traveled down innumerable pathways that have carried them from whatever infatuations and attractions first drew them together through the exhausting, demanding, and humbling years of child rearing. The passage from lovers to co-parents is not an easy one to survive, and, as we know, not all couples do it, and those who do may not always be doing it very well. As one mother succinctly put it: "Now that the kids are gone, my husband and I just stare at each other across the table and ask each other, 'What now?' and 'What next?'"

When we work with families in which the two parents of the young adult are still married, we must remember that the spouses have shared countless moments of intimacy, warmth, affection, and gratitude, but that their marital landscape is also littered with at least two decades' worth of injuries and reconciliations, insults and truces. The affianced couple has fought numerous battles—some resolved thoughtfully and respectfully, others left unresolved, like running sores—battles about money and sex, about in-laws and distribution of labor, about fidelity and betrayal, honesty and deceit, justice and injustice, generosity and stinginess, and, certainly—often *constantly*—about child rearing.

As noted in an earlier chapter, parents were not raised in identical homes, so they come at parenting from different angles. In some marriages, a steady alignment between the partners is the norm, while in other marriages, areas of agreement and overlap occur quite rarely. Most reside somewhere between, with plenty of congruence but much incongruence as well.

We originally marry because, among other things, we wanted another person to help us to improve and straighten out our lives. And of course that expectation, we all eventually find out (some of us more quickly than others), can never be met. Instead, we each find that we steadfastly maintain some of our crookedness, and even maneuver our partners into displaying the behavior that justifies it. This pattern can become so entrenched that it is difficult for couples to recognize it, let alone alter it.

As family therapists working on the ledge of the launching stage, we will find ourselves listening to couples who are long past the phase in which a spouse's weaknesses and vulnerabilities seemed endearing and appealing—these same weaknesses and vulnerabilities now feel aggravating and burdensome at best, if not outright unbearable. We will find ourselves taking care of couples who are experiencing great difficulty recalling the happiness that drew them together, the qualities that swept them off their feet in the presence of this new and scintillating counterpart.

We will find ourselves counseling spouses who are not only angry with their partner but also angry with themselves for still expecting their partner to change, knowing that this is unlikely to ever happen. Meanwhile, time has moved on, and 20, 30, 40 years have passed like the blink of an eye in the vast face of their relational eternity.

Marriages commence and advance themselves in many different ways—some begin passionately, and some begin in a more obligatory way, seemingly based more on negotiation than romance. Some are unhappy before they even commence, others hit their stretches of unhappiness down the road. But no matter how they start, they are all destined to stumble and falter. Spouses can complete each other, and, as a result, make each other very happy at times, but they cannot live together without at other times making each other absolutely miserable.

Because of this, most midlife couples whom I have treated feel the intense urge to enter a time machine and return to the era when they first met, giving them the opportunity to either start over and prevent the ruinous mistakes that set the marriage veering off course, or never to have married in the first place. Everybody wants what they once had, or what they thought that they *deserved* to have and were surely *destined* to have.

But what we need to help them to remember is that no marriage follows the path that its initiators want it to follow, and *all* marriages eventually skid and swerve in unanticipated ways—the question is not whether this happens but whether the couple is able to steer into the skids and swerves in ways that ultimately bring them and keep them together, even though their emotional travels have brought them to relational regions that they never anticipated exploring.

An enduring marriage does not endure because there are no awful parts, or because the awful parts are skipped over or forgotten; it endures because the couple makes a concerted effort to survive the awful parts together and to learn from what was awful so that they grow closer and more trusting of each other as a result of having survived. When a husband and wife can do this, they will gradually experience more that is awesome and less that is awful.

And when that journey is traveled well, it can leave spouses feeling more passionate about and appreciative of each other than ever before, able to chart directions that take them to places that they once dreamed of or never even imagined. The couple who has successfully slalomed between the jagged rocks of family life and come coasting down to the base of the mountain intact will experience a majestic sense of splendor and triumph.

So when we are working with married parents of young adults, we need to help them to understand the importance of reassessing the significance, relevance, and potential of their marriage in the face of their children increasingly needing them less.

We want them to loosen the strictures that have tightened around them as a result of child rearing and begin stretching their relational limbs and flexing their emotional muscles after years of parent-based confinement. We want to abet their efforts to cultivate an enlivened marriage between still-interesting, still-compelling, and, perhaps even still-mysterious and intriguing peers.

We have to help them look candidly at the ways in which their relationship has become interpersonally imbalanced or lopsided over the years and to help them understand that both of them need to make changes if they're going to revamp and rebalance their marriage and move forward in healthy ways. We want to them to reassess their sense of fulfillment within the marriage—fulfillment both in regard to feeling gratified and satisfied but also in regard to how they did and did not fulfill their roles as spouses to the extent that they had hoped, wished, or planned to.

And we want them to ask each other not only what is left *of* their marriage but also what is left *for* their marriage.

Marital issues are particularly relevant at the launching stage, because we have seen how frequently a young adult returns to the family, or comes to a screeching developmental halt, because of his desire to renovate or solidify his parents' marriage or because of how difficult it is for him to even sketch out a leave-taking if the marriage has been characterized by increasing conflict or remoteness between the partners.

Marital issues are also important to pay attention to at this phase of the family life cycle because young people will invariably choose a romantic (and possibly marital) partner with whom they can replicate some of the relational dynamics that they have witnessed taking place between their parents. Children will seek to experience that which is familiar—whether what is familiar is satisfying or unsatisfying—and what is familiar is the kind of relationship that looks, for better or for worse, like certain aspects of their parents' marriage do.

Finally, because children have usually been one of the most significant of marital stressors, their departure can be capitalized on by a couple as they contemplate marital rejuvenation and renewal. The father of a very challenging 21-year-old was intending to tell me that, "My son took my life away from me," but it came out as, "My son took my *wife* away from me." Children by their very nature take their parents away from each other, so when they begin to separate from the family, their parents can begin the exciting process of finding each other again, and becoming reacquainted in ways that will carry them forward.

MARITAL FORCE FIELDS

Back in chapter 5, I described three types of family dynamics and the ways in which they sometimes produce stiff headwinds that prevent a young adult's successful leave-taking. Centripetal families make it difficult for the young adult to depart because departure is made to feel like a betrayal. Centrifugal families eject her prematurely and thus fail to provide her with the psychological nutrients she needs to become self-reliant. Mission Impossible families, while supportive of the young adult's departure, burden him with responsibilities that are either so incongruent or overwhelming that the departure eventually knuckles under beneath the strain.

When I work with couples who are trying to empty their nest and wind down their parenting apparatus, I usually see echoes of these dynamics in their marital life.

CENTRIPETAL MARRIAGES

In Centripetal marriages, there is often an ongoing relational deadlock, a chafing under overly restrictive rules, making it difficult for one or both partners to develop fully as individuals and establish the kind of sturdy intimacy that can only come about when there is a healthy amount of independence in place. As I often explain to couples, you can only be as married as you are separate—it is the balance between the two that keeps an enduring relationship vigorous and resilient.

Centripetal spouses seem bound together like downcast twins in a sterile uterine environment that will never release them. Their spavined relationship seems to have just about died under the weight of routine, disappointment, guilt, and weariness—exhausted by predictability and suffocated by domesticity, it is inertia rather than movement that defines their moribund minuet. They may appear to get along with each other, and even treat each other respectfully and politely, but it is a grim respect and a tight-lipped politeness that they exhibit.

The challenge that Centripetal marriages present to the young adult is that the centripetal forces may extend to him—just as his parents are not allowed any kind of healthy separation from each other, he is not allowed any kind of healthy separation from them. Or he may be intuitively aware that his departure will throw their asphyxiating relationship into disarray, that it has been his (and perhaps his siblings') presence that helped to create the black hole that the marriage now disconsolately resides in.

CENTRIFUGAL MARRIAGES

In Centrifugal marriages, a growing distance between the two partners that began either before or after they started their family can become a seemingly unbridgeable gorge, making intimacy of any sort—emotional or physical—a challenge. While a legal divorce may or may not be spoken of, they may have been psychologically divorced for years. The hairline fractures that began to reveal themselves in the early stages of parenthood never healed and gradually widened over the years, and the couple became entombed as spouses despite their ability to stay alive as co-parents.

The Centrifugal marriage is characterized by interminable stretches of real indifference, or by an indifference that is actually an uneasy, brittle truce, a thin veil for underlying acrimony and irritability. Dimly lit by the dying embers of the fire that first might have drawn them toward each other, each spouse participates in a carefully choreographed two-step of avoidance and accommodation, close enough on the marital stage that they still appear to others (and maybe even to their children) like partners but not so close that they ever actually reach each other to any extent.

Orphaned of passion, sexual ardor becomes an unwanted weed in the chaste garden of their marriage, and one or both of these stony spouses work diligently to ensure that it never has the opportunity to push through the surface—and if, perchance, it does so, efforts are quickly made on one or both of their parts to smother it or tear it out. As the wife in a Centrifugal marriage told me during our initial couples session, "Honestly, I really don't have any desire to even see if we have any desire."

The challenge that Centrifugal marriages present to the young adult is that she may believe that her ongoing availability is necessary to keep her parents in contact with each other, threadbare as their contact actually is. She fears that if she moves on or moves out, the diaphanous threads that enjoin her parents may vanish altogether, resulting in the end of their relationship.

MISSION-IMPOSSIBLE MARRIAGES

More than once, I have seen the words "martial arts" misspelled as "marital arts" and the words "marital therapy" misspelled as "martial therapy." In Mission-Impossible marriages, there is a combative, pugnacious climate as a result of an embittered couple having arrived at a recent, or long-standing, impasse. Their original marriage contract has metamorphosed into a combination suicide-homicide pact. Trapped in a thicket consisting of each other's needs, compulsions, and unmet yearnings, they goad each other into blistering fight after blistering fight, shrieking at each other from their nearby branches like enraged blue jays. The suppressed, malignant anger swells between them like a dangerous, unlanced boil, and they scald each other in a thunderous or silent lava of unobtainable expectations.

Not only have they been furious and unhappy with each other for years, but each insists that the other should experience just as much, if not more, than that share of fury and unhappiness. They tend to their marital ire and indignation like a mourning widow or widower, with perpetual care and attentiveness. They harbor and nourish the conviction that they would be happier alone, and perhaps that would be the case, but in the meantime, they don't do anything to make that happen. They can't live together and they can't imagine living apart, so their ongoing presence in each other's lives simply serves to distill the hostility that they stir up in each other into a more and more concentrated poison.

The challenge that Mission-Impossible marriages present to the young adult is that he may believe that unless he sticks around to play a mediating role, or to be a marital lightning rod and draw off their electrifying current, his parents will destroy each other, and possibly the entire family as well.

THE IMPACT OF IMBALANCE

In any of these three uneven marriages, we will see one or both partners tending to rely on self-destructive behavior patterns, such as abusing alcohol or prescription drugs or turning to infidelity in an attempt to dilute the rage and frustration engendered by a relationship that has become torpid and unhappily transfixed. Or one or both may engage in other kinds of behavior patterns that are not necessarily self-destructive (although they can be) but that still keep them safely at arm's length from any intimate engagement with their partner. Endeavors such as going to the gym or becoming involved in community service or political activism are without question potentially vitalizing when undertaken with a marital or family equilibrium in mind, but when taken to an extreme, they can easily preclude the likelihood of more personal encounters with one's spouse and the possibility of an emancipated marriage.

Likewise, we will see young adults sacrifice themselves in one way or another that sabotages their growth and compromises their capacity to become autonomous. Marriages that are acutely, if not gravely, imbalanced in these ways don't, by themselves, prevent young adults from leaving home or becoming autonomous, but they certainly don't incite these processes, either.

However, when couples are able to rebalance their marriage during the launching phase, it always helps, in both direct and indirect ways, to resolve a young adult's hesitancy and ambivalence about moving on. And just as importantly, the young adult's ability to move on invariably gives couples the opportunity to make important marital adjustments, producing a positive feedback loop wherein growth displayed in one part of the family augments and supports growth in another.

A comprehensive examination of couples therapy is beyond the scope of this chapter or book, but here are several issues that may need to be at least touched upon by the clinician treating families with struggling young adults. Couples get socketed into these unhealthy imbalances at midlife because they remain hostages to old patterns that originated in each partner's desire to be loved, respected, and treasured in the way that he or she had hoped to be. That is why the only way to release themselves from being hostages is to request *from* each other, and display *toward* each other, the love, respect, and treasuring that each one deserves. The family therapist can inspire and instigate this request for and display of caring marital behavior in the way that he engages with the couple, whether he is working with their marriage directly (through couples work) or indirectly (through family therapy).

FORGIVENESS

Just as parents have to forgive their children for being less than perfect, spouses need to do the same, particularly as they begin to migrate into a relationship that pivots on the axis of just the two of them, without the distractions and diversions of child rearing.

We have to help couples to define and abide by their statute of limitations regarding old hurts and resentments, because marinating in these hurts and resentments can quickly torpedo a couple's efforts to come together and join in a new and more satisfying clasp. We want them to understand that the best way to dissolve the glue of bad memories is to create a new glue composed of good and fond memories.

When spouses are able to truly forgive each other for the pain that they have inflicted on each other, their feelings of acceptance and affection expand to encompass the revelation of flaw after flaw, year after year, and they experience a sense of cherishing, and being cherished by, each other that is unmistakable and irreplaceable.

RECALIBRATING

Once the fulcrum of child rearing has been removed from beneath the marital teeter-totter, it will require both parents to find a way to recalibrate their relationship with each other.

The essence of much marital conflict is that couples vacillate between being competitive and complementary when it comes to their relationship with each other, and every healthy marriage needs some of both (Madanes, 1990). It is important to establish a complementarity of roles, a respectful distribution of labor, so that spouses don't exhaust themselves trying to do everything, or trying to do everything better than their spouse does. However, sometimes that complementarity becomes so rigidified that there is no longer any significant serenade between the two of them—they function like a well-oiled machine, but a good marriage cannot survive on machinery alone—it comprises a duet, not two unaccompanied solo melodies.

Likewise, while too much competition results in endless squabbles and pointless battles, making it appear as if the couple comprises two siblings rather than two lovers, too little competition results in boredom and stagnation—competition, when not destructive, prompts us to encounter each other and excel, and efforts to do so always pay handsome dividends in the course of a marriage.

Other inequalities have to be managed as well. For example, when spouses lose the constant affection of and connection with a child who has left home, they may or may not feel that they can turn to their marital partner to experience that affection and connection, which can throw the relationship off-kilter. Or if one spouse experienced power in the marriage through being the more influential parent, the loss of the child who is being influenced may mean the spouse's loss of power, and the couple will have to find a way to recalculate their power differential.

Even if you are not doing marital therapy per se, many couples will need assistance finding ways to align and square up their relationship as they are attempting, or being forced, to leave behind their significance as parents.

SEXUALITY

What I have observed in many marriages is that a husband's libido decreases with age while his wife's increases with age. This gradual regression to the mean on both of their parts can sometimes result in a couple's sexual relationship becoming increasingly satisfying for the two of them. Much better matched in their level of desire, they merrily embark on a new stage of sexual intimacy that floats them onward into their senior years.

On the other hand, these physical changes sometimes create problems. The husband may confuse his diminishing level of desire with a diminishing level of desire *for his wife* and assume that a younger, or differently attractive, partner is necessary for him to reinvigorate or maintain his vigor. Or he may feel embarrassed or ashamed of his lowered libido and pull away from his wife sexually, not wanting to be exposed and afraid of how she might hurt or humiliate him were she to know.

While I have treated many women whose sexual desire seems to be decrease upon reaching menopause, I have worked with many more women who experience an increased level of desire, which might prompt her to realize that she could do better than her husband, who may have been an inexpert or inattentive lover. Or if he begins to turn his sexual attention to another woman (or man), she may naturally seek out a better-suited, more like-minded erotic partner as well.

No matter what their sexual history and what brought them into treatment, we may be in the position of needing to help the parents to cultivate or recultivate a romantic love that may be more patient and tender than frenzied and intense but that still leaves them feeling more connected to each other as their connections with their children are being downgraded.

AFFAIRS

One of the not unsurprising marital occurrences during the launching phase is a second kind of launching—the launching of an affair. After all, the nature of children leaving home is that the parents are being, or are threatened with being, jilted, and when we are jilted, it is all too human to turn to others for comfort, solace, affection, and support. Ideally, the individual that the jilted parent turns to is his or her spouse, but, as we've noted above, a couple's history over the previous years may work against this optimal upshot.

Affairs are common at this stage not only because one or both spouses yearn to replace the lost attachment to their separating and departing child but also because one or both spouses are yearning for a last gasp of youth and erotic excitement or because one or both spouses are simply seeking a fantasied escape from the sodden clay of their quotidian lives, and it may be easier to arrange this now that they are no longer so consumed by the duties of intensive child rearing.

An affair is often nothing more than a frantic flailing about in an effort to stay aloft and not be sunk or submerged by hurts from the past or fears of the future. But many times these liaisons, short-lived and sexually gratifying as they may be, are damaging, if not devastating, to the marriage, particularly at such a vulnerable point in the conjugal expedition. The misguided effort to live out the kind of in-fatuation that one may no longer feel capable of and restore an inwardly doubted sense of vitality, attractiveness, or purpose generally creates prodigious feelings of pain and rejection in the betrayed spouse (and sometimes in the betraying spouse, as well, if he or she is eventually spurned by the sought-after extramarital paramour).

On rare occasions, I have seen these kinds of launching-stage affairs ultimately evolve into loving and stable relationships or remarriages, but most of the time that does not happen. The copious conglomerate of deception and self-deception entailed with initiating and maintaining the affair precludes the possibility of per-sonal or relational growth, and what is left is a seething trail of resentment and bitterness that becomes yet another challenge to an already challenged marriage. Sometimes, of course, infidelity pushes a faltering (or even a relatively stable) marriage right over the edge and into a separation or divorce.

There are occasions, however, when, painful as they may be, these amorous ventures do serve to awaken and animate partners—psychologically and/or sexually—who have become quiescent. This outburst of passion, illogical and hurtful as it may be, takes the form of a courageous final stand against prematurely tossing in the marital towel and the couple consigning themselves to an arid, stagnating marriage. Sometimes an affair will call attention to long-neglected issues and conflicts that have hindered individual and marital growth and prompt a couple to bravely broker conversations—or even fights—that have been avoided for far too long, at both of their expense. The result is that the marriage is resuscitated and revivified, and a new and fulfilling relational chapter can now begin to be written.

I have worked with many couples for whom an emotional affair on one of their parts—an affair that did not have a physical component and that remained well-bounded—injected added zest into the marriage. In these cases, the experience of feeling attractive to and adored by another adult and of dancing the exquisite dance of dalliance and flirtatiousness—a dance whose steps may have been all but forgotten—is re-energizing, and he or she is able to feed that energy back into the marriage and enliven both of them as a result.

It is obviously intoxicating to fall in love again, whether that love is real or imagined, and to experience the heightened state of well-being that love lends to life, particularly when life has been overly dominated by the mundane and the ordinary. Love so instantly and generously provides us with a sense of purpose, of drama, of possibility, of suspense—everything seems to matter more, and we occupy our lives with renewed intensity and passion.

On the other hand, when the emotional affair does become physical or when the boundaries of the emotional affair become more diffuse and that relationship takes up so much energy and time that the other spouse begins to feel secondary and neglected or betrayed and humiliated, the results are rarely positive. Sometimes even the nonsexual affair will take a central, or overly prominent, role in a marriage, behaving like an ungovernable field fire that continues to flare up again after each attempt to dampen it or stamp it out. In these situations, the marital renaissance that might have been initially spurred by the once-harmless flirtation caves in on itself, breeding animosity and outrage.

Of course, not all affairs involve other people. Sometimes, when a marriage has lost its sense of drama and excitement, when there is no longer anything that is in the least bit surprising, unpredictable, or adventurous taking place between the two partners, other kinds of affairs will be embarked upon—an affair with a substance, with gambling, with spending, with the latest technology, perhaps with psychogenic discomfort and an endless series of medical consultations. Any of these can provide the powerful sense of relatedness—albeit with an object or experience rather than with a subject—that is missing, but still longed for, in the marriage.

If the couple is going to work things out, they have to learn to talk to each other about the affair and what led up to it. A patient of mine who had started up a brief affair with another woman shortly after he and his wife had emptied their nest joined his wife in couples treatment with me in an effort to heal the rupture in their relationship. He tearfully confessed to her that he felt tremendous regret about having had the affair and told her that, "I want you to know that I talk to God about it every single day."

Her understandable response was, "You didn't humiliate God, you humiliated *me*—shouldn't you be talking to your *wife* about this more than talking to God?"

He replied, "I don't want to talk to you about this, because it upsets you so much—it's like opening up the wound again, I don't want to do that to you."

"The wound never *closed*, Rob," she said, her voice now quivering tremulously. "You never gave it a chance to close because you won't talk to me about it. All you did is announce that you're sorry and then start praying to God. That may help *you*, but it sure doesn't do anything for *me*. How can you reopen a wound that never closed?"

The key to a marriage thriving in midlife is the couple learning, or relearning, the ability to converse with each other about important matters. These kinds of conversations may have rarely, if ever, taken place at all in the marriage, or they may have gradually fallen to the wayside over the years under the pressure of other matters, such as child rearing, health issues, or finances.

But when a young adult child is struggling on the precipice of leaving home, it is an opportunity (whether intended by the young adult or not) for the parents to talk to each other in novel and perhaps unaccustomed ways, and these newly conveyed words become the basis for their salvaging, resuscitating, or even finally creating the marriage that they dearly yearn to foster.

DEATH OF A SPOUSE

A couple's reinvestment in their marriage as their children separate will be tragically truncated if one of the spouses dies. The death of a marriage partner at a point in time when the couple was making plans for the next stage of their lives instantly shatters the remaining spouse's hopefulness and optimism about the future. He or she is consumed by feelings of sorrow, loss, and injustice. Friends who are still married may pull away, perhaps afraid to confront the reality of their own or their spouse's mortality and the enormity of this kind of loss.

As a result, the launching process will often be affected as one or more of the children feel compelled to turn their attention backward, to their bereaved parent, rather than forward, to their personal pursuits. In these situations, the clinician can help the widow or widower to determine what is and is not realistic to ask his or her children for, and to help the children find a workable balance between caring for their parent without abandoning their own, evolving objectives.

For example, Anne-Marie lost her husband to leukemia when she was 53 and when her two sons, Sammy and Luke, were 25 and 23. Sammy was still living at home when the father died, while Luke had graduated from college and was now in his first year of law school several states away.

Luke was the more confidently differentiated of the two siblings and tried to be attentive to his mother from a distance, calling her a couple of times a week to check in and e-mailing her with updates on his classes and what he was up to. However, there were limits to how available he could be, based on his geographical distance as well as his demanding curriculum.

Sammy had already made two attempts to disembark but had miscarried on both. He had gone away to college after high school but returned home after failing his classes. A year later he had made an attempt to live independently as a snowboard instructor at a ski resort but wasn't able to make ends meet and returned home again. These two failed departures, along with his father's illness and death, appeared to have cemented Sammy in for good—he was a lost soul living an aimless life, drifting from girlfriend to girlfriend without holding on to a job or making plans for another foray toward self-sufficiency.

Anne-Marie, feeling lonely and lost, wanted to draw Sammy closer—he was, she told me, the one who looked and sounded most like her husband. "I can't ask for any more support from Luke than he's already giving me—he's hundreds of miles away and he's busy with law school. But Sammy . . . Sammy, I feel like you should be taking more time to be with me. But you're never around . . . or it's more like you make *sure* that you're never around. Where do you go, anyway? It's not like you have a regular job," she wondered, with just a hint of sarcasm.

"I go out, Mom, I go out. What exactly do you need to know? I'm twenty-five years old, what do you expect me to do, wait around the house all day for you to come home from work so we can have a dinner date together?"

"But Sammy, this is a very hard time for me. I'm not asking you to wait on me hand and foot; I'm just asking you to be a little more available, like when I need help."

"What kind of help do you need? Just let me know what kind of help you need, and I'll take care of it."

"I don't know, it's not like I need anything in particular. Sometimes I just want to know that you're around—that *someone's* around. This isn't easy for me, you know."

"It's not easy for me either," Sammy snapped.

Sammy, of course, was extremely resentful that he was stuck with the family caretaking obligations. Not only, from Sammy's perspective, was Luke unfairly off the hook when it came to filial responsibilities, but Sammy was also fighting not to lose what little ground he had gained in his thus far stunningly unsuccessful march toward autonomy. Giving in to his mom's request for more closeness and assistance was tantamount to giving up on what scant freedom he had. Not yet having established any trust in his own individuation, he remained committed to maintaining as much individualism as he could maintain—*self-absorption* had become a poor replacement for actual *selfhood*. This meant that Sammy felt compelled to do everything in his power to escape his mother's clutches and keep himself removed from her as much as possible—no matter how unproductive he had to become—which in turn prompted her to become more clutchy with him.

Our work together focused on helping Anne-Marie to find other sources of support and care besides Sammy and helping Sammy to get his life back into gear so that he felt more confident in his ability to separate, which would in turn enable him to more easily toggle back and forth between appropriate care of his mom and appropriate momentum for himself.

We included Luke in sessions by way of conference calls, making sure that he was willing to maintain the level of closeness that he had already established, a necessary step in the process of Anne-Marie ameliorating her dependence on Sammy. Finally feeling like the potential life sentence of caring for his mother was being commuted, Sammy was able to respond to the clemency that had been granted by pulling himself together and preparing for another concerted effort to gain a foothold in the world outside of his family.

MULTIGENERATIONAL MARRIAGES

Particularly in lower-income families, it is not infrequently the case that the birth parents have never married, so there is no relationship between a mother and father to be revived or renegotiated during the launching stage—child rearing has been taken care of in a single-parent arrangement. However, the young adult may also have been raised in a multigenerational home, so that the "marriage" that needs to be renegotiated is one between, for example, a parent and a grandparent rather than between two parents. This relationship, just like a marriage between spouses, has to evolve in response to the child's sendoff.

In one family that I worked with, the departure of 18-year-old Jonquille was a welcome relief for Jonquille's grandmother, Syreeta, who, along with Jonquille's mother, Lavonya, had raised her since she was born, when Lavonya was 17. Jonquille's father, who was serving a life sentence in prison for first-degree murder, had never married Lavonya and had met his daughter only once, as a newborn.

Jonquille had put the family through the wringer many times during her adolescence as a result of numerous drug and theft infractions, but she had finally settled down by the end of high school and enlisted in the marines. Syreeta, who was single, overweight, and trying to manage her diabetes and high blood pressure over these last few years, almost instantly began to feel better once Jonquille left home for basic training. Now 43 years old, she had the sense that she finally could have her life back after back-to-back sequences of challenging, hands-on child rearing and was looking forward to taking care of herself physically, getting some additional training so that she could make more money in her data entry position, and dating.

Jonquille's mother, Lavonya, did not adapt to Jonquille's parting as well as Syreeta did, however. Jonquille's life as an 18-year-old—leaving home in a successful way and laying the groundwork for a productive career and world travel, despite the attendant risks—was in stark contrast to Lavonya's life as an 18-year-old, when she was a new mother and trying to beat an addiction to crack cocaine (which, to her credit, she did).

Without her daughter around to mobilize and stabilize her, and forced to come to terms with how little she had made of her life, Lavonya became depressed and resumed her drug habit, and Syreeta once again found herself in the mothering role. Our work together focused on helping Syreeta to disentangle herself from this role and on Lavonya responding to her daughter's growth by becoming more, rather than less, functional. In other words, their "marriage," like any marriage, had to be reconditioned and refurbished in the face of a child leaving home.

Chapter 10

Money Matters at the Launching Stage

H. L. Mencken once noted that if someone insists, "It's not about the money," then you know it is, in fact, about the money. Over the years, I have found it impossible to discuss young adults' departure from home without, at some point, discussing money.

Many currencies are fungible within the commercial institution known as the family—love, power, sex, guilt, anger, resentment, to name a few—but there is one currency that is versatile and malleable enough that it can serve as a stand-in for any of them, and that currency is money.

Sometimes, I have found that the family's focus on money obscures more painful issues—the ones that really need to be talked about. Sometimes, the family has become mired in an endless discussion of painful issues because they are avoiding the topic that *really* needs to be talked about, which is money. Money and all that money represents in and for a family often seem as if they've been cooked together into an indissoluble stew, and it's difficult to tease out whether money is a substitute for other issues, or whether other issues are a substitute for money. In any of these situations, however, a therapist who is treating families with struggling young adults has to help them to explore and understand the role that money has played, and is currently playing, in their development.

When young adults are not separating effectively from their families, I generally find that somewhere along the line they have not been paying close enough attention to the way in which they discuss, earn, exchange, and spend their money. Money fulfills many purposes in human relationships, and especially in family relationships its role is chameleonic. Here are some examples:

- Money can be requested, offered, and/or accepted as an expression of love or hostility.
- Money can be withheld or spent profligately as an expression of anger, disappointment, or resentment.
- Money can be actively or passively demanded in an effort to exact retribution or revenge or to engage in extortion.
- Money can be given in an effort to restrict growth and freedom.

- Money can be tendered to make a child feel good or to make a child feel patronized or diminished.
- Money can be administered or withdrawn to demonstrate who does and doesn't have power in the family.
- Money can be offered as a surrogate for love or to expiate the guilt associated with not being very loving.
- Money can bring family members close to each other or alienate them from each other.

Depending on how it is acquired and managed, money can solve problems or create problems. It can provide access to many important possessions and endeavors, such as a nice place to live or a college or postgraduate education, and it can imprison people in their greed or immobilize them with the fear of losing what they have.

One of the hallmarks of self-reliance for young adults is inescapably fiscal in nature: the ability to earn enough to live on their own without needing the financial support of their parents or others. And one of the hallmarks of continued maturity is eventually developing the capacity to take care of one's parents as they age, which often entails financial expenditure. The slow, lifelong shift from being taken care of by one's parents to one day taking care of one's parents—be it financially based care or not—is one of the processes that makes us distinctly human. As sociobiologists have noted, we are the only animal species in which the younger generation at some point takes care of the older generation.

While children learn about many aspects of life in school, in religious institutions, on the playground, and in the community at large, they mostly learn about money at home. This takes place when they watch their parents work or balance the checkbook or pay their bills or donate to charity or spend their money on leisure pursuits. This takes place when they are provided with an allowance or rewarded for good grades or given gifts for birthdays and holidays. This takes place when their mother and father fight with each other about money because one overspends and the other is too stingy, or because one earns more than the other, or because one has a large inheritance and the other doesn't, or because they can't agree on alimony and child support during a divorce.

When parents give children money or subsidize them in some way, there is always some expectation attached to it. For instance, when I am working with middle- and upper-class families, I often hear parents of adolescents complain bitterly because their teenager no longer wants to pursue an activity that the parents have spent a significant amount of money on over the years.

"I invested thousands of dollars in ice-hockey equipment and league fees for the last ten years, and now you want to stop playing? Now, when you're in tenth grade and college scouts start looking for recruits and you could get a scholarship and save *me* some money?"

"How many years have I paid for your clarinet lessons now? How much money did we spend getting you the best clarinet that we could? Do you know how expensive those summer music camps were? And now you're telling me that you're done with the clarinet, that you just don't feel like playing anymore?"

In these situations, there is an unspoken contract between parent and child—"I will make a significant investment in *you*, in return for which you need to pay me back in a currency that is meaningful to *me*," which, in this case means continued pursuit of excellence in the activity that the parent has been underwriting. The parents will ultimately have to realize, however, that their child never signed that contract and feels no particular obligation to uphold his or her end of the so-called bargain.

SUPPORT AND LACK THEREOF

With some families who have difficulty setting financial limits with their young adults, I am reminded of a half-humorous comment made by the late owner of the Washington Redskins, Edward Bennett Williams. After several lackluster seasons, Williams had hired the well-known former coach of the Los Angeles Rams, George Allen, to take over the Redskins because he wanted to quickly expedite his team's success. When it came to acquiring the players necessary for a championship team, the owner admitted ruefully, "I gave Coach Allen an unlimited budget, and, somehow, he exceeded it."

All parents have to determine the extent to which they are going to financially bankroll their children—how much support they are willing to provide, what will and will not be supported, and how long support can be expected. The goal will be for them to find the golden mean that encourages children's growth—not so much or so little that the young adult is prevented from being able to, or being motivated to, achieve independence.

This calculation will be complicated by each parent's personal financial history, and by the fiscal psychodynamics that take place between the parents, which is where family therapy can be helpful. Some parents, for example, do not want their children to suffer through any of the deprivation that they suffered through and do anything they can to prevent distress—whatever their child wants, their child gets. Other parents *want* their child to suffer through deprivation, so that their child understands them and their personal experience better, or because the parents feel that this better prepares the child for life. Either of these approaches, taken to an extreme, can hobble the separation process.

In many families, there has been a division of financial labor during the years of childhood and adolescence, in which one parent makes significantly more money than the other. Sometimes this means that the spouse making less money takes on more of the budgeting and spending responsibilities. Sometimes this means that the spouse making more money has greater power and is entitled to make all of the final decisions regarding how money will be managed.

When the imbalance in pecuniary clout becomes overly rigid or severe, it is not uncommon for the financially disempowered spouse to look for other sources of power, such as by building a coalition with one or more of the children that is designed to neutralize or dilute the more financially empowered spouse. This dynamic displayed itself in the O'Riordan family. Mr. O'Riordan was a workaholic entrepreneur with Scrooge-like tendencies who was the financially successful founder of a computer software company, but a man who was emotionally neglectful of his wife and two sons. Ms. O'Riordan had chosen to be a stay-at-home mom but tired of her husband's constant and, from her perspective, demeaning supervision of her household spending. He would look over the grocery bill and wonder why she couldn't find cheaper milk. He would question the amount of money spent on the children's clothing. When she encouraged him to go shopping for food or clothes so that he could see that she was being reasonable with her purchases, he begged off, citing his work commitments—"I don't have time to do that; I work hard so that *you* have time to do that," was his rationale.

Ms. O'Riordan eventually began turning to her sons with her complaints about her husband. She recruited them to be on her side when it came to fighting the family's financial battles:

"I'd like for us to take a trip during your winter break, but it doesn't look like your father wants to spend the money."

"Boy, if your father wasn't such a penny-pincher, we wouldn't be watching this lousy TV; we'd have one of those nice flat screens."

"I know you want to go to that soccer camp this summer, but you know how your father is when it comes to money."

The O'Riordans contacted me because their eldest son, 18-year-old Sean, was running into trouble with the law as a result of drug dealing and had been arrested twice. Mr. O'Riordan began having to spend significant amounts of money bailing Sean out and financing the high-priced attorney that he retained in an effort to keep Sean out of jail. But the more money the O'Riordans spent, the more expensive Sean became. Shortly after Sean's second court hearing, which resulted in a three-year probation, he totaled one of the family cars in a crash while under the influence of pot and shattered his femur and pelvis in the process, resulting in a two-week hospitalization. He needed two additional operations over the next several months to reset the broken bones, and then required additional months of physical therapy.

In our family therapy discussions, it quickly became obvious that the imbalance of financial dominion between the parents was at least partially at the root of Sean's behavior. One interchange went as follows:

"We've spent over seventy-five thousand dollars this year on lawyer bills and doctor bills, and we're not even done yet! This is absolutely ridiculous! I should be planning for retirement, and all I'm doing is spending money on our son, who's technically already an adult!" Mr. O'Riordan shouted.

"Sure, you don't like spending *money* on your son, and you don't like spending *time* with him, either," replied Ms. O'Riordan, frostily.

"What does that have to do with anything? He's eighteen years old, he's not a little kid—*I* wasn't doing the drug deals! *I* wasn't driving the car into a guardrail! Why are you blaming *me*?"

"Because it's like all of a sudden you're waking up and seeing that we have a son! Now that he's causing problems, it's suddenly occurring to you that you never paid him any mind."

"I'm paying *plenty* now, I'll tell you that! This kid is gonna break us!"

"Maybe if you were willing to pay for more when he was younger, he wouldn't be so involved with drugs."

"What exactly didn't I pay for? We have a nice house, we have three cars—or at least we *had* three cars, now we're down to two—we've taken some nice trips . . . please refresh my memory, did anyone in this family ever go hungry? Did anyone in this family ever miss a meal?"

"But everything was a fight, Michael, it was always a fight. I had to fight with you about anything that we spent on the kids; you questioned every last nickel that I spent! I wanted Sean to get tutoring, and you said it wasn't worth it. I wanted Sean to get counseling when he was having a hard time in middle school, and you said it wasn't worth it. And look what it got you! Now you're spending hundreds of times the amount of money that we were fighting about. Congratulations, you made sure I bought the least expensive clothes and the least expensive food, and now we're spending far more than we saved. What exactly was the point?"

"Well, at least I've made enough money to pay for all of these lawyer and doc-tor bills! Where would we be if I didn't?"

"Maybe we wouldn't be *here*! Maybe if you weren't always at work and were a better father, maybe if you weren't so busy scrutinizing my spending habits, Sean wouldn't be in such trouble!"

"Oh, so once again it's my fault. Please explain to me how I caused all this to happen."

"I'm not saying you caused it; I'm just thinking that maybe we could have prevented it."

It began to occur to me that Sean was helping his mother out by punishing his father—in this case, by psychologically forcing him to finally spend the money that he had resisted spending all these years. What better way to support his mother than by putting his father in the position of having to "pay up" and to finally realize how much it can really cost to raise a child?

Our subsequent work confirmed this hypothesis, as I learned that Ms. O'Riordan had become aware of Sean's drug use early in high school and of his drug dealing at least a year before but had chosen not to tell her husband, because she didn't want him to "over-react like he always does—what would be the point, so that he could come down on him like a ton of bricks?" With no real consequences in place other than his mother's gentle warning to discontinue his drug using and dealing behavior, and with his father remaining (and choosing to remain) in the dark, Sean continued on the path that eventually led to his getting arrested.

While he was clearly aligned with his mother, it was interesting also to note the ways in which Sean aligned himself with his father—after all, he was making money by starting and running his own business of sorts, which is exactly what his father had done.

Finances during the launching stage will also be complicated by the fact that most adults in their middle years are sandwiched between their children and their parents, so the issue of where their financial loyalties and priorities should lie can be a perplexing one. If one of the grandparents needs to be supported financially at the same time as some steep college tuition bills are due, what form of fiscal triage is organized?

And this ever-shifting allocation of resources is made even more recondite by the often inexcusable desire to establish fairness, which is a constant pursuit within any web of human relationships, especially within the web of the family. Particularly when there is more than one child, parents have to constantly determine what is fair when it comes to financial dispensation, and children will often howl in protest when they believe that unfairness has taken root, that their personal system of financial justice has been violated. Should parents commit the exact same amount of subsidy to each of their children, or should they give according to each child's needs, or should they give according to how much emotional support or involvement they receive from each child? There is no perfect solution to this calculation—one or more individuals are going to say or believe that it's just not fair.

In one family, the parents were paying their 26-year-old daughter's credit card bills, often close to $2,000 per month, because she insisted she was unable to work full-time due to fighting an illness that countless clinicians had been unable to pin down and treat. When their 30-year-old son and daughter-in-law, who were healthy and had been financially independent for years, asked them for $10,000 to help them make a down payment on a house now that they were expecting their second child, the parents were in a quandary because they couldn't meet both children's requests. The son, who knew that his younger sister remained financially dependent on their parents, felt that he was being "punished" for having become as self-sufficient as he had become and that it was "his turn" for a parental allocation. The daughter believed that she needed the money more than her brother, since he was married and both he and his wife were healthy enough to earn solid incomes, while she felt perpetually handicapped by the misfortune of her perpetual malady.

One common predicament when it comes to the role of money in the family is that the motives and emotions associated with the individual who is giving money are rarely identical to the motives and emotions associated with the individual who is requesting or receiving money. Money can be offered with kindness and generosity or with anger and disappointment. Money can be received and spent with gratitude and respect or with resentment and guilt.

I often see caring parents who are surprised and upset that their generosity is not acknowledged with appreciation by their young adult children, particularly if the capacity to be generous in the first place is the result of significant effort on the parents' part. The reality, though, is that generosity often elicits resentment and envy rather than appreciation. Being on the receiving end of generosity can make us feel diminished, particularly in response to our munificent benefactor. It may indeed be better to give than receive, but it doesn't always *feel* better to give, since giving stirs up complicated feelings in the recipient that can get misdirected to the one who gives.

On the flip side, resentment on one generation's part may also arise if generosity is *not* extended. One 20-year-old patient of mine was so hurt that her father did not call her on her birthday that she went online with his credit card (which she had a copy of) and purchased hundreds of dollars of clothes at his expense.

Most parents hope that their children are able to accomplish at least as much as they have accomplished, if not more. But for various reasons, parents sometimes sabotage or undermine their children and subtly or explicitly set them up to fail financially, sometimes without even knowing that they are doing so. There are ways to provide financial support to young adults that spur their growth and trigger their moves toward self-reliance, and there are ways to provide financial support that hobble and stunt them, that dissolve their natural motivation and capacity to achieve self-reliance. And the more well off the family is, the more ways there are to do the latter rather than the former. As clinicians, we have to be attentive to the ways in which parents might encourage their children's dependence through financial means.

Conversely, children of middle- and upper-class parents often reject a path that will carry them toward substantial income, because they can't help but notice how devoid of pleasure their parents' lives may be. Countless adolescents and young adults have shared with me their fear that if they take on the yoke of achieving financial success, they will be unhappily burdened by it for life, just as their parents appear to be.

ADDRESSING COLLEGE EXPENSES

One father observed, "I've worked very hard to make enough money to tell Shane that he can afford to go to college wherever he wants to, but, frankly, now that he's a junior, I'm starting to really hesitate at the thought of spending $50,000 a year when he's kind of just strolled through high school, getting his lackadaisical Bs and Cs. I'm sure that one of these expensive private schools that he's applying to is going to admit him—I mean, he's done decently—but the thought of spending a quarter of a million of my hard-earned dollars when he's never really worked very hard himself, and doesn't even know what he wants to do, is a little hard to stomach. On the other hand, it's kind of what I always dreamed I'd be able to do for him—my parents were certainly never able to do that for me."

I suggested to this father that it was important for him to have a frank conversation with his son and to make it clear that their original agreement would need to be revised in light of the son's relentlessly relaxed approach to his high school curriculum.

"I kind of agree, but I feel like I'm going back on my word."

"You are," I concurred, "but that's an important lesson for Shane to learn, as well. Part of being an adult is evaluating decisions carefully, and changing them based on changing data and circumstances."

"What if he hates me?"

"He very well may be unhappy with your decision, that's for sure. But he also may be relieved. After all, it would certainly be sending him a mixed message to agree to endow an education that he hasn't really demonstrated that he's worthy of. How much worse would he feel if he went to an expensive school which you used your hard-earned money to pay for, and he did no better, or perhaps worse, than he's done in high school? And how resentful you might feel if that's what happened."

"I do sometimes feel that resentment, I have to say. I feel like life has been handed to him on a platter, and sending him to a fancy university without him ever having pushed himself very hard . . . well, I guess resentment's the best word for it."

"He'd probably be better off going to a less expensive college and being free of some of that resentment rather than going to a more expensive college and having to pay off the steep price of your resentment," I offered.

A mother I worked with came to the same conclusion, although for different reasons. "Carolyn has been a steady student, all As and Bs since middle school, and with all of her athletic accomplishments, there are a lot of colleges she could get into. But what she really wants to do is to be a PE teacher. Now I think that's great, she's just a natural teacher, and I'm all for her pursuing this career.

"But the fact is that she can get her education credits at the University of Maryland for a whole lot less than she can at some of the private colleges she and her friends are looking at. And I hate to tell her she can't go to one of those expensive schools, but the fact is, it would be a stretch for us because we've got two other kids. And the reality is that she'll surely be as good a gym teacher as a result of going to the University of Maryland as she would if she went anywhere else—and with a whole lot less debt to pay off."

With this family, also, it was important for the parent to overcome whatever guilt she was feeling about putting restrictions on her daughter's college plans and revise her plans so that they were better aligned with the reality of their financial circumstances.

"I'm afraid that she'll think I don't value her career choice."

"That's possible," I nodded, "and because of that you'll have to clarify the basis for your revision of the original agreement and emphasize that it is not meant to diminish her decision but is simply a way to help her get started off in life on the right foot."

"But her younger sister talks about being a dentist, and I'll feel awful if I allow *her* to go to a high-prestige school simply because a dentist is likely to make more money than a gym teacher and be better able to help pay off loans."

"But that is up to you and her sister to figure out when *she* is ready for college. All you can do right now is help Carolyn think practically about her next step and to help ensure that that step doesn't create too many problems down the road."

SAYING NO OR GOING SLOW

I recently saw a brief clip from a TV sitcom in which an adolescent asks her father for spending money and he declines. "Does this mean that we're poor?" she asks, fretfully. "No," replies the father, matter-of-factly, "it means that *you* are—we're doing quite well, actually."

Declining a request for financial assistance is painful, but it is often necessary to sympathetically, albeit firmly, say no. Certainly, I have found it best for parents to not answer quickly when their young adult asks them for money, either in the form of a loan or gift, but to give the matter careful reflection. I have worked with many families for whom the delay results in the young adult rescinding his request as he thinks about the complexity of borrowing money from his parents or finds other resources to tap into.

And I have certainly worked with many families for whom the delay clarifies the parents' decision-making process. Encouraging parents to stall for time is never a bad idea, since it:

1   Demonstrates to the young adult that this is a serious matter and deserving of careful scrutiny
2   Models thoughtful deliberation rather than an impulsive, crisis-driven mentality when it comes to financial matters, something that many young adults need to learn to do
3   Gives the parents the opportunity to sort out their mixed emotions and come to a decision that they are more likely to feel comfortable with
4   Buys some time and provides the parents with the opportunity to determine whether their help (if they agree to help) should be a gift or a loan
5   Provides the parents with a chance to determine what their financial expectations are when it comes to terms of fiscal repayment
6   Provides the parents with a chance to determine what their emotional expectations are when it comes to the terms of psychological repayment

Sometimes, helping parents to find ways to be of assistance that are not purely monetary is useful as well. This might entail preparing regular meals, lending a car for a period of time when one is needed, or helping out with child care if a grandchild is in the picture. I have seen that the less fiscal the support that is proffered, the less that resentment builds up if that support cannot promptly (or ever) be fully reciprocated.

If parents *do* decide to lend money and expect to be paid back, I have found it valuable to ask them to put together a simple contract that describes the terms of the arrangement and that specifies matters such as a repayment schedule or any interest that will be charged (this is actually useful for legal reasons, too, because if the money surpasses the $12,000 threshold currently established by the Internal Revenue Service for gifts, the gift money becomes taxable).

When parents loan money to young adults and it is paid back according to expectations, this can be a very positive experience for both generations. The parents feel good about their altruism, about their having supported their child's initiative or gotten her through a tough time, and about their having trusted their young adult to be responsible when it comes to repayment. The young adult feels good about having gotten the support and what it enabled her to do, and also about having been given the opportunity to prove and redeem herself in her parents' eyes.

On the other hand, the reality is that family loans are often not paid back, and this can exert a significant strain on family relationships, which is why parents should be encouraged to think carefully about the ways in which they subsidize their young adult. This prompts me to recall the astute comment, "If someone owes you a thousand dollars, then he's got a problem. But if someone owes you a million dollars, then *you've* got a problem."

FINANCIAL ASSESSMENT

Despite our sense that it is intrusive or voyeuristic, it is often crucial to delve into and examine the details of a young adult's and a family's pecuniary life to obtain an accurate read on the financial exchanges and interchanges that take place. This is often a dicey endeavor—I treat many patients who are much more willing to discuss with me their sex lives and other very personal matters than they are to discuss their finances. And, as with any sensitive area, what family members *say* is happening is not always what is *actually* happening.

For example, a father proudly told me that he was forcing his 23-year-old son to become more independent by not giving him any more money, but it did not take me long to figure out that he was continuing to cover many of his son's expenses, including his college loan payments, auto and health insurance premiums, cell phone contract, athletic club membership, and a large auto repair bill. There was, indeed, no actual cash outlay to his son, but this young man was still being quite comfortably endowed.

I recently had two different young adult patients, both of whom had applied for food stamps. One was a 21-year-old with two children who was working as a medical receptionist, making about $25,000 a year and living with her mother, who was assisting her with child care. One was a 24-year-old without children or income who was paying for her first year of law school with loans. However, she was living in a tony apartment in a gentrified area of downtown Baltimore that her parents were covering the rent for and driving a relatively new car that had been given to her by them as a college graduation gift two years before. Both young adults qualified for federal aid, but they were obviously on very different financial paths.

Here are some of the questions that should either be asked directly by the clinician or that the clinician should at least consider privately:

- What does money represent in this family?
- To what extent is any financial support that the parents are offering spurring their young adult's growth, and to what extent might it be hobbling that growth? What metrics are being used to determine this?
- What are the expectations behind fiscal exchanges in the family? What are the parents expecting in return for what they give, and in what coinage? What does the young adult think, know, or imagine that the psychological price for financial support is going to be?
- What are the various family members' roles when it comes to money? Who is the miser? Who is the philanthropist? Who is the hoarder? Who is the spender?
- In what ways are one or more family members demonstrating an irrational or inappropriate use of money?
- Who is overspending or secretly spending (on alcohol/drugs, clothing, gambling, etc.)?
- Who is refusing to earn money, or earning money below his or her capacity, and how is that being responded to by other family members?
- Who is the most expensive member of the family, and what expenses does he or she typically run up? Who steps in to call attention to this, and who attempts to reduce or alleviate these expenses? Is this family member expensive because of the money he or she spends or because of the money that needs to be spent by the family *on* him or her (such as for legal or medical expenses, credit card debts, loan payments, etc.)?
- Is any form of stealing taking place in the family?
- In what ways are monetary conflicts about control and power? How long have power or control imbalances been in place?
- Are family members trying to make relational purchases such as love, connection, trust, or commitment using money?

SOLUTIONS

In addition to clarifying the family's financial issues and conflicts with the questions noted above, here are some guidelines that clinicians can offer:

- Encourage the parents to make joint decisions between them regarding when and when not to financially support their young adult.
- Make sure that agreements having to do with financial transactions are written down and signed, so that everyone is clear on the terms and expectations.
- Maintain flexibility on the part of both generations should some kind of renegotiation become necessary.
- Help parents communicate well with each other, and help parents and young adults communicate well with each other when it comes to what is entailed with anything financial.
- Encourage parents to be candid about their financial concerns and limitations.
- Maintain some sort of statute of limitations for financially based conflicts. At a certain point, the family's "fiscal year" has to end and the ledger book for a developmental phase close. For example, the young adult's successive car accidents when he was 17 cannot continue to be brought up in negotiations that are taking place more than several years later (unless, of course, he is continuing to get into car accidents that are still draining the family's finances). Likewise, the fact that the parents chose not to co-sign on their daughter's off-campus apartment during her senior year of college cannot be brought up by her in negotiations that are taking place when she's in her mid-20s or older.

Countertransference

I endured a very complicated experience with a therapist whom I began consulting with shortly after completing my doctorate. After a long period of productive collaboration, I expressed a desire to cut back on the frequency of our sessions, especially because my own practice was growing and my wife and I had recently had our first child.

Despite my progress, however, and my burgeoning personal and professional responsibilities, he insisted strongly that I should continue coming on a weekly basis. I could not understand why he was not more enthusiastic about my growth, why he wasn't proudly endorsing a healthy yearning to begin pulling away from him and "leave home." In fact, his adamant stipulation that I remain in weekly treatment began to trigger much self-doubt. Was I not growing in the way that I thought I was? Was the progress that I was seeing in so many dimensions of my life simply delusional, or perhaps fraudulent?

As a result of this conflict, our relationship grew increasingly contentious, and he seemed to become (or at least I imagined that he became) more and more disparaging. At one point during this difficult phase, I jubilantly told him that I had been offered my first book contract after many discouraging months of repeatedly receiving rejection letters from publishers, a dispiriting process that I had intently focused on in treatment. His stunningly deflating comment was, "As a practicing clinician, you should be careful about that, because patients usually don't like it when their therapist starts writing books—it can make them uncomfortable." (It did not occur to me at the time what the corollary to his observation might be, which is that therapists—like him—who are *not* authors may not like it when their *patients* start writing books because they might feel as if they're being rivaled or surpassed.)

After much struggle, I ceased attempting to convince him that it made sense to cut back on the frequency of our sessions and chose to finish up altogether. My therapist responded with a predictably gloomy prognosis for my future if I followed through on this decision. With tremendous trepidation (because I had, indeed, learned a lot from this clinician and still trusted his judgment), I stuck to my guns and was very relieved and reassured to discover that I somehow survived, and even thrived, without his ongoing presence.

In looking back at this therapeutic crossroads that I had gotten stuck at early in my professional life, I can easily see that the act of leaving home—no matter what, where, and who the home might be—remains an act of daring and courage. Interestingly and coincidentally, I learned several years later that my therapist had left his wife after a long marriage while his two children were young adults. This news was quite a revelation, being that he had spoken to me about his marital and family life in only the most glowingly positive terms during our work together.

It prompted me to wonder if perhaps, during the time that he was insisting that I stay in treatment, that he was also insisting to himself that he stay in his unsatisfying marriage or that his *wife* was insisting that he stay. Was I absorbing some countertransferential edict and paying the price for a contemplated or torturous separation that he was struggling with in his personal life? And to what extent did the departure of his young adult children influence his feelings about *my* leaving, or about his decision to leave his wife?

I will, of course, never know the answers to these questions, but this painful experience certainly taught me about the clinical danger of not attending carefully to the conflicts and concerns that show up in a therapist's own life. When it comes to working with young adults who are struggling to separate and differentiate from their families, and the families who are struggling to manage that separation and differentiation, the more we are aware of our *own* current and historical difficulties with these knotty processes, the better equipped we will be to help them to understand and manage theirs.

There are invariably ways in which our separation from our own family of origin parents was difficult, anguished, or impeded, and we need to be alert to the dynamics of this separation so that we don't ask our patients—either the young adult or the parents—to replicate components of this drama on our behalf, to play out scenarios that have much more to do with us than with them.

Of course, one of the great challenges of managing countertransferential responses while doing family therapy is that there are so many countertransferential threads to observe and monitor. We can count on having strong emotional responses to every member of the family, not only the ones who show up in our office, but even the ones who don't or won't.

Part of managing our countertransference involves an examination of our own leave-taking. Here are some questions that clinicians should ask themselves, questions that are, of course, similar to some of the questions for parents that were discussed in the chapter on assessment.

- What was the hardest part of my leaving home?
- What was the easiest part?

- What work do I need to continue to do when it comes to my own differentiation from my family of origin?
- Which leave-taking issues do I still struggle with or agonize over?
- What makes it difficult for me to leave something or someone, even if it's time, or past time, to do so?
- When have I felt developmentally stuck, and what is my understanding of what got me or kept me stuck?

If you have children of your own of any age who are still living at home, additional questions are worth exploring, such as:

- What aspects of my children's separation from me do I struggle with?
- What are the most painful components of my children's growth and development?
- In what ways have I found myself not supporting their autonomy?
- What feels most daunting about their eventual departure?

And if you have children who have already left home, you might ask yourself:

- What are the best and worst ways in which I managed my children's separation?
- In what ways is additional separation/differentiation between us still warranted?
- What are the challenges to our being able to achieve a higher level of separation/differentiation within our family?

Family theorist Helm Stierlin (1977) outlined a useful framework for examining clinicians' countertransferential tendencies during family treatment, which I have adapted and modified so that it is more specifically relevant to our work with families in the launching stage of the life cycle.

The scaffolding is that family therapists will tend to over- or underidentify with certain actors in the family drama in ways that inhibit their clinical maneuverability. The four actors are:

- The Victimized Young Adult
- The Rebellious Young Adult
- The Victimized Parent
- The Ineffective Parent

OVERIDENTIFYING WITH THE VICTIMIZED YOUNG ADULT

When a clinician overidentifies with the Victimized Young Adult, he believes that the parents are projecting all of their negativity onto the child, making him pay the price for their unaddressed issues. He tends to side with the young adult when it comes to family conflict and has difficulty acknowledging the ways in which the child is contributing to the dysfunctional family dynamic, and to notice the ways in which he is eliciting the victimization.

The subconscious hope behind this form of overidentification is that the therapist will somehow symbolically make the parents feel badly for the ways in which his own parents projected family negativity onto him or onto one or more of his siblings, and thus retroactively restore justice in his own family of origin.

To manage this overidentification and not get waylaid by it, the therapist must pay close attention to the ways in which the young adult patient still wields power over the parents, rather than focusing exclusively on how the parents wield power over the child, and attend to the mutuality that is an inherent part of any family relationship.

OVERIDENTIFYING WITH THE REBELLIOUS YOUNG ADULT

When a clinician overidentifies with the Rebellious Young Adult, she believes that the child is unjustly imprisoned and has the right to battle family oppression with whatever tools she has at her disposal, productively or counterproductively, using anything from aggression to passivity, from denunciation to extortion.

The subconscious hope behind this form of overidentification is that, in siding with the child's rebellion, the therapist's own muted or foreclosed rebellious struggles will be vicariously reinvoked and reinvigorated.

To manage this overidentification and not get waylaid by it, the therapist must understand that the young adult patient may not really be rebelling at all, but simply resonating and conforming to her parents' disowned rebellious impulses—in other words, rather than successfully rebelling against the family order, the struggling child is, in actuality, succumbing to it.

OVERIDENTIFYING WITH THE VICTIMIZED PARENT

When a clinician overidentifies with the Victimized Parent, he believes that the parents are oppressed by their mean-spirited, ungrateful, and incorrigible child.

The subconscious hope behind this form of overidentification is that, in siding with the parents, he will feel better about the ways in which he is oppressed by his *own* mean-spirited, ungrateful, incorrigible child, or he will feel less guilty about the ways in which he was mean-spirited, ungrateful, and incorrigible to his parents when he was a child or young adult.

To manage this overidentification and not get waylaid by it, the therapist (much like the therapist who overidentifies with the Victimized Young Adult) must pay close attention to the reciprocal behaviors that each generation engenders in the other rather than pointing the finger solely at the younger generation.

UNDERIDENTIFYING WITH THE INEFFECTIVE PARENT

When a clinician underidentifies with the Ineffective Parent, she concludes that she is better equipped than the parents are to launch the young adult toward autonomy and self-reliance and attempts to co-opt the launching while relegating the feckless mother and father to the margins of family life.

The subconscious hope behind this form of underidentification is that the therapist's own self-regard will be supported and augmented as she compares herself favorably with the parents, whom she needs to (and thus is inevitably able to) envision as ineffectual.

To manage this underidentification and not get waylaid by it, the therapist needs to find more authentic ways to expand her self-esteem other than by displacing the parents, and instead empower them so that they are the ones who can finish the launching on their own.

SHEDDING LIGHT

There are, of course, other ways to understand our countertransferential tendencies, but I have found this framework to be particularly useful when I consider my own work and when therapists consult with me for supervision.

The reality is, though, that none of us are capable of managing the complexity of countertransference entirely on our own, which is why it's important to avail yourself of personal therapy or individual or group consultation with an experienced clinician. No matter how self-aware we may be, there are always going to be blind spots and trapdoors that await us as we traverse any family's rocky terrain. The commitment to talking about our experience as clinicians with other clinicians is the best way to illuminate those blind spots and trapdoors so that we can sidestep them and remain present to our patients as we accompany them on their journey toward growth and healing.

GETTING OFF TRACK

Here are some questions that you might want to ask yourself that may help you to understand when you are getting clinically deflected and losing your systemic perspective:

- To what extent am I buying into a linear treatment model and beginning to believe that the patient's problem exists exclusively within him, rather than emerging as an outcome of the family's web of relationships, and that the answer ultimately lies in some form of individual treatment (medication, individual psychotherapy, etc.)?

- To what extent have I lost hope and settled for an attitude of, "This is as far as they're going to get, this is the best that they can do with their limitations"?
- To what extent have I begun to lose interest in the family and their struggles?
- To what extent am I dreading the family's appearance in my office due to the feelings of helplessness and unpleasantness that generally arise?
- To what extent do I feel supremely confident and overly comfortable in my work with this family? What would this suggest that I am missing when it comes to their dynamic?
- Does one family member seem much more enamored with me than any other? If so, in what ways am I not expending enough effort to connect with the other family members? What about them might I find less appealing?
- Is anything surprising about this family and our work together, or has it become completely predictable, if not mechanistic? Am I experiencing a false sense of divinatory clarity, or is there any mystery still lurking in the family's story/history?
- What should be happening in these sessions that is not happening, and what am I doing or not doing that is getting in the way of that happening?

TERMINATION

Just as a parent's paramount job is to make herself obsolete, our job as therapists is to make ourselves obsolete as well, to allow our patients to supersede us. We certainly want them to treasure what we have offered them, but we also want them to be able to transcend our offering, to carry it with them and leave us behind.

Young adults' stories will continue pulsing out toward eternity without their parents and grandparents being able to see how it all finally turns out. So, too, will our patients' stories pulse outward once they have finished with us. In the face of this reality, we have to somehow summon the courage and trust to let go, to grieve, and to find pleasure in the loss.

EMPATHY

While none of us can possibly experience all that a family has experienced, we are not excused from imagining what their experience is or has been like. This may necessitate our coaxing and convening personal experiences that may not be as troubled or traumatic as those of our patients but that contain within them a germ of the human experience that enables us to empathize with them, which provides the foundation for our connection with and compassion for them.

For example, my wife and one of my sons have both, at different times, been beset by harrowing medical ordeals. I am fully aware that we were able to obtain the best care possible in both situations—care that enabled both of them to recover well and for which I remain boundlessly thankful. I am just as fully aware that most citizens of the United States and many around the world who are suffering through similar conditions are not able to avail themselves of that kind of care, and, as a result, probably don't come through it as quickly or fully.

When these medical crises hit, the helplessness, terror, injustice, and rage that I experienced were immense and, to some extent, surely indistinguishable from the helplessness, terror, injustice, and rage that any parent or spouse would feel in a similar situation. Those feelings, as a result of my privilege and good fortune, surely did not last as long as they do for those who don't have access to the kind of resources that our family did. But they remain very close to the surface and easy to call upon when I am working with families who are in the midst of any ordeal that triggers a similarly profound response. Being privileged does not inoculate anyone against the awful susceptibilities that we are all confronted with.

To believe that we can thoroughly and exhaustively identify with everyone we work with and understand the depth and entirety of their pain would be irresponsible, but so would surrendering to this reality and not making the effort to bridge that gap. It is the compassion and love that actuate that effort that unmistakably come across to our patients. Wealth and privilege indeed buffer us from certain dreadful realities and make life much easier to live, but there is an elemental humanity—a humanity shadowed by vulnerability, tragedy, and, ultimately, mortality—that all of us share, no matter what the circumstances of our birth.

FINAL THOUGHTS

No matter how experienced and enlightened we may be, we will still run into what I call "flagship cases"—patients who painfully remind us of everything that we don't know but who, in the process, teach us some of the things that we *ought* to know. With some families, I still feel like an unarmed matador about to enter a bullring, nervously eyeing all of the possible exits I can pursue when the angry, snorting bull starts charging after me. Even after three decades of practice, I am often left scratching my head after sessions, feeling titanically ineffective, overcome by deep, weary feelings of desolation and dejection, trying to determine what to do next and wondering if I have anything meaningful to offer, any way to break the circular, unbearable, and debilitating family patterns that seem resolutely unbreakable.

Our task in these situations is to remind ourselves that it is not our job to solve the family's problems but to instead change their *relationship* with the problem by helping them to look at it from different angles and perspectives. Doing so requires us to focus on the family's dignity and humanity rather than on their psychological symptoms and to envisage treatment not as an intervention that we coolly administer to our patients from a distance but as the process of coauthoring a new and more interesting family story that changes *their* lives, as well as *our* lives, for the better.

I have referenced throughout this book the many clinicians and theorists who have influenced my work, but the most profound influence on the evolution of my clinical voice has been my patients, the ones who "patient-ly" sit with me and school me in the melancholy, suffering, and grief that are the handmaidens to change, growth, and healing. I can only hope that they have learned as much from being with me as I have learned from being with them.

Conclusion

Dim light, deathly silence, and a hanging body. These three realities assailed me very early one misty September morning—the September that began my youngest child's senior year, the last year that my wife and I would be likely to have a child living at home. I was in the midst of the run with which I begin each day, chugging down a path that wended its way through the athletic fields of the neighborhood high school that my three children had attended, a route that I had navigated literally thousands of times before. Being a man of many rituals, this was my Tuesday peregrination—each day of the week has its own distinct course. On my left rose the steel underside of the football field's bleachers. On my right were the school's outdoor basketball courts.

As I scooted along, I suddenly noticed a man dangling by his neck from a rope that was attached to the top row of the bleachers. There was no one else around—it was just the two of us. I continued on for a few steps, trying to shake the image out of my head. Then I frowned, slowed, stopped completely, and ran backward a few steps. I experienced a strange, momentary urge to laugh. Yes, there was a body hanging from a thick rope that was looped around the top row of the bleachers. The body was very still, as still as the morning air. All was quiet.

My first thought was the typical thought that crosses one's mind in the face of an intimate encounter with death—this simply cannot be. As a chill rose through my chest, I frenetically spun off the best explanations I could come up with. A high school prank, perhaps the effigy of an opposing team's quarterback. A practical joke, one of those clever street actors who can hold still like a statue for minutes at a time, prompting passersby to wonder if he's real. Where were the videographers and photographers who were surreptitiously filming my surprised response, ready for a humorous upload to YouTube? Where, indeed . . .

Meanwhile, the body hung there, almost completely motionless except that, as I stared, I noticed just the slightest swing back and forth in the cool dawn—an infinitesimal sway to the left, an infinitesimal sway to the right. It was just him and me. A young African American male, wearing a blue hooded sweatshirt, neon green shorts, dark socks, white running shoes. Shoes that were at least a foot off the ground. Shoes that shod feet that were now treading air.

I always run with my cell phone, comforted by the somewhat irrational thought that if I were ever threatened with attack by some lurking perpetrator in the half-light of dawn, I would be better able to protect myself by making a call. This morning that reality had, in fact, occurred, but it was a different kind of attack than I had ever anticipated. I punched in 911, staring at the body, still in complete disbelief. I did not recognize my voice as I spoke. It sounded thin and weak, with a quaver. I was hearing myself say words, and they were words that I had never uttered before—"There is a body hanging from the bleachers here at the high school."

I remember the voice on the other end asking me questions, and I remember answering those questions in the same tremulous voice. I remember her asking me to go up to the body to see if there was any condensation coming off of the skin or out of the mouth. I remember telling her that I was afraid to get too close. I remember that I felt ashamed of my cowardice. My feet felt like they were frozen to the ground. I remember hearing the first faint wail of sirens in the distance—and I remember that they made me want to cry.

"Stay where you are until the police arrive," I was instructed by the dispatcher. She was direct and calm, but not unkind. "I have to apologize if this is just a mannequin," I recall mumbling embarrassedly at one point. "I am so sorry if I fell for a prank." It was odd how there was a part of me that was actually hoping that the body turned out to be real so that I could spare myself the embarrassment of having been duped. What did it say about my complete absence of humanity that I momentarily preferred that this was an actual young man who had hung himself to death rather than a scarecrow stuffed with straw, simply so that I wouldn't be humiliated, simply so that I could be certain that I hadn't been made a fool?

"Better safe than sorry," she reassured me. In that moment I felt profoundly grateful for her kind words, the deep gratitude that one experiences when offered the first small comfort in the face of devastating peril and loss.

The police cars and fire trucks arrived, rolling like caissons into the parking lot near the bleachers. I waved vigorously toward them with one arm and pointed to the body with my other, desperate to be helpful. I was struck by the way that the officers, EMTs, and firefighters seemed to casually saunter down the slope from the parking lot to the field. No sprinting with stretchers, no shouts and hollers for medical equipment. "They know," I muttered to myself. "They've seen this before and they know."

I told the dispatcher that the police had arrived, and I don't remember anything else about our conversation. I then called my wife, who was home exercising. I told her to get off the machine, I explained what had happened, and I asked her to come and get me. In a daze, I wandered up toward the parking lot where I had told her to pick me up. A police officer stopped me, asking if I was the person who had made the call to 911. "Yes, that was me," I acknowledged woodenly.

"You need to stay here for some questions," he said, with just the slightest hint of firmness. Funny thing was that, at that moment, I wanted to be noticed. I didn't want to be able to roam away, unaccountable—I wanted to be significant. Had this really happened, or had I made up the entire gruesome scene? Worse . . . had I actually somehow created it?

"Sure," I agreed, "but can I sit in my wife's car?"

"Of course."

I sat and waited until a young officer came over, introduced himself, and asked some questions. I now have no idea what he asked or how I answered. I know that I was released and told that someone would be contacting me later that day. My wife drove me home, a part of me wishing I had been questioned in a more forceful fashion, wishing that I had been required to prove my innocence, that I had been forced to struggle to exonerate myself in the face of insistent accusations. In reality, I suspect that he simply asked me for my contact information and rapidly eliminated me as a suspect. Nobody ever called to follow up. I apparently was not that interesting. This vaguely troubled me.

In the coming days I learned a bit more about Richard, the young man who had hanged himself (and to whom I have dedicated this book). He was a drifter, an 18-year-old who had withdrawn from high school in a nearby state and had recently moved to my city in an attempt to make a fresh start. He had gotten a job at a nearby shoe store, but his Facebook entries had grown increasingly morose and elegiac during the previous weeks. He had, in fact, attended a football game at the high school just a few nights before his death, probably trying to make some friends in his new community. I imagined him that evening, alone on the top row of the bleachers, eventually ignoring the contest on the field below while peering down and mentally working out the mechanics of his own demise.

I will tell you that I have led a very sheltered life—this was the first time that I had ever seen a corpse outside of a funeral home or cemetery. I had never before come across someone who had died a violent death. Experiences like these remove the fig leaf from our existence, expose our raw nakedness in the face of a vast universe and its unknowable, unpredictable whims.

But I will also tell you that this experience hung like a veil over the subsequent year. The reality is that, by then, I was already preoccupied with my daughter's impending departure for college and the final emptying of the nest, the nest that my wife and I had been so carefully constructing and cultivating since starting our family 24 years before, with the birth of our eldest son.

As we have been discussing throughout these pages, there are many losses associated with the launching of children into young adulthood. There is the loss of the young adult's childhood, and there is the loss of the parents' essential relevance and worth. So in a way it seemed dreadfully appropriate that this year—one that would be colored by the anticipation of these losses—had been rung in by a disquieting encounter with a stunningly vivid loss: an actual—rather than a symbolic—loss of life.

In the subsequent weeks, I continued my morning runs but made sure to travel other routes. Eventually, though, I allowed myself—perhaps *forced* myself—to take the one that led me down the path past the bleachers. Richard was not there, of course. Yet I realized that I was half expecting him to greet me, and these days—more than a year since our encounter—it is as if he still waits for me any morning that I pass by the silver stands. In my mind, the two of us remain entwined in a peculiar embrace, the young man who could not bear the pain of his lonely, tormented life and who believed he needed to end it because he had lost hope, and the middle-aged father who was coming to grips with the pain that heralded the unavoidable end of a *stage* in his life and the accompanying loss of his identity as a parent, an identity that had pulsed steadily for more than two decades and had generously supplied him with a sense of purpose, direction, and motivation. *My* painful story is, of course, far less devastating and tragic than Richard's painful story, but both are stories that are defined and determined by the arc, the ache, and the echo of loss.

****

Families are the streams that add the richest nutrients to the vast river of human life. They are composed of an extraordinary confluence of ancestors and ghosts, myths and memories, blessings and curses, triumphs and defeats. When a child enters a family—through birth, through adoption, through remarriage, through foster care—that child deepens and broadens the family stream, which in turn further enriches the river of which we are all a part.

Even when children leave home, their relationship with their family continues, like water flowing through viaducts that have been built above ground or through tunnels that have been dug below ground that convey shipments of fondness, longing, and affection back and forth across the generations. The family is where time and timelessness entwine, where the finite and the infinite clasp, where history and future cradle each other.

We all live such tangled, fraught lives and somehow must struggle to wrest meaning from life's complexity. We all try to make sense, however gossamer that sense may be, of life and death, attempting to maintain hope and love in the face of the grim recognition of the futility and brevity of existence.

The rituals and relationships that we engage in console us in the face of passing time and awaiting death, and psychotherapy is an act that is both ritual and relationship. That is why, to my way of thinking, it decidedly remains, and *best* remains, more art than science, an enterprise that is not dependent on answers, diagnoses, and certainty but on questions, conflict, and doubt.

Doggedly helping the family to discover and inhabit the oases of care and tenderness that have been deserted due to the pain and loss that have become their stubborn tenants is a responsibility of enormous magnitude and requires the therapist to acknowledge his or her own lack of immunity to that very pain and loss, to suffering and strife.

When therapist and family join hands in the face of the human predicament, we open each other up to our unique destiny and all the blessings that accompany it. We are put here to inhabit our lives, to heroically step through the doorway that our soul has opened up for us, and the therapeutic encounter can be one of the most compelling and enduring ways to ensure that those heroic steps are taken.

****

I have coached an inestimable number of soccer games in my life—high school, travel, recreational league, peewee. Being a meticulous planner, I always prepared a careful scheme prior to each match, enthusiastically laying out for my players the sequence of strategies that would surely lead us to victory. And, invariably, as soon as the game started, it seemed that my painstaking game plan would quickly collapse in the competitive chaos on the pitch, and it was just one version after another of a mad scramble for the ball. We won plenty and we lost plenty, but rarely did my game plan maintain its original integrity in the heat of battle. This may be because I was not a particularly sophisticated coach or because of the unpredictable nature of any athletic battle, since my opposing coach was surely doing the same thing I was.

What I have just described is, for me, an apt metaphor for writing a book. In my head, and before I actually start composing, every book that I write is elegant and coherent, gracefully and persuasively conveying my thoughts and ideas in carefully turned phrases and paragraphs—just like my hundreds of earnestly designed soccer game plans. But when the writing finally begins, chaos invariably ensues, and it always seems, at the end, as if it's just a mad scramble for me to get down on paper what I want to say in whatever clumsy way I am able to do so, fiercely hoping that I salvage some sort of victory—in this case, the victory of my words carrying some measure of meaning to the reader.

When it comes to this particular book, I am hoping that my modest attempt to add to the literature on the psychological treatment of young adults and their families will at least encourage you to think a little bit differently not only about your work but also about your life, since in the field of psychotherapy, our lives and our work are inextricably interlaced. I have expressed myself in words, but as we have seen throughout these pages, words do not always convey the worlds that lie behind them. But if you have been able to glimpse some new region of your personal or clinical world as a result of reading my words, then I can take heart that I have not written completely in vain.

I have studied the science of goodbyes,
The bareheaded laments of night.
Osip Mandelstam, *"Tristia"*

Bibliography

Arnett, Jeffrey Jensen. (2004). *Emerging Adulthood: The Winding Road from the Late Teens through the Twenties*. New York: Oxford University Press.

Boszormenyi-Nagy, I. (1987). *Foundations of Contextual Therapy: Collected Papers of Ivan Boszormenyi-Nagy, M.D.* New York: Brunner/Mazel.

Bowen, M. (1978). *Family Therapy in Clinical Practice*. New York: Jason Aronson.

Bowlby, F. (1969). *Attachment*. New York: Basic Books.

D'Augelli, A. R. (2006). "Developmental and Contextual Factors and Mental Health among Lesbian, Gay and Bisexual Youths." In A. M. Omoto and H. S. Kurtzman (Eds.), *Sexual Orientation and Mental Health: Examining Identity and Development in Lesbian, Gay and Bisexual People* (pp. 37–53). Washington, DC: American Psychological Association.

Deci, Edward. (1996). *Why We Do What We Do*. New York: Penguin Books.

Dweck, Carol. (2007). *Mindset: The New Psychology of Success*. New York: Ballantine Books.

Fishman, H. Charles. (1988). *Treating Troubled Adolescents: A Family Therapy Approach*. New York: Basic Books.

Haley, Jay. (1980). *Leaving Home: The Therapy of Disturbed Young People*. New York: McGraw-Hill.

Haley, Jay. (1985). *Problem Solving Therapy: New Strategies for Effective Family Therapy*. San Francisco: Jossey-Bass.

Madanes, Cloe. (1981). *Strategic Family Therapy*. San Francisco: Jossey-Bass.

Madanes, Cloe. (1990). *Sex, Love and Violence: Strategies for Transformation*. New York: W. W. Norton.

Madanes, Cloe. (1998). *The Secret Meaning of Money*. San Francisco: Jossey-Bass.

McGoldrick, M., Carter, B., and Garcia-Preta, N. (2011). *The Expanded Family Life Cycle: Individual, Family and Social Perspectives*. Boston: Allyn & Bacon.

McGoldrick, M., and Hardy, K. (2008). *Re-Visioning Family Therapy: Race, Culture and Gender in Clinical Practice*. New York: Guilford Press.

Minuchin, S. (1974). *Families and Family Therapy*. Cambridge, MA: Harvard University Press.

Savin-Williams, R. (2001). *Mom, Dad. I'm Gay. How Families Negotiate Coming Out*. Washington, DC: American Psychological Association.

Settersten, R. A., Furstenberg, F. F., and Rumbaut, R. G., eds. (2005). *On the Frontier of Adulthood: Theory, Research and Public Policy*. Chicago: University of Chicago Press.

Stierlin, H. (1977). *Psychoanalysis and Family Therapy: Selected Papers*. New York: Jason Aronson.

Stierlin, H. (1981). *Separating Parents and Adolescents*. New York: Jason Aronson.

Walsh, Froma. (2002). *Normal Family Processes: Growing Diversity and Complexity.* New York: Guilford Press.

Walsh, Froma. (2006). *Strengthening Family Resilience* (2nd ed.). New York: Guilford Press.

White, M., and Epston, D. E. (1990). *Narrative Means to Therapeutic Ends.* New York: W. W. Norton.

Winnicott, D. W. (1952). *Through Paediatrics to Psychoanalysis.* New York: Basic Books, 1975.

Index